"A great how-to for teachers!"—*Washington Post*

"Offers ways to change bullying behavior and prevent potential victims from being bullied; provides teacher and parents with tools to help students learn to resolve conflicts appropriately and effectively."—National P.T.A.'s *Our Chil*

THE

BULLY

FREE

CLASSROOM

Over 100 Tips and Strategies for Teachers K–8

ALLAN L. BEANE, PH.D.

free spirit
PUBLISHING®

Works for kids®

Library of Congress Cataloging-in-Publication Data
Beane, Allan L., 1950–
The bully free classroom: over 100 tips and strategies for teachers K–8 / by Allan L. Beane.
    p.   cm.
Includes bibliographical references and index.
ISBN 1-57542-054-6
1. School violence—United States—Prevention—Handbooks, manuals, etc. 2. Bullying—United States—Prevention—Handbooks, manuals, etc. 3. Classroom management—United States—Handbooks, manuals, etc. 4. Activity programs in education—United States—Handbooks, manuals, etc. I. Title.
LB3013.3.B43   1999
371.102'4—dc21

98-47202
CIP

At the time of this book's publication, all facts and figures cited are the most current available; all telephone numbers, addresses, and Web site URLs are accurate and active; all publications, organizations, Web sites, and other resources exist as described in this book; and all have been verified. The author and Free Spirit Publishing make no warranty or guarantee concerning the information and materials given out by organizations or content found at Web sites, and we are not responsible for any changes that occur after this book's publication. If you find an error or believe that a resource listed here is not as described, please contact Free Spirit Publishing. Parents, teachers, and other adults: We strongly urge you to monitor children's use of the Internet.

Cover design by Percolator
Book design and production by Jessica Thoreson
Index prepared by Kay Schlembach

10 9 8 7 6 5
Printed in the United States of America

Free Spirit Publishing Inc.
217 Fifth Avenue North, Suite 200
Minneapolis, Minnesota 55401-1299
(612) 338-2068
help4kids@freespirit.com
www.freespirit.com

The following are registered trademarks of
Free Spirit Publishing Inc.:

FREE SPIRIT®
FREE SPIRIT PUBLISHING®
SELF-HELP FOR TEENS®

SELF-HELP FOR KIDS®
WORKS FOR KIDS®
THE FREE SPIRITED CLASSROOM®

DEDICATION

This book is dedicated to my wife, Linda, for her unconditional love and support
throughout the writing of this book, and to my son and daughter,
Curtis and Christy Beane, for their shared experiences and insights regarding the
importance of peer acceptance.

ACKNOWLEDGMENTS

I wish to recognize the teachers who, in the initial stages of this book, freely shared their
experiences and made suggestions for promoting peer acceptance.

I also want to thank Free Spirit Publishing for believing in this book, and especially Ms.
Jessica Thoreson for her help and encouragement during writing, editing, and production.

Thank you!

CONTENTS

LIST OF REPRODUCIBLE PAGES

INTRODUCTION

Say the word "bully" to almost anyone you know, and the stories will start pouring out. About the fourth-grade bully who regularly tripped kids walking to their desks or down the hall. The second-grade bully who made girls cry. The sixth-grade bully who lay in wait around the corner for kids walking home from school, ready to bloody noses or toss books in a gutter. If bullying is, as some people claim, a "normal, natural" part of childhood, why do our memories of bullying incidents remain so vivid—and so universally painful?

Bullying has been a problem since a jealous Cain murdered his brother, Abel . . . or since the first caveman hit another over the head. Because kids spend much of their time in school, that's where a lot of bullying takes place—usually out of adults' sight and hearing. Despite recent efforts to publicize the problem, most bullying still goes unnoticed and unreported.

We hear and read many stories about bullying in the media (enough to cause considerable alarm among parents and educators), but those stories are the tip of the iceberg. They also tend to be sensational—guns, knives, children so hopeless and desperate they commit suicide. Those are the exceptions to everyday life in most schools, where bullying is less dramatic but far more common.

Bullying starts in preschool, seems to peak during the middle school years, and declines during high school. Except for hazing, we don't hear much about bullying in colleges and universities. We do hear about abusive spouses and workplace bullies, however, which underscores the fact that bullying is a learned behavior that must be unlearned. Bullies don't just grow up and grow out of it. They must be taught better ways of relating to others.

And that's where you come in. As a teacher, you know children who are bullied daily or weekly. You've witnessed the bullying yourself, or you've heard the reports or rumors. You believe that young people have the right to feel safe, secure, accepted, and valued at school—free from teasing, name-calling, harassment, threats, intimidation, violence, and fear.

This book can help you create that kind of experience for your students. The focus throughout is on your classroom—your immediate environment, and the students you work with every day.

It's possible that your school or district is using one or more programs on bully prevention, conflict resolution, peer mediation, social skills training, self-esteem, safety, stress management, and/or other topics aimed at helping students get along and realize their full potential. *The Bully Free Classroom* is not a program. Rather, it's a collection of tips, strategies, and activities designed to address and ameliorate the multifaceted problem of bullying in schools. You might use this book to complement or supplement a program already in place, to take purposeful action in the absence of a program, or to plan and develop a program that meets the unique needs of your classroom or school.

With or without a program, you can have a profound impact on your students' behavior—and on the school climate as a whole. Never underestimate your ability to make a difference. As a classroom teacher, you're shaping young lives. When you notice your students, reach out to them, and treat them with kindness and respect, you're giving them what all children need: positive attention from a caring adult. When you model acceptance and tolerance, you're leading the way for them to do the same. In large part, that's what this book is about: interacting with students and showing by example what you want and expect from them.

Because this book spans a broad range of grades (K–8), not all activities are appropriate for all

1

classrooms. Some are simple and take just a few moments to do; others take more time to introduce, present, and follow through. Most are easy to understand and implement, requiring little or no advance preparation and few or no special materials.

"Creating a Positive Classroom" (pages 15–76) features tips, strategies, and techniques designed to change everyone's attitudes and behaviors for the better. "Helping Victims" (pages 77–113) focuses on students who are current or potential victims of bullying. "Helping Bullies" (pages 115–148) zeroes in on kids who seem to delight in tormenting others. They need your help as much as victims do, and you'll find lots of ideas for turning them around.

Many activities include a variety of options or approaches to try with your students. Throughout, "Go Farther" suggestions present ways to expand an activity or explore a topic in greater depth. You'll also discover dozens of handouts, ready to use and reproducible for your classroom.

You know your students better than anyone. Please feel free to adapt any of these activities or handouts to meet your needs and theirs. Some might need "aging up" or "aging down"; specific age levels are not assigned, because what students are ready for and capable of doing seldom depends on age alone.

Give this book a quick scan, then dip in anywhere you want to start. A few of the strategies have a recommended sequence, but most stand alone. Some include "see also" references to strategies elsewhere in the book; because bullying is a complex problem—environment, victims, and bullies are interrelated—some activities in one section might just as easily fit into another.

If you'd like some background before you start trying these strategies with your students, read "The Top Ten Facts About Bullying" (pages 5–14). When you're ready, you may find it most effective to begin with strategies from "Creating a Positive Classroom." These help to set the stage and give everyone a common language and shared understanding of bullying. But if you think it's more important to help a victim right away or stop a bully immediately, turn to those sections first. It's up to you.

Throughout this process, it's vital to communicate with parents and caregivers. On page 3, you'll find a letter you can copy and use to announce that you're using this book and why. Stay in touch with parents at various points along the way; you might give them copies of handouts you're using with your students, send brief notes home, or pick up the phone for a quick update. It's especially important to communicate with parents of students you've identified as bullies or victims.

Whenever you'd like more information, turn to "Resources" at the end of the book (pages 149–161). This section lists and describes books, videos, other materials, organizations, and Web sites to enhance your teaching and support your efforts to make your classroom bully free.

This book has a dual emphasis: intervention and prevention. It's not enough to stop the bullying that's already happening; we also need to keep students who aren't yet bullies or victims from starting down that road. If you don't have a bully problem in your classroom, you'll be improving the chances that one doesn't develop. If you do have a bully problem, you'll be taking concrete steps to counter the attitudes, actions, and perceptions that have caused it and sustain it.

I hope this book can help make your classroom a place where all students are free to learn without fear—and you're free to teach without worrying about bullies and their victims. I'd love to hear how these strategies and tips work for you; I welcome your comments, letters, stories, and emails. You may contact me in care of my publisher:

Free Spirit Publishing
217 Fifth Avenue North, Suite 200
Minneapolis, MN 55401-1299
email: help4kids@freespirit.com
Web site: www.freespirit.com

Allan L. Beane, Ph.D.

Dear Parent/Caregiver,

As I look back on my school days, I can remember times when kids were bullied. You probably can, too. Bullying has been getting a lot of attention recently, but it's hardly a brand-new problem. Bullies (and their victims) have been around forever.

What's new is our attitude toward bullying. What used to be accepted as "kids will be kids" (or "boys will be boys," though girls are bullies, too) has changed. We know now that bullying is serious. Young bullies grow up to be abusive adults. Young victims get hurt. In very rare cases, bullying escalates into violence. And it's not just the bullies and victims who are affected. People around them are distracted, intimidated, and upset. Bullying in the classroom prevents students from learning and teachers from teaching.

What's also new is our commitment to do something about bullying. If it's not a problem, we want to make sure it doesn't start. That's called prevention. If it is a problem, we're determined to stop it. That's called intervention.

As your child's teacher, I'm committed to prevention and intervention in my classroom. That's why I've started using a book called *The Bully Free Classroom.* It's designed to help teachers create a positive environment where everyone feels safe, accepted, and valued.

From time to time, I'll send home materials related to what we're doing in the classroom, and your child might tell you about some of the activities and discussions that are happening in class. If you ever have questions or concerns, I hope you'll contact me personally.

Sincerely,

_____

(Name)

_____

(Telephone)

THE TOP TEN FACTS ABOUT BULLYING

This research-based section provides a broad, general overview of what bullying is, who is affected by bullying, and why it's important for adults—including you—to get involved in prevention and intervention. You might read this before you jump into the main sections of this book, then refer to it periodically for answers, insights, and inspiration as you work with your students to create a bully free classroom.

1. BULLYING IS MORE THAN JUST TEASING

In their article entitled "Overcoming Bullying Behavior," Ellen R. Clore, R.N., and Judith A. Hibel, R.N., describe bullying as "one or more individuals inflicting physical, verbal, or emotional abuse on another—includes threats of bodily harm, weapon possession, extortion, civil rights violation, assault and battery, gang activity, attempted murder, and murder." Other experts add sexual harassment to the list of bullying behaviors.

For both girls and boys in elementary and middle school, the most common form of bullying is, in fact, teasing. However, physical abuse (for boys) and social ostracism (for girls) are in second place.* Most researchers believe that bullying involves an imbalance of physical or psychological power, with the bully being stronger (or perceived to be stronger) than the victim.

According to the National Association of School Psychologists (NASP), approximately one in seven schoolchildren is a bully or a victim, and the problem directly affects about five million elementary and junior high students in the United States. For fourth through eighth graders, 22 percent report academic difficulties resulting from peer abuse.

2. ANYONE CAN BE A BULLY

Bullies are kids who need to feel powerful, and they have learned that bullying works. What distinguishes them from someone who teases occasionally is a pattern of *repeated* physical or psychological intimidation.

There is no one reason why a child may become a bully, but environmental factors can lead to the development of bullying behaviors. Because this behavior is learned, it can also be unlearned. The pattern of behavior can begin as early as age two; the older the child becomes, the more difficult change will be. Child bullies are at a greater risk for problems in the future. For example, by age thirty, 25 percent of the adults who had been identified as bullies as children had a criminal record, as opposed to 5 percent of the adults who hadn't been bullies.* Early intervention is essential.

Some environmental factors that contribute to the development of bullying behavior include the following:**

- *Too little supervision of children and adolescents.* Children need to get the message that bullying behavior is not okay.

* SOURCE: *Bullies and Victims* by SuEllen Fried, A.D.T.R., and Paula Fried, Ph.D. (New York: M. Evans and Company, 1994).

** SOURCE: "Bullying Fact Sheet" by George Batsche and Benjamin Moore, in *Helping Children Grow Up in the '90s: A Resource Book for Parents and Teachers* (Bethesda, MD: National Association of School Psychologists, 1992). Used with permission.

* SOURCE: *The Bullying Prevention Handbook* by John H. Hoover and Ronald Oliver (Bloomington, IN: National Education Service, 1996).

- A "payoff." When parents or other adults give in to an obnoxious or aggressive child, the child learns to use bullying to get what he or she wants.

- *Aggressive behavior in the home.* Some children are more likely than others to imitate aggressive behavior. Watching adults bully each other gives children the tools they need to become bullies themselves.

- *Harsh physical punishment.* Bullies often attack smaller, weaker children to model what happens to them in their homes. The worst possible punishment for bullies is physical.

- *Abusive peers.* Children may be bullied by their "friends" or may be encouraged to bully to be part of the group.

- *Constant negative feedback.* Bullies feel that the world around them is more negative than positive. As a result, they use negative behavior to feel important and get attention.

- *Expecting hostility.* In many ways, the bully's philosophy is "the best defense is offense." They attack before they are attacked, and assume hostility where none may exist.

The school environment also influences the development of bullying behaviors. Environmental factors can include the following:*

- Larger schools report a greater percentage of violence.

- Schools with clear rules of conduct enforced by the principal report less violence.

- Schools with students that report fair discipline practices report less violence.

- Small class size relates to less violence.

- Schools where students mention that they are in control of their lives report less violence.

- A principal who appears to be ineffective or invisible to students reports more violence in school.

- Schools with principals who provide opportunities for teachers and students to participate in decision-making report less violence.

- Cohesiveness among the teaching staff and the principal relates to less violence.

3. ANYONE CAN BE A VICTIM

In general, less is known about victims than about bullies. Children are victimized because of their physical appearance, mannerisms, or just because they don't fit in. In fact, one survey shows that "not fitting in" is the most common reason why a child is abused by peers.* Children who have a disability or a chronic illness are common targets. Other victims are the children of overly protective or domineering parents.

Most victims are either *passive* (anxious, insecure, etc.) or *provocative* (hot-tempered, restless, etc.). Provocative victims are also at risk of becoming bullies themselves. A few children who are victimized don't fit either category—talented or popular children are also victimized. Some students see high achievers as "sucking up" to teachers and decide to torment them into changing their behaviors. Of course, this kind of bullying may be based on jealousy.

Research shows that children who are frequently victimized are more likely to "reward" bullies physically or emotionally (by giving up their lunch money or bursting into tears, for example) and less likely to fight back.

---

* SOURCE: "Bullying Fact Sheet" by George Batsche and Benjamin Moore, in *Helping Children Grow Up in the '90s: A Resource Book for Parents and Teachers* (Bethesda, MD: National Association of School Psychologists, 1992). Used with permission.

---

* SOURCE: *The Bullying Prevention Handbook* by John H. Hoover and Ronald Oliver (Bloomington, IN: National Education Service, 1996).

In the short term, victims may feel afraid and lonely and often attempt to avoid situations in which they may be bullied. In the long term, children who are victimized begin to see themselves as unworthy or inferior, and their academic performance suffers. Some children eventually believe that they deserve the abuse; this phenomenon is also common in victims of domestic abuse. Over time, a victimized person can develop a victim mentality as a permanent part of his or her psyche. This type of victim needs help from a professional therapist or counselor.

Victimized children are also at a greater risk for depression and suicide than their non-bullied peers. They may see suicide as their only way to escape.

4. BULLYING ISN'T A MODERN PROBLEM

Bullying in schools is nothing new. In the 1850s English novel *Tom Brown's Schooldays*, author Thomas Hughes vividly described how a younger boy at an English boarding school was forced by a group of older bullies to undergo a painful and sadistic roasting in front of an open fire.*

Unfortunately, adults have been relatively slow to protect the rights of children. The role of child as obedient servant without rights was unquestioned in America until the case of Mary Ellen McCormack came to light in 1874. The ten-year-old, who was beaten almost daily, was discovered in ragged clothes, imprisoned in an apartment, and allowed outside only at night. Unable to save Mary Ellen by herself, the woman who found her turned to the American Society for the Prevention of Cruelty to Animals (ASPCA), which had been founded in 1868 to protect abused animals from their cruel owners. Because there were no laws in place to protect children at the time, Mary Ellen was tried as a

member of the animal kingdom, under ASPCA legislation. She was removed from the home in less than twenty-four hours and placed in an orphanage.*

After this case, interest in children's rights ebbed and flowed. A major modern step in child protection was the Child Abuse Prevention and Treatment Act, passed by Congress in 1973.

Some people may claim that with all the violence in our culture today, "peer abuse" is the least of a child's worries. However, bullying can be put to rest only when it is recognized and steps are taken to prevent it. Ignoring the problem will not make it go away.

5. BULLYING AFFECTS EVERYONE

Children who watch other children being bullied are often afraid to speak out, perhaps thinking "That could be me!" A child who is victimized may be rejected by his or her peers as if the victim had some sort of disease. (One common variation of this is the childhood game in which one child has "cooties" that he or she attempts to pass on to others.) Some children who witness a great deal of bullying react as many victims do—they attempt to avoid the situation and may even develop headaches, stomachaches, or other physical symptoms to handle the stress. An atmosphere where children worry "who will be next" encourages absences, truancy, and dropping out of school.

Studies with English and Australian schoolchildren and adolescents showed that most students were opposed to bullying and tended to be supportive of victims. Half tried to help victims, and nearly one third regretted not helping.

However, children become less sympathetic to victims as they grow older; almost one third of the adolescents surveyed said they could understand why the bully chose the victim.

* SOURCE: *Set Straight on Bullies* by Stuart Greenbaum with Brenda Turner and Ronald D. Stephens (Malibu, CA: National School Safety Center, 1989).

* SOURCE: *Bullies and Victims* by SuEllen Fried, A.D.T.R., and Paula Fried, Ph.D. (New York: M. Evans and Company, 1994).

In an American study, children in grades four through seven were asked to imagine aggressive acts against victims and nonvictims. In their minds, hurting the victims was less upsetting than hurting the nonvictims.*

Blaming the victim is a common reaction among children. Like many adults, children may believe that bad things don't happen to good people, so the victim must be doing something wrong to deserve the abuse. They may also feel that the abuse makes the victim "tougher." These attitudes help them justify their inaction.

Not every child, of course, ignores the mistreatment of their peers, but intervention can have a high cost. In England, a sixteen-year-old girl who went to the police and identified one of a group of twenty boys who had severely beaten a Pakistani student was both praised and vilified. In the year after the incident, she received death threats, was verbally abused by total strangers, was bullied at school, and suffered a concussion and minor injuries when she was attacked by another student.**

6. BULLYING IS A SERIOUS PROBLEM

The law protects adults against crimes like theft, extortion, slander, and assault and battery. An adult who throws rocks and shouts obscenities at another adult will probably be arrested. This protection should extend equally to children, who generally are considered more vulnerable and less able to defend themselves. Unfortunately, this isn't the case. It's estimated that only about one third of all violent crimes against youths are ever reported to authorities, so it's difficult to determine the true scope of the problem.***

According to Dr. Dan Olweus, one of the world's leading authorities on bullying, "a person is being bullied or victimized when he or she is exposed, repeatedly and over time, to negative actions on the part of one or more persons." This *repeated* nature is most disturbing to some researchers. Bullying is a consistent pattern of disrespect for others, accepted and even created by the environment.

This might explain the popularity of television shows in which children watch people falling down, getting hit by baseballs or bitten by dogs, and the laughter of others convinces them that these things are funny. Students who become bullies don't see other people as people and can't see the consequences of their own actions.

Many bullies often object to being disciplined, claiming "We were just having fun." The difference between playful teasing, hurtful teasing, bullying, and abuse isn't always clear. Because much of the pain of being victimized is emotional or social, it is less evident than a cut or a bruise. A student can be in a great deal of pain without having a visible injury. Words can hurt, and verbal abuse can lead to physical abuse with frightening ease. Experts suggest watching our language for violent metaphors ("The thought struck me," "I'll take a shot at that," etc.) and eliminating them from everyday use. "Think before you speak" is a useful phrase. Calm words may lead to calm actions.

Turning the trend of violence around isn't easy. As one New York City student said:

> Violence has been a problem in our city for a long time, and in recent years it has spread to our schools. Some schools have even installed metal detectors hoping to stop violence. But weapons aren't the only problem. No metal detector on earth can stop people from bringing fear, prejudice, and conflict to school, and no metal detector can prevent students from bringing that fear, prejudice, and conflict back to the street at 3 P.M.*

---

* SOURCE: *Childhood Bullying and Teasing* by Dorothea M. Ross, Ph.D. (Alexandria, VA: American Counseling Association, 1996).

** Ibid.

*** SOURCE: *Set Straight on Bullies* by Stuart Greenbaum with Brenda Turner and Ronald D. Stephens (Malibu, CA: National School Safety Center, 1989).

---

* SOURCE: *Waging Peace in Our Schools* by Linda Lantieri and Janet Patti (Boston: Beacon Press, 1996).

7. WE CAN WORK TOGETHER TO FIND SOLUTIONS

Simply enrolling a victim in karate classes is not the answer. Because bullying has a variety of causes, we need to find a variety of ways to deal with it.

Obviously, many situations in which bullying occurs involve some sort of conflict. Young people (and their adult role models) need to learn conflict management and resolution skills, which can help stop these bullying problems from developing.

Schools can create an atmosphere where healthy choice-making is encouraged. "The new three R's" can make a difference in the school environment:*

- *Rules.* Parents and school personnel must demonstrate that they are in charge and won't tolerate any student hurting another student, either physically or psychologically.

- *Rights.* Every student has the right not to be hurt and the right to learn in a safe environment.

- *Responsibilities.* Educators must be responsible for better supervision and more observant monitoring. By eliminating fear from the lives of students, teachers are able to do their jobs more effectively. Also, students must be responsible for respecting the rights of their classmates and themselves.

The involvement of parents, teachers, administrators, students, and the community is essential in stopping bullying in schools. Research on school climate suggests that the principal is the single most important person to have involved in the program. School staff will follow the lead of an effective, motivated principal.** The larger the group of concerned parents, teachers, and community members, the better off the school will be.

In peer mediation, all students (or just a few, depending on the model) are trained to help students work out their differences by leading them through a series of steps or an outline. Here's one example of a series of mediation steps:

- *Relax.* Take a step back from the problem and admit how you feel.
- *Choose to solve the problem.* Let the other person know that you are ready to talk things through. Stay calm and don't make the problem worse.
- *Share your feelings.* Talk about the situation using "I statements." Be honest and specific about your feelings. Answer any questions the other person may have.
- *Listen.* Without interrupting, listen to the other person's point of view. When the other person is finished, you can ask a few simple questions to find out more.
- *Find a solution.* Together, agree on a way to solve the problem. Then put the plan into action.
- *Make a plan for the future.* Think of some better ways to handle the situation if it happens again. Agree to try one of these ideas next time.

Many modern conflict resolution programs stress peer mediation, a concept found in many cultures. In ancient China, people practiced the Confucian way of resolving disputes by using moral persuasion and agreement. In Japan, the village leader was expected to use mediation and conciliation to help community members

---

* SOURCE: *Set Straight on Bullies* by Stuart Greenbaum with Brenda Turner and Ronald D. Stephens (Malibu, CA: National School Safety Center, 1989) *(http://www.nssc1.org)*. Used with permission.

** SOURCE: *The Bullying Prevention Handbook* by John H. Hoover and Ronald Oliver (Bloomington, IN: National Education Service, 1996).

settle their disputes. In parts of Africa, a neighborhood meeting, or "moot," assembled, and a respected member helped disputants resolve their conflict without involving a judge.*

Holocaust survivor Victor Frankl saw the importance of taking responsibility for our own actions when he said, "Everything can be taken from us but one thing, which is the last of the human freedoms—to choose one's attitude in any given set of circumstances, to choose one's own way."

People who solve problems without resorting to violence seldom make the evening news. Getting along just isn't that exciting. But learning conflict resolution skills can increase a child's EQ ("emotional quotient"), which some experts claim is as essential to success as IQ. Assertiveness training, character education, and a consistent, organized approach to discipline are other important aspects that should be included in a bully prevention plan. Concerned adults *can* make a difference.

8. A COMPREHENSIVE PLAN WILL PRODUCE THE BEST RESULTS

An effective bullying prevention program will include short-term actions and activities that relate to long-term goals. Identifying specific areas for action helps educators recognize and address overlapping goals, conflicting messages, and missed opportunities. It can also suggest community partners that schools want or need to enlist.

Some state education departments have built plans around several key areas of the school environment that affect safety. These areas may include:

- school climate
- student monitoring and discipline

- policies and planning
- prevention and intervention programs
- leadership and staff development
- communications
- facilities
- transportation
- partnerships
- school neighborhood and community

The National Crime Prevention Council suggests building a program using these guidelines:*

- Establish Zero Tolerance policies for weapons and violence. Spell out penalties in advance. Adopt the motto "If it's illegal outside school, it's illegal inside." Educate students, parents, and staff about policies and penalties. Include a way for students to report crime-related information that does not expose them to retaliation.

- Establish a committee to develop a safe school plan. Include students, if you feel it's appropriate, and invite law enforcement officers to be part of your team. Policies and procedures for both day-to-day operations and crisis handling should cover such subjects as identifying who belongs in the building, avoiding accidents and incidents in corridors and on school grounds, reporting weapons or concerns about them, working in partnership with police, and following up to ensure that troubled students get help.

- Work with juvenile justice authorities and law enforcement officers on how violence, threats, potentially violent situations, and other crimes will be handled. Meet regularly to review problems and concerns. Develop a memorandum of understanding with law enforcement on access to the school building, reporting of crimes, arrests, and other key issues.

---

* SOURCE: *Reducing School Violence Through Conflict Resolution* by David W. Johnson and Robert T. Johnson (Alexandria, VA: ASCD, 1995).

* For a copy of the National Crime Prevention Council's *Safer Schools*, write or call: National Crime Prevention Council, 1700 K Street, NW, Second Floor, Washington, DC, 20006-3817; (202) 466-6272; toll-free telephone (orders only) 1-800-627-2911. On the Web, go to: *http://www.ncpc.org/*

- Offer training in anger management, stress relief, mediation, and related violence prevention skills to staff and teachers. Help them identify ways to pass these skills along to students. Make sure students are getting training.

- Involve every group within the school community—faculty, professional staff, custodial staff, students, and others—in setting up solutions to violence. Keep lines of communication open to all kinds of student groups and cliques.

- Develop ways to make it easier for parents to be involved. Provide lists of volunteer opportunities; ask parents to organize phone trees; hold events on weekends as well as weeknights. Offer child care for younger children.

- Work with community groups and law enforcement officials to create safe corridors for travel to and from school. Help with efforts to identify and eliminate neighborhood trouble spots.

- Reward good behavior. Acknowledging students who do the right thing—whether it's settling an argument without violence, helping another student, or apologizing for bumping into someone—helps raise the tone for the whole school.

- Insist that your faculty and staff treat each other and students the way they want to be treated—with respect, courtesy, and thoughtfulness. Be the chief role model.

- Develop relationships with health care, mental health, counseling, and social work resources in your community. Make sure that teachers, counselors, coaches, and other adults in the school know how to connect a needy student with available resources.

- Ensure that students learn violence prevention techniques throughout their school experience. Don't make it a one-time thing. Include the training in an array of subjects. Draw from established, tested curricula whenever possible.

- Consider establishing policies such as mandatory storage of outerwear in lockers (to reduce chances of weapons concealment), mesh or clear backpacks and duffel bags (to increase visibility of contraband), and limited entry to the building (to reduce inappropriate visitors).

9. CHILDREN AT RISK CAN BE HELPED

Effective schools recognize the potential in every student to overcome difficult experiences and to control negative emotions. Adults in these school communities use their knowledge of early warning signs to address problems before they escalate into physical or emotional violence. These warning signs (which may be exhibited by bullies or their victims) include:*

- *Social withdrawal.* In some situations, gradual and eventually complete withdrawal from social contacts can be an important indicator of a troubled child. The withdrawal often stems from feelings of depression, rejection, persecution, unworthiness, and lack of confidence.

- *Excessive feelings of isolation and being alone.* Research has shown that the majority of children who are isolated and appear to be friendless are not violent. In fact, these feelings are sometimes characteristic of children and youth who may be troubled, withdrawn, or have internal issues that hinder development of social affiliations. However, research also has shown that in some cases feelings of isolation and not having friends are associated with children who behave aggressively and violently.

- *Being a victim of violence.* Children who are victims of violence—including physical

* SOURCE: *Early Warning, Timely Response* by K. Dwyer, D. Osher, and C. Warger (Washington, DC: U.S. Department of Education, 1998).

or sexual abuse—in the community, at school, or at home are sometimes at risk of becoming violent toward themselves or others.

- *Feelings of being picked on and persecuted.* The youth who feels constantly picked on, teased, bullied, singled out for ridicule, and humiliated at home or at school may initially withdraw socially. If not given adequate support in addressing these feelings, some children may vent them in inappropriate ways—including possible aggression or violence.

- *Excessive feelings of rejection.* In the process of growing up and in the course of adolescent development, many young people experience emotionally painful rejection. Children who are troubled often are isolated from their mentally healthy peers. Their responses to rejection will depend on many background factors. Without support, they may be at risk of expressing their emotional distress in negative ways—including violence. Some aggressive children who are rejected by nonaggressive peers seek out aggressive friends who, in turn, reinforce their violent tendencies.

- *Low school interest and poor academic performance.* Poor school achievement can be the result of many factors. It is important to consider if a drastic change in performance and/or poor performance becomes a chronic condition that limits the child's capacity to learn. In some situations—such as when the low achiever feels frustrated, unworthy, chastised, and denigrated—acting out and aggressive behaviors may occur. It is important to determine the emotional and cognitive reasons for the academic performance change to understand the true nature of the problem.

- *Expression of violence in writings and drawings.* Children and youth often express themselves in their drawings and in stories, poetry, and other written expressive forms. Many children produce work about violent themes that for the most part is harmless when taken in context. However, an over-representation of violence in writings and drawings that is directed at specific individuals (family members, peers, other adults) consistently over time may signal emotional problems and the potential for violence. Because there is a real danger in misdiagnosing such a sign, it is important to seek the guidance of a qualified professional—such as a school psychologist, counselor, or other mental health specialist—to determine its meaning.

- *Uncontrolled anger.* Everyone gets angry; anger is a natural emotion. However, anger that is expressed frequently and intensely in response to minor irritants may signal potential violent behavior.

- *Patterns of impulsive and chronic hitting, intimidating, and bullying behaviors.* Children often engage in acts of shoving and mild aggression. However, some mildly aggressive behaviors such as constant hitting and bullying of others that occur early in children's lives, if left unattended, might later escalate into more serious behaviors.

- *History of discipline problems.* Chronic behavior and disciplinary problems both in school and at home may suggest that underlying emotional needs are not being met. These unmet needs may be shown in acting out and aggressive behaviors. These problems may set the stage for the child to violate norms and rules, defy authority, disengage from school, and engage in aggressive behaviors with other children and adults.

- *History of violent and aggressive behavior.* Unless provided with support and counseling, a youth who has a history of aggressive or violent behavior is likely to repeat those behaviors. Aggressive and violent acts may be directed toward other individuals, be expressed in cruelty to animals, or include fire setting. Young people who show an early pattern of antisocial behavior frequently and across multiple settings are particularly at risk for future aggressive and antisocial behavior. Similarly, youth who engage in overt behaviors such as bullying, generalized aggression and defiance, and covert behaviors such as stealing, vandalism, lying, cheating, and fire setting also are at risk for more serious aggressive behavior. Research suggests that age of onset may be a key factor in interpreting early warning signs. For example, children who engage in aggression and drug abuse at an early age (before age twelve) are more likely to show violence later on than are children who begin such behavior at an older age. In the presence of such signs it is important to review the child's history with behavioral experts and seek parents' observations and insights.

- *Intolerance for differences and prejudicial attitudes.* All children have likes and dislikes. However, an intense prejudice toward others based on racial, ethnic, religious, language, gender, sexual orientation, ability, and physical appearance—when coupled with other factors—may lead to violent assaults against those who are perceived to be different. Membership in hate groups or the willingness to victimize individuals with disabilities or health problems also should be treated as early warning signs.

- *Drug use and alcohol use.* Apart from being unhealthy behaviors, drug use and alcohol use reduces self-control and exposes children and youth to violence, either as perpetrators, as victims, or both.

- *Affiliation with gangs.* Gangs that support antisocial values and behaviors—including extortion, intimidation, and acts of violence toward other students—cause fear and stress among other students. Youth who are influenced by these groups—those who emulate and copy their behavior, as well as those who become affiliated with them—may adopt these values and act in violent or aggressive ways in certain situations. Gang-related violence and turf battles are common occurrences tied to the

use of drugs that often result in injury and/or death.

- *Inappropriate access to, possession of, and use of firearms.* Children and youth who inappropriately possess or have access to firearms can have an increased risk for violence. Research shows that such youngsters also have a higher probability of becoming victims. Families can reduce inappropriate access and use by restricting, monitoring, and supervising children's access to firearms and other weapons. Children who have a history of aggression, impulsiveness, or other emotional problems should not have access to firearms and other weapons.

- *Serious threats of violence.* Idle threats are a common response to frustration. Alternatively, one of the most reliable indicators that a young person is likely to commit a dangerous act toward self or others is a detailed and specific threat to use violence. Recent incidents across the country clearly indicate that threats to commit violence against oneself or others should be taken very seriously. Steps must be taken to understand the nature of these threats and to prevent them from being carried out.

When warning signs indicate that danger is imminent, safety must always be the first and foremost consideration. Take action immediately. Emergency intervention by school authorities and possibly law enforcement officers is needed when a child:

- has presented a detailed plan (time, place, method) to harm or kill others—particularly if the child has a history of aggression or has attempted to carry out threats in the past

- is carrying a weapon, particularly a firearm, and has threatened to use it.*

---

* SOURCE: *Early Warning, Timely Response* by K. Dwyer, D. Osher, and C. Warger (Washington, DC: U.S. Department of Education, 1998).

In situations where students present other threatening behaviors, parents should be informed of the concerns immediately. School communities also have the responsibility to seek assistance from appropriate agencies, such as child and family services and community mental health. These responses should reflect school board policies and be consistent with the violence prevention and response plan.

Effective school communities support staff, students, and families in understanding the early warning signs. Support strategies include having:

- school board policies in place that support training and ongoing consultation. The entire school community knows how to identify early warning signs, and understands the principles that support them.

- school leaders who encourage others to raise concerns about observed early warning signs and to report all observations of imminent warning signs immediately. This is in addition to school district policies that sanction and promote the identification of early warning signs.

- easy access to a team of specialists trained in evaluating and addressing serious behavioral and academic concerns.

Each school community should develop a procedure that students and staff can follow when reporting their concerns about a child who exhibits early warning signs. For example, in many schools the principal is the first point of contact. In cases that do not pose immediate danger, the principal contacts a school psychologist or other qualified professional, who takes responsibility for addressing the concern immediately. If the concern is determined to be serious—but poses no immediate danger—the child's family should be contacted.

The family should be consulted before implementing any interventions with the child. In cases where school-based factors are determined to be causing or worsening the child's troubling behavior, the school should act quickly to modify them.

10. SCHOOLS ARE RESPONSIBLE FOR PROTECTING STUDENTS

Children cannot learn effectively if they fear for their safety. Troubled young people—both bullies and victims—need a supportive environment to learn and grow. In the words of Dr. Dan Olweus, "Every individual should have the right to be spared oppression and repeated, intentional humiliation, in school and in society at large."

Federal and state legislation is helping to support the idea of bully free schools. Some experts have suggested that prevention of bullying may become a legal obligation of schools.* Part of President Clinton's "Call to Action for American Education in the 21st Century" (delivered to Congress on February 4, 1997, as part of the State of the Union address) calls for "strong, safe schools with clear standards of achievement and discipline." The Clinton administration strongly encourages a Zero Tolerance policy for classroom violence and weapons in school.

The Gun Free Schools Act requires that each state receiving federal funds under the Elementary and Secondary Education Act (ESEA) must have put in effect, by October 1995, a state law requiring local educational agencies to expel from school for a period of not less than one year a student who is determined to have brought a firearm to school.

Each state's law also must allow the chief administering officer of the local educational agency to modify the expulsion requirement on a case-by-case basis. All local educational agencies receiving ESEA funds must have a policy that requires the referral of any student who brings a firearm to school to the criminal justice or juvenile justice system.

---

* SOURCE: *The Bullying Prevention Handbook* by John H. Hoover and Ronald Oliver (Bloomington, IN: National Education Service, 1996).

CREATING A
POSITIVE CLASSROOM

Our classroom is a place where...
1. We all feel respected.
2. We all work together.
3. We accept our differences.

The tips and strategies in this section will help you create a classroom environment where everyone feels safe, accepted, and appreciated. In a positive classroom, students can learn, teachers can teach, and education—not behavior—is the focus.

As you try these ideas with your students, your classroom environment will change for the better. If you *don't* have a bully problem, you'll be making sure that one doesn't develop down the road. If you *do* have a bully problem, you'll be taking concrete actions to reduce and ultimately eliminate most of the negative attitudes, actions, and perceptions that have caused it and sustain it.

These tips and strategies benefit everyone. Here are some good things you can expect to happen along the way:

Your students will learn how to:

- think and talk positively about themselves and others
- notice similarities and appreciate differences
- work together
- treat each other with kindness and respect
- give each other support and encouragement
- respond to bullying in ways that work
- resolve conflicts appropriately and effectively
- build empathy and realize that other people have feelings, wants, and needs that are just as real and valid as their own.

You'll discover how to:

- clearly communicate a zero-tolerance policy for bullying in your classroom
- reinforce your students' positive behaviors
- get to know and understand your students even better
- treat your students with greater kindness and respect
- model accepting, appropriate behavior in all kinds of situations
- teach your students skills that will help them resolve conflicts, affirm themselves and each other, manage anger, make friends, and be more assertive.

EXPOSE THE MYTHS

There are many myths about bullying. The "True or False?" handout (page 17) will expose some of the myths and start students thinking about what bullying is and how it affects everyone. Answers with brief explanations are given on page 18.

You might read the answers aloud, and/or have students come up with their own reasons why each statement is a myth. Allow time for discussion. Make copies of the answers to give to students during or after the discussion.

DEFINE BULLYING

Before you can solve (or prevent) a problem, you first have to define it. If you and your students did the "Expose the Myths" activity (above), everyone should have a general idea of what bullying *isn't*. (It isn't "just teasing," "normal," a "boy thing," etc.) You also want your students to agree on what it *is*. The process of defining it will help you arrive at a shared understanding and common language about bullying.

You might do this as a class, or divide the class into small groups and give them 10 minutes to work on a definition. Each group can choose one person to write down the group's ideas, and another to read the group's definition aloud when the class reconvenes.

Write students' definitions on the chalkboard. Then work together to come up with a class definition of bullying. Here are some concepts you can introduce into the discussion to keep students on track:

- Bullying takes at least two people: the bully and the victim.
- Bullies like to feel strong and superior.
- Bullies enjoy having power over others.
- Bullies use their power to hurt other people.

Your class definition might use different words but should include these basic ideas:

> **Bullying is when a stronger, more powerful person hurts or frightens a smaller or weaker person deliberately (on purpose) and repeatedly (again and again).**

You might write the class definition on the chalkboard and leave it there indefinitely. Or have students write the definition in the notebook they use in your class.

BUILD ACCEPTANCE

When students accept each other, they are less likely to bully each other and more likely to defend victims of bullying. Here are three ways you can build acceptance in your classroom.

ACCEPTANCE STATEMENTS

Work with your class to come up with a list of "acceptance statements" everyone (or most) can agree on. (*Example:* "We are all unique. Our differences make us interesting.") Have students make posters, collages, bulletin boards, or displays illustrating the statements.

ACCEPTANCE PROJECTS

Ask your class to brainstorm ways to help people become more accepting of each other. What do they think everyone should know? How can they get their message across? Through songs? Skits? Stories? Poems? Posters? Announcements over the P.A. system? Articles in the school paper?

Let your students make the important decisions about what types of projects to do. Be available to offer support and advice (and to suggest alternatives to projects that are clearly inappropriate), but try to let your students go wherever their creativity takes them. They might work individually or in small groups.

TRUE OR FALSE?

1. Bullying is just teasing.   T   F

2. Some people deserve to be bullied.   T   F

3. Only boys are bullies.   T   F

4. People who complain about bullies are babies.   T   F

5. Bullying is a normal part of growing up.   T   F

6. Bullies will go away if you ignore them.   T   F

7. All bullies have low self-esteem.   T   F
    That's why they pick on other people.

8. It's tattling to tell an adult when you're being bullied.   T   F

9. The best way to deal with a bully   T   F
    is by fighting or trying to get even.

10. People who are bullied might hurt for a while,   T   F
    but they'll get over it.

Answers to TRUE OR FALSE?

1. Bullying is just teasing. **FALSE**

Bullying is much more than teasing. While many bullies tease, others use violence, intimidation, and other tactics. Sometimes teasing can be fun; bullying *always* hurts.

2. Some people deserve to be bullied. **FALSE**

No one ever deserves to be bullied. No one "asks for it." Most bullies tease people who are "different" in some way. Being different is not a reason to be bullied.

3. Only boys are bullies. **FALSE**

It seems that *most* bullies are boys, but girls can be bullies, too.

4. People who complain about bullies are babies. **FALSE**

People who complain about bullies are standing up for their right not to be bullied. They're more grown-up than the bullies are.

5. Bullying is a normal part of growing up. **FALSE**

Getting teased, picked on, pushed around, threatened, harassed, insulted, hurt, and abused is *not* normal. Plus if you *think* it's normal, you're less likely to say or do anything about it, which gives bullies the green light to keep bullying.

6. Bullies will go away if you ignore them. **TRUE** and **FALSE**

Some bullies might go away. But others will get angry and keep bullying until they get a reaction. That's what they want.

7. All bullies have low self-esteem. That's why they pick on other people. **FALSE**

Some bullies have *high* self-esteem. They feel good about themselves, and picking on other people makes them feel even better. Most of the time, bullying isn't about high or low self-esteem. It's about having power over other people.

8. It's tattling to tell an adult when you're being bullied. **FALSE**

It's smart to tell an adult who can help you do something about the bullying. It's also smart to tell an adult if you see someone else being bullied.

9. The best way to deal with a bully is by fighting or trying to get even. **FALSE**

If you fight with a bully, you might get hurt (and hurt someone else). Plus you might get into trouble for fighting. If you try to get even, you're acting the same as the bully. And the bully might come after you again to get even with *you*. Either way only makes things worse.

10. People who are bullied might hurt for a while, but they'll get over it. **FALSE**

Bullying hurts for a long time. Some kids have dropped out of school because of bullying. Some became so sad, desperate, afraid, and hopeless that they committed suicide. Many adults can remember times when they were bullied as children. People don't "get over" being bullied.

When the projects are finished, show them off at an open house or Parents' Night. Invite family members, other teachers, and members of the community and the media to see what your students have accomplished and how they feel about acceptance.

"OUR CLASSROOM IS A PLACE WHERE . . ."

Distribute copies of the handout "Our Classroom Is a Place Where . . ." (page 20) and discuss each statement. If students agree with the statements, they can sign and date their handouts. Post them around the room to show that your classroom is a place where people accept each other.

 Go farther: Send copies of the handout home so students can share them with their families.

When it's time to take down the handouts display, make a poster-sized copy of the original handout, hang it on a wall in your classroom, and leave it there. Refer to it often throughout the year. Discuss it with your students, with parents and caregivers at conferences, and with visitors to your classroom.

TALK ABOUT BULLYING

Have a class discussion about bullying. You might use the questions that follow. *But first:* Tell students not to name names or point fingers. This should be a *general* discussion, not a time for blaming or accusing.

1. Who can tell me what bullying is?

   If you and your students did the "Define Bullying" activity (page 16), someone can read the class definition.

2. What happens to people who are bullied? How do you think they feel?

3. How do you think bullies feel?

4. What happens to people who are around bullies and victims? What's it like to see someone get bullied? How does that make you feel?

5. Is there anyone who thinks bullying is a problem in our school? What makes you think that?

6. Is there anyone who thinks bullying is a problem in our classroom? What makes you think that?

7. Who would like to have a bully free classroom?

8. What would it take to make our classroom bully free? Who has ideas for doing this?

 Go farther: Write students' ideas on the chalkboard. Then have them vote for the top 5. Try their ideas for a week or two. Let students assess their own progress toward making your classroom bully free.

SHARE FACTS ABOUT BULLYING

If bullying is a problem in your classroom or school, you're not alone. Share and discuss these facts with your students:*

- About *one in seven* schoolchildren is either a bully or a victim. (To illustrate this, you might have your students count off by sevens. Every seventh student can come to the front of the room or stay standing.)

- Bullying affects about 5 *million* elementary and junior high students in the United States.

- Ten to fifteen percent of *all* children report being bullied on a regular basis.

---

* SOURCES: National Association of School Psychologists (NASP); *Education Week;* National Crime Prevention Council.

We don't all have to be the same.

We don't all have to think the same.

WE DON'T ALL HAVE TO ACT THE SAME.

We don't all have to talk the same.

We don't all have to dress the same.

We don't all have to believe the same things.

WE HAVE THE RIGHT TO BE OURSELVES.

We like it that people are different.

We know that our differences
make us interesting and UNIQUE.

We honor different ways of being, acting,
and believing—even when we don't agree with them.

We do our best to solve problems peacefully.

We speak up if we see others being treated unfairly.

We treat each other the way we'd like to be treated.

We treat each other with respect.

- Bullying is more than beating people up. There are three basic types of bullying: physical, verbal, and emotional. Most bullying is verbal.

- Most bullying happens at school where there is little or no supervision. *Examples:* on the playgrounds, in the hallways, in the cafeteria and bathrooms.

- Bullying hurts everyone. *Victims* feel sad, afraid, anxious, and bad about themselves. They may have social problems (a hard time making friends), emotional problems (low self-esteem, loneliness), and academic problems (their schoolwork suffers). *Witnesses* (people who see or hear others being bullied) may feel afraid and anxious. *Bullies* often get into serious trouble as adults; statistics show that one in four bullies will have a criminal record before the age of 30, and many have problems with relationships throughout their lives.

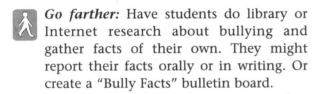 *Go farther:* Have students do library or Internet research about bullying and gather facts of their own. They might report their facts orally or in writing. Or create a "Bully Facts" bulletin board.

NAME BULLYING BEHAVIORS

What do bullies do? Your students—whether victims or bullies—probably know the answer(s) to this question. Ask them and list their responses on the chalkboard. Your list might include several (or all) of the following. If your students focus mostly on physical bullying (hitting, kicking, etc.), introduce some of the other behaviors listed here (act rude, embarrass people, ignore people, etc.). Students need to understand that bullying encompasses a broad spectrum of behaviors, none of which are "normal" or acceptable.

- act like they rule the world
- act mean
- act rude
- attack people
- boss people around
- brag about being tough
- break people's things
- carry weapons
- cheat
- damage people's things
- embarrass people
- force people to hand over their money
- force people to hand over their possessions
- frighten people
- gossip
- harass people
- haze people
- hit
- humiliate people
- hurt people's feelings
- ignore people
- insult people
- intimidate people
- kick
- laugh at people
- make fun of people
- make obscene gestures
- make racist or sexist comments
- make people feel helpless
- make people feel inferior
- make people feel invisible
- leave people out
- lie
- make people do things they don't want to do
- make people feel uncomfortable
- name-call
- pick on or attack people because of their race, religion, gender, family background, culture, etc.
- pick on or attack people because they're different in some way
- push
- put people down
- refuse to talk to people
- reject people
- say nasty things about people
- say sarcastic things to people

- scare people
- scream
- shove
- spread rumors
- steal
- swear
- take people's things
- taunt
- tease
- tell mean jokes
- threaten
- touch people in rude or abusive ways
- use physical violence
- use verbal taunts
- write nasty things about people
- yell

 Go farther: Turn the list into a class pledge. Provide an extra-large piece of posterboard or butcher paper, markers, magazines (for cutting out pictures), tape, glue, scissors, etc. Write across the top in big letters: "As a class, we pledge NOT to. . . ." Then let students add words, phrases, illustrations, pictures, etc. to create a colorful poster for your classroom wall—or the hall outside your classroom. They can all sign their names across the bottom.

SHARE STORIES ABOUT BULLYING

Distribute copies of the handout "Bullying Stories" (page 23). Tell your students that they will use the handouts to write about their own experiences with bullying—as someone who was bullied; as someone who bullied another person; as someone who witnessed a bullying incident and did nothing about it; and as someone who witnessed a bullying incident and either got help or tried to stop it.

Call attention to the "No Names Rule" at the top of the handout. If some students don't understand how they can tell their stories without using names, give examples. ("Someone called me a bad name." "I knocked someone's books off his desk on purpose." "I saw one person trip another, but I didn't say anything." "I told someone to stop pushing my friend.")

Divide the class into small groups (no more than 5 students each).

 Important: If you're aware that one student in your classroom has been bullying another, make sure those two students aren't in the same group.

Allow quiet time for students to write their stories. Then allow time for them to share their stories within their groups. Reconvene the class and ask a spokesperson from each group to briefly summarize the stories.

Have a class discussion about the stories. You might ask questions like these:

- Did we hear stories about people getting bullied? How did those stories make you feel?

- Did we hear stories about people bullying others? How did those stories make you feel?

- If you saw or heard someone being bullied, what would you do?

- Did we hear good ways to stop bullying or get help? Are there any ideas you might try if you see or hear someone being bullied in the future?

You might end by saying, "To all of you who saw or heard bullying and did something about it—congratulations! You're Bully Busters!"

TAKE A SURVEY

How much bullying goes on in your classroom, and what kinds? You've probably noticed specific instances, and students might have told you about others. But most bullying goes *unnoticed* and *unreported.*

BULLYING STORIES

Use the spaces below to write about experiences from your life.
NO NAMES RULE: Don't use anybody's name.

Describe a time when someone's words or behavior hurt you.	Describe a time when you said or did something to hurt another person.
Describe a time when you saw/heard bullying but didn't do anything about it.	Describe a time when you saw/heard bullying and either got help or tried to stop it.

It goes unnoticed because:

- Bullies tend to hurt or abuse others when adults aren't around to see it.
- Bullies act in ways that adults aren't aware of or don't notice.

It goes unreported because:

- Victims are ashamed of being bullied, afraid of retaliation, or worried that adults can't or won't help them.
- Witnesses don't want to get involved, or they don't interpret what they're seeing as bullying, but as "teasing" or "normal" or "kids being kids" behavior.

If you want to know what's happening in your classroom, ask your students. One of the best, simplest, least intimidating ways to do this is by taking a survey.

You might use one or both of the surveys on pages 26–30. Or invite your students, their parents, and other teachers and staff to help you create a survey. If your school or district is using a bully prevention program, a survey instrument might already exist.

The primary purpose of the surveys on pages 26–30 is to gather information about the types of experiences your students are having, not to point fingers at specific individuals. If you want a survey to help you identify students who are being bullied, have students write their names on it. Otherwise, keep it anonymous. When you ask students to sign their names, some might be reluctant to admit to certain items. Anonymity might lead to more honest responses.

Depending on your students' age(s) and reading level(s), you might want to read a survey aloud. Some students might need individual assistance completing the survey.

Give each student as much privacy as possible when completing a survey. Tell students that the survey *isn't* a test (they won't be graded), but it's *like* a test in two important ways: No looking at anyone else's survey. No talking during the survey.

ABOUT "THIS WEEK IN SCHOOL" (pages 26–27)

This survey describes things that might happen to a student during a typical week. About half of the things described are pleasant or neutral; about half are unpleasant. This keeps the focus on students' experiences in general, not just bullying.

Introduce the survey with a brief explanation. *Example:*

> "This checklist lists things that might or might not happen to you in school. Like: 'This week in school, another student in my class called me names.' Or: 'This week in school, another student in my class said something nice to me.' Read each statement and think about the past week. How often did this happen to you? Never? Once? More than once? Answer by putting a checkmark in that column."

Since the survey asks about "this week," it's best to give it on a Friday. If your students are very young, you might want to ask them what happened to them yesterday or even today; their memories of an entire week might be sketchy or inaccurate.

Use the survey as is or adapt it to meet the needs of your students. If you adapt it, make sure to include a balance of positive, neutral, and negative items. Also make sure to include these six key statements:

4. tried to kick me
8. said they'd beat me up
10. tried to make me give them money
23. tried to hurt me
36. tried to break something of mine
38. tried to hit me

For these six statements:

- Add up the number of times a checkmark was placed under "more than once." Do this separately for each statement. (*Example:* For "4. tried to kick me," 3 students said "more than once.")

- Divide the score for each statement by the number of surveys completed to get the percentage of student responses. (*Example:* 3 students divided by 25 in the class = 12%.)

- Add all six percentages. (*Example:* 12 + 8 + 12 + 20 + 5 + 10 = 67%.)

- Divide this number by six. (*Example:* 67 divided by 6 = 11.16%.)

This gives you an idea of how many students in your classroom are being bullied or at risk of being bullied.

You can do the same math for checkmarks placed under "once" for the six key statements. This gives you an idea of the level of aggression in your classroom.

The survey asks students to indicate their gender. You'll probably notice gender differences when you look at the results. The six key statements have a bias toward physical bullying, which seems to be more common among boys. If you want to get a sense of bullying among girls, pay special attention to girls' responses to these six statements:

1. called me names
6. was mean to me because I'm different
34. laughed at me in a way that hurt my feelings
35. said they would tell on me
37. told a lie about me
39. made me feel bad about myself

ABOUT THE "BULLYING SURVEY" (pages 28–30)

You might give this survey to the whole class, use it to interview individual students you suspect of being bullied, or use it to interview small groups of students to get a feeling for what types of bullying and how much goes on in your classroom.

Introduce the survey with a brief explanation. *Example:*

"Bullying is when a stronger, more powerful person hurts or frightens a smaller or weaker person deliberately (on purpose) and repeatedly (again and again). Often, students who are bullied don't tell other people about it. They feel bad inside, or they're afraid that the bully might get back at them for telling, or they're worried that no one will help them if they tell.

"Everyone has a right not to be bullied. No one deserves to be bullied. This survey is a safe way to tell me if you're being bullied at school. You don't have to give anyone's name. You don't even have to sign it unless you want to. If you do sign it, I'll arrange to talk with you in private. So you can answer the questions honestly."

Use this survey as is or adapt it to meet the needs of your students. For example, you might want to:

- limit it to questions about bullying in your classroom (skipping those about recess, lunch, the bathroom, and the halls)

- expand it with questions about bullying on the way to and from school (at the bus stop, on the bus, while walking or biking, etc.), at school-sponsored events (sporting events, assemblies, fairs, concerts, club meetings, etc.), and elsewhere in the school building or on the grounds (in the locker room, between buildings, in the gym, etc.)

- add questions about specific types of bullying (teasing, name-calling, pushing, shoving, hitting, kicking, shouting, tripping, intimidating, ignoring, rejecting, threatening, taking possessions, excluding, swearing, spreading rumors, lying, harassing, etc.)

- gather additional demographic information (race, ethnic background, religion, etc.) to try to determine whether bullies are targeting a particular group of students.

THIS WEEK IN SCHOOL

Read each statement and think about the past week. Put a checkmark in the column that describes how often that happened to you during the week. When you're through with the checklist, give it to the teacher.

Today's date: _____

Check this box if you're a boy ☐   Check this box if you're a girl ☐

This week in school, another student in my class:	Never	Once	More than once
1. called me names			
2. said something nice to me			
3. said something rude or mean about my family			
4. tried to kick me			
5. treated me with kindness and respect			
6. was mean to me because I'm different			
7. gave me a present			
8. said they'd beat me up			
9. gave me some money			
10. tried to make me give them money			
11. tried to scare me			
12. loaned me something I wanted to borrow			
13. stopped me from playing a game			
14. was mean about something I did			
15. talked about clothes with me			
16. told me a joke			
17. told me a lie			
18. got other kids to gang up on me			

CONTINUED →

This week in school, another student in my class:	Never	Once	More than once
19. tried to make me hurt someone else			
20. smiled at me			
21. tried to get me in trouble			
22. helped me carry something			
23. tried to hurt me			
24. helped me with my schoolwork			
25. made me do something I didn't want to do			
26. talked about TV with me			
27. took something away from me			
28. shared something with me			
29. said something rude or mean about the color of my skin			
30. shouted at me			
31. played a game with me			
32. tried to trip me			
33. talked with me about things I like			
34. laughed at me in a way that hurt my feelings			
35. said they would tell on me			
36. tried to break something of mine			
37. told a lie about me			
38. tried to hit me			
39. made me feel bad about myself			
40. made me feel good about myself			

BULLYING SURVEY

Read each question and answer it as honestly as you can.
Keep this definition in mind when answering the questions:

BULLYING IS WHEN A STRONGER, MORE POWERFUL PERSON
HURTS OR FRIGHTENS A SMALLER OR WEAKER PERSON DELIBERATELY
(ON PURPOSE) AND REPEATEDLY (AGAIN AND AGAIN).

Today's date: _____

Your name (if you want to give it): _____

Check this box if you're a boy ☐   Check this box if you're a girl ☐

1. Is anyone mean to you when you're in our classroom?   yes ☐   no ☐
   If *yes,* what do they do to you?_____
   _____
   _____

   How often does this happen? (Once a day? Twice a day? Several times a day? Once a week? Once a month?) Your answer:
   _____

2. Is anyone mean to you at recess?   yes ☐   no ☐
   If *yes,* what do they do to you?_____
   _____
   _____

   How often?_____

3. Is anyone mean to you at lunch?   yes ☐   no ☐
   If *yes,* what do they do to you?_____
   _____
   _____

   How often?_____

CONTINUED →

4. Is anyone mean to you in the bathroom?   yes ☐   no ☐

If *yes*, what do they do to you?_____

_____

_____

How often?_____

5. Is anyone mean to you in the halls?   yes ☐   no ☐

If *yes*, what do they do to you?_____

_____

_____

How often?_____

6. Without naming the bully (or bullies), describe him or her by checking statements in this list:

The bully is . . .

☐ about my age   ☐ younger than me   ☐ a girl

☐ older than me   ☐ a boy   ☐ a whole group

☐ what else?_____

7. Have you ever told anyone at school that you're being bullied?   yes ☐   no ☐

If *no*, why don't you tell someone?_____

_____

If *yes*, who did you tell?_____

_____

What did the person do to help you?_____

_____

After you told, did the bullying stop?   yes ☐   no ☐

After you told, did the bullying get worse?   yes ☐   no ☐

CONTINUED →

8. How has the bullying affected you personally? Has it changed your life in any way? Think about how you feel (good? okay? bad? sick? scared?); how you feel about yourself; how you're doing in school; who your friends are; and anything else you think might relate to being bullied.

_____

_____

_____

9. How long have you been bullied? (A week or less? Two or three weeks? A month? A few months? Half a year? A year? More than a year? A few years? Many years? Your whole life?) Your answer:

_____

10. Have you ever bullied someone else?   yes ☐   no ☐

If *yes*, what did you do?_____

_____

Why did you do it? _____

_____

How did it make you feel?_____

_____

11. Are you bullying anyone now?   yes ☐   no ☐

If *yes*, would you like to stop?   yes ☐   no ☐

12. What can we do to stop or prevent bullying in our classroom?

_____

_____

_____

_____

_____

SET RULES

Establish and enforce class rules about bullying and behavior. Rules clearly communicate a zero tolerance for bullying and an expectation of positive behavior. They also meet students' physical and psychological needs for safety; it's hard to learn when you're intimidated, threatened, and scared, or when you're a witness to intimidating, threatening, and scary behavior.

For rules to be effective, they should be:

- created with student input
- short and simple
- easy to understand
- specific
- agreed upon and accepted by everyone
- enforceable
- enforced consistently and fairly
- communicated to and supported by parents, other teachers, and staff
- reviewed periodically and updated when needed

Note: If your school or district has already established rules about bullying and behavior, share these with your students. If the language seems too complicated, have students put the rules in their own words.

If you're free to make your own class rules, get everyone involved. Have a class discussion or break up into small groups. Ask students to come up with answers to these questions:

- What kind of classroom do you want to have?
- What can everyone do to make this happen?

When students set their own rules (instead of being told to follow rules imposed by adults), they learn to manage their own behaviors. Work together to come up with a list of rules; depending on the age of your students, you might limit the total number to 5 or 10 (the fewer the better). *Examples:*

1. **Bullying is not allowed in our classroom.**
2. **We don't tease, call names, or put people down.**
3. **We don't hit, shove, kick, or punch.**
4. **If we see someone being bullied, we speak up and stop it (if we can) or go for help right away.**
5. **When we do things as a group, we make sure that everyone is included and no one is left out.**
6. **We make new students feel welcome.**
7. **We listen to each other's opinions.**
8. **We treat each other with kindness and respect.**
9. **We respect each other's property. (School property, too.)**
10. **We look for the good in others and value differences.**

You might write the rules on a poster headed "Our Class Rules" and have everyone sign their names.

What will be the consequences of breaking the rules, and how can you enforce them? This might depend on existing school or district rules. Or work with your class to determine fair and reasonable consequences.

Post the rules in your classroom where everyone can see them. For a time, you might start each day by reading the rules aloud (or having a student read them). Once you feel confident that your students know the rules—and you've seen evidence that they're following them—you can read them weekly. Every month or so, review the rules with your class to see if any changes are needed. Don't hesitate to revise the rules. Tell your class that the rules aren't written in stone and there's always room for improvement.

Go farther: Communicate the rules and consequences to parents in a letter home, and share them with other teachers and staff.

DESIGNATE YOUR CLASSROOM BULLY FREE

If you and your students did the "Talk About Bullying" activity (page 19), chances are they all agreed that they would like to have a bully free classroom (question #7).

Ask if they're willing to designate their classroom bully free—a place where people accept each other, value each other, and treat each other with kindness and respect. If they are, brainstorm ways to formalize and publicize your class commitment. *Examples:*

1. Make a poster or banner announcing "This Is a Bully Free Classroom." Display it in the hall outside the classroom.*

2. If your class publishes a newsletter or newspaper, devote an issue to the topic of what it means to be a bully free classroom. Invite students to write articles, draw cartoons, do interviews, etc.

3. Write a press release announcing that your classroom has decided to be bully free. Send it to your local media (newspapers, magazines, radio stations, TV stations). They might follow up with a story about your students.

 Go farther: Have students visit other classrooms and encourage them to become bully free. They can also meet with the principal, explain what your class is doing, and ask him or her to announce that your whole school is committed to being bully free.

---

* If you like, you can order a big, bright "Bully Free Classroom" poster that looks like the cover of this book. Contact Free Spirit Publishing at 1-800-735-7323 for ordering information. See the poster on the ad page near the back of the book.

TEACH ANGER MANAGEMENT SKILLS

What happens to most of us when we're in danger or under stress? We experience the "fight-or-flight" response. We battle the cause of the danger we perceive or the stress we experience . . . or we run as fast as we can to get away.

When students are bullied, running away is an option; sometimes it's the only option. Your students need to know that fighting is not an option, except in cases where self-defense is essential.

What can they do instead of fighting or trying to hurt someone back? They can learn and practice other ways to manage their anger.

Distribute copies of the handout "20 Things to Do Instead of Hurting Someone Back" (page 33) and go over it with the students. Explain that this handout gives them 20 *different* ways to manage their anger. Ask if they know other ways that work, and list them on the chalkboard.

 Go farther: The National Center for Violence Prevention has many excellent resources available on anger management. Several are listed in "Resources" at the end of this book (pages 149–161). Or you can contact the Center and request a catalog. Write or call: The National Center for Violence Prevention, PO Box 9, 102 Highway 81 North, Calhoun, KY 42327-0009; toll-free telephone 1-800-962-6662.

RESPOND EFFECTIVELY TO REPORTS OF BULLYING

Much (even most) bullying occurs where adults can't see it and intervene. Bullies don't want adult audiences. You need to rely on students for information about bullying you don't witness personally. How can you encourage them

20 THINGS TO DO INSTEAD OF HURTING SOMEONE BACK

When someone hurts you, it's normal to feel angry. You might even want to get back at the person by hurting him or her. But you can choose not to do that. You can do one (or more) of these things instead.

1. STOP and THINK. Don't do anything right away. Consider your options. Think about what might happen if you try to hurt the other person.

2. Know that what you do is up to you. You can decide. You are in charge of your actions.

3. Tell yourself, "It's okay to feel angry. It's not okay to hurt someone else. Even if that person hurt me first."

4. Tell the person, "Stop that! I don't like that!"

5. Keep your hands to yourself. Make fists and put them in your pockets.

6. Keep your feet to yourself. Jump or dance or stomp.

7. Walk away or run away.

8. Tell the person how you feel. Use an "I message." *Example:* "I feel angry when you hit me because it hurts. I want you to stop hitting me."

9. Take a deep breath, then blow it out. Blow your angry feelings out of your body.

10. Find an adult. Tell the adult what happened and how you feel.

11. Count slowly from 1 to 10. Count backwards from 10 to 1. Keep counting until you feel your anger getting smaller.

12. Think cool thoughts. Imagine that you're sitting on an iceberg. Cool down your hot, angry feelings.

13. Think happy thoughts. Think of something you like to do. Imagine yourself doing it.

14. Treat the other person with kindness and respect. It won't be easy, but give it a try. This will totally surprise the other person, and it might end the conflict between you.

15. Draw an angry picture.

16. Sing an angry song. Or sing any song extra loud.

17. Remember that getting back at someone never makes conflict better. It only makes it worse.

18. Take a time-out. Go somewhere until you feel better.

19. Find another person to be with.

20. Know that you can do it. You can choose not to hurt someone else. It's up to you.

to come forward? You might want to post these suggestions in your classroom:

- If you *see* someone being bullied, tell the teacher.

- If you *know* that someone is being bullied, tell the teacher.

- If you *think* that someone might be bullied, tell the teacher.

- If you *do nothing* about bullying, you're saying that bullying is okay with you.

- We have the power to stop and prevent bullying in our classroom, but we have to work together!

How can students tell you about bullying? Give them several options. If they're comfortable doing this, they can tell you face-to-face—before or after school, in private (especially if they fear reprisals from the bully). Or they can write about bullying in their journals (see "Weekly Journaling," pages 38–39). Or they can write you a note (see "Use a Notes-to-the-Teacher Box," pages 41 and 45).

No matter how much you encourage your students to keep you informed about bullying in your classroom, *reporting will stop* if you don't respond quickly and effectively. Your students need to trust that if they risk telling you about bullying, you'll do something about it. Anything less compromises or destroys that trust.

Your school or district might already have procedures in place for intervening with bullying and responding to reports of bullying. If so, follow these procedures. You'll find additional tips and suggestions in the "Helping Victims" and "Helping Bullies" sections of this book.

INTERVENE IMMEDIATELY WHEN YOU WITNESS BULLYING

You're the teacher. It's your classroom—and your responsibility to intervene immediately with any bullying you witness, whether it's physical (pushing, shoving, hitting, tripping), verbal (teasing, name-calling, racist or bigoted remarks), or emotional (intimidating, ignoring, excluding). When you intervene effectively, you accomplish four important goals:

1. You put a stop to that particular bullying incident.

2. You make it clear that you won't tolerate bullying in your classroom.

3. You show that you're an adult who will do something about bullying, not just ignore it.

4. Your behavior encourage other victims and witnesses to tell you about bullying you don't witness personally.

You'll find intervention tips and strategies in the "Helping Victims" and "Helping Bullies" sections of this book.

TEACH FRIENDSHIP SKILLS

Some kids become bullies because they don't have friends, feel lonely, and seek attention by bullying. Some kids become victims because they're isolated and easier to pick on. All students—bullies, victims, and everyone else—can benefit from learning and practicing friendship skills. Here are two activities you can try with your students.

FRIENDSHIP TIPS

Distribute copies of the handout "12 Tips for Making and Keeping Friends" (page 35). Read and discuss each tip in turn. During the discussion, you might ask students to give examples

12 TIPS FOR MAKING AND KEEPING FRIENDS

1. **Reach out.** Don't always wait for someone else to make the first move. A simple hi and a smile go a long way.

2. **Get involved.** Join clubs that interest you. Take special classes inside or outside of school. Be a volunteer.

3. **Let people know that you're interested in them.** Don't just talk about yourself; ask questions about them.

4. **Be a good listener.** Look at people while they're talking to you. Pay attention to what they say.

5. **Risk telling people about yourself.** When it feels right, let them in on your interests, your talents, and what's important to you. BUT . . .

6. **Don't be a show-off.** Not everyone you meet will have your abilities and interests. (On the other hand, you shouldn't have to hide them—which you won't, once you find friends who like and appreciate you.)

7. **Be honest.** Tell the truth about yourself, what you believe in, and what you stand for. When asked for your opinion, be sincere. Friends appreciate truthfulness in each other. BUT . . .

8. **Be kind.** There are times when being tactful is more important than being totally honest. The truth doesn't have to hurt.

9. **Don't just use your friends as sounding boards for your problems.** Include them in the good times, too.

10. **Do your share of the work.** That's right, *work*. Any relationship takes effort. Don't always depend on your friends to make the plans and carry all the weight.

11. **Be accepting.** Not all of your friends have to think and act like you do. (Wouldn't it be boring if they did?)

12. **Learn to recognize the so-called friends you can do without.** Some people get so lonely that they put up with anyone—including friends who aren't really friends at all.

Adapted from *The Gifted Kids' Survival Guide: A Teen Handbook* by Judy Galbraith, M.A. and Jim Delisle, Ph.D., copyright © 1996 Free Spirit Publishing Inc., for *The Bully Free Classroom* by Allan L. Beane, Ph.D., copyright © 1999 Free Spirit Publishing Inc., Minneapolis, MN; 800/735-7323 (*www.freespirit.com*).
This page may be photocopied for individual, classroom, or group work only.

from their own experience of how they have used these friendship skills. You might also comment on times when you've seen students use these skills with each other.

 Go farther: Challenge your students to choose one friendship tip to work on during the next week. Then, at the end of a week's time, ask them to report on their progress. They might do this orally or in writing.

FRIENDSHIP BOOSTERS AND BUSTERS

Ask your students, "What makes someone a good friend?" Invite them to think about their own friends and what they like most about them. Write their ideas on the chalkboard under the heading "Friendship Boosters." *Examples:*

> - **A good friend is always there for you.**
> - **A good friend is someone who listens.**
> - **A good friend is someone who likes you for who you are.**
> - **A good friend is someone you can trust.**
> - **A good friend is someone who trusts you.**
> - **A good friend is honest.**
> - **A good friend encourages you to do and be your best.**
> - **A good friend is someone who understands you.**
> - **A good friend is someone who shares with you.**
> - **A good friend respects your property.**
> - **A good friend respects your rights.**
> - **A good friend is fair.**
> - **A good friend is someone who sticks up for you.**
> - **A good friend doesn't try to get you to do things you shouldn't do.**

Next, ask your students, "What kinds of things can hurt a friendship or keep people from making friends?" Write their ideas on the chalkboard under the heading "Friendship Busters." *Examples:*

- bragging
- name calling
- being bossy
- teasing
- making fun of others
- being stuck-up
- lying
- spreading rumors
- stealing
- being rude
- being sarcastic
- ignoring people
- making people feel left out
- cheating
- hitting
- being mean
- embarrassing people
- trying to get people to do things they don't want to do or shouldn't do

If you and your students did the "Name Bullying Behaviors" activity (page 21–22), someone will probably notice the similarities between these "Friendship Busters" and bullying behaviors. If not, point it out. You might ask questions like these:

- Can acting like a bully ruin a friendship?

- Can acting like a bully get in the way of making friends?

WELCOME NEW STUDENTS

New students are more likely to be accepted if they join your class at the start of the school year. If a new student arrives during the year, make a special effort to welcome him or her.

A day or two before the new student is scheduled to arrive, alert your class. If you have any information about the new student (has the family recently moved from another town, city, or state? does the student have any special talents, interests, abilities, or needs?), share it with the class. Ask questions like these:

- How would you feel if you were new in our school? If you were new in our class?

- How would you want us to treat you?

- What would make you glad to be in our class?

- What can we do to make (student's name) feel welcome?

Brainstorm ideas with your class. Here are a few starter ideas:

- Create a colorful "Welcome (Student's Name)!" banner to hang in your room.

- Make greeting cards to give the new student.

- For the first week or two, ask for volunteers to be the new student's "buddy"—showing him or her around, making introductions, sitting with him or her at lunch, etc. *Tip:* Change buddies every day or every other day. Make sure that buddies come from different groups within the class.

- Create a "welcome kit" to give the new student. Include a student handbook, a map of the school, a class directory (see the next activity), a school calendar, a map of your town or city, information about school clubs and activities (with contact names and telephone numbers), a special treat of some kind (a candy bar, a coupon for an ice cream cone at a local business), and anything else you and your students can think of that might be useful and fun.

CREATE A CLASS DIRECTORY

Using a computer (so you can easily update the information as new students arrive), create (or have your students create) a class directory. List students' names, home addresses, and telephone numbers; include email addresses for students who have them. Print out copies for every student in your class. *Tip:* You might want to send a note home to parents asking permission for their children to be included in the directory.

 Go farther: Invite each student to write a one-paragraph description of himself or herself. Students might include their likes, dislikes, talents, interests, club memberships, goals, hopes for the future, or anything else they'd like other people to know about them. Include these descriptions in the directory.

EXPLORE EXPECTATIONS

Sometimes other people behave in ways we expect them to behave. We communicate our expectations—in words, actions, and body language—and other people respond in kind. Similarly, how we treat others is often based on our expectations. Does this mean that changing our expectations can change someone else's behavior—or our own behavior? It's worth exploring.

As a class, talk about the power of expectations. You might ask questions like these:

- Where do our expectations come from? Our own experiences? Things other people have told us? Or a combination of the two?

- Do you think expectations can influence our behavior? Why or why not?

- If you expect someone to treat you with kindness and respect, how do you act toward that person?

- If you expect someone to be mean or rude to you, how do you act toward that person?

- If someone has high or positive expectations of you, how do you know? How does that make you feel?

- If someone has low or negative expectations of you, how do you know? How does that make you feel?

- Do you think that changing your expectations of another person might change the way you treat him or her?

- Do you think that changing your expectations of another person might change the way he or she treats you?

You might illustrate these concepts with examples from your own experiences. Or use examples like these:

- "[Student's name], imagine that each day when you come to class, I expect you to interrupt me, tease people sitting near you, and refuse to do your schoolwork. How will I treat you? How will you act then?"

- "[Student's name], imagine that each day when you come to class, I expect you to be polite, helpful, and ready to work. How will I treat you? How will you act then?"

Suggest that students try this activity:

1. Think of someone you don't usually get along with. How do you expect him or her to treat you? How do you communicate your expectations?

2. Try changing your expectations for a few days or a week. See if that makes a difference in how the person treats you—and how you treat him or her.

If your students are keeping journals (see the next activity), you might ask them to record their thoughts and experiences.

Summarize by asking the class:

- What might happen if we all came to school each day expecting the *worst* from each other? How would we treat each other? How would we act? What kind of classroom would we have?

- What might happen if we all came to school each day expecting the *best* from each other? How would we treat each other? How would we act? What kind of classroom would we have?

- What if we all expected our classroom to be bully free every day? Would we work to make it that way? To keep it that way?

LEARN MORE ABOUT YOUR STUDENTS

The more you know about your students, the better you can meet their learning needs—and their needs to belong, feel accepted, and get along with each other. This all contributes to a positive classroom environment.

You're probably doing many things already to know your students better: greeting them by name when they enter your classroom, communicating with them one-on-one, asking about their days and weeks, listening when they come to you with a problem, concern, or exciting news. Here are two more ideas you may want to try.

WEEKLY JOURNALING

Reading your students' journal entries can give you insight into their actions and help you understand the problems they face each day. Commenting on their entries—with brief, encouraging notes, never criticisms—can strengthen your relationship and improve two-way communication.

If possible, provide your students with spiral-bound notebooks or small blank journaling books. Then introduce the activity by saying something like this:

"Each week, I'll give you a topic to write about in your journal. I'll ask you to write about your thoughts or feelings, something you care about, or something important to you. Your entries can be as long or as short as you want, but I'd like you to write at least a paragraph. I'll collect the journals and keep them between journaling times. I'll be reading your journals as a way to get to know you better. I'll also be writing back to you with my own thoughts and responses. Your journals will never be graded or criticized. Think of this as another way for us to communicate with each other."

Here's a short list of sample topics to start with. Create your own topics based on what you learn about your students and what you'd like to know.

- a time when I felt happy
- a time when I felt sad
- a time when I felt proud
- a time when I felt scared
- the last time I helped someone
- the last time I got into trouble
- my definition of a friend
- my definition of caring
- my greatest achievement
- my hopes for the future

Consider keeping your own journal and sharing your entries with your class as you see fit.

MY FAVORITE THINGS

Distribute copies of the handout "My Favorite Things" (page 40). When students complete them, you can either collect the handouts to review privately, invite students to tell the class about some of their favorite things, or post the handouts around the room and give students time to read them. *Tip:* Tell your students ahead of time which option you'll choose, in case they prefer to keep their responses private.

If the handouts are shared, you might have a class discussion about them. Ask questions like these:

- Did you discover that you have things in common? What things?

- Were there any surprises?

- Did you learn anything new? What did you learn?

- Are there things that everyone likes?

- Are there things that no one likes?

 Go farther: Have students create a poster or bulletin board listing and/or illustrating things they have in common.

IDENTIFY ROLE MODELS

Who are your students' role models? Celebrities? Family members? Other adults they know and admire? Friends? This is an excellent topic for a class discussion—and it reveals a great deal about who your students look up to and are likely to want to emulate.

When more than 1,000 young people ages 13–17 were asked "If you could pick one person to be your role model, which of the following categories would your role model be in?" here's how they responded:*

Family members	40.7%
Friends/family friend	14.4%
Teaching/education	11.1%
Sports/sports-related	10.3%
Entertainment industry	4.9%
Religious leader	4.3%
Business leader	1.9%
National political leader	0.5%
International political leader	0.4%
Local political leader	0.0%
Other	11.6%

* SOURCE: *The State of Our Nation's Youth 1998–1999* (Alexandria, VA: Horatio Alger Association of Distinguished Americans, Inc., 1998).

MY FAVORITE THINGS

Today's date: _____

Your name: _____

My favorite TV show	My favorite place to go	My favorite thing to do in my free time	The thing I like MOST about school	The thing I like LEAST about school
My favorite athlete/sports personality	My favorite radio station	My favorite food	My favorite place to eat	I like people who
I don't like it when people	My favorite magazine	My favorite book	My favorite movie	My favorite Web site
The job I'd like to have when I grow up	My favorite game	My greatest hope	My biggest worry	If I could go anywhere in the world, I'd go to
My favorite type of music	My favorite singer/group/ musician	My favorite actor/actress	The person I admire most	My favorite time of the day

Ask your students to name their role models. So they don't all "follow the leader" and name the same person (or someone a friend names), have them write their role models' names on a piece of paper, sign them, and give them to you. You might also ask them to list one or two reasons why they admire these people. Encourage them to think about people they know, not just the usual sports figures, actors, singers, and other celebrities.

Set aside time to talk about role models. You might ask questions like these:

- What makes someone a role model?

- Why is it important to have role models?

- Why do you admire your role models? What special qualities do they have? Are these qualities you would like to have someday?

- Are your role models a positive influence on you? In what ways?

- Are your role models people who accept others? How can you tell?

You might also identify your own role models and tell your students why you admire them.

EXPLORE WAYS TO DEAL WITH BULLIES

What should you do when someone bullies you? Many students don't know the answer to that question. Of course, there isn't just one right answer; it depends on the specific situation. But certain responses are generally more effective than others.

The "What Should You Do?" handout (page 42) invites students to consider several possible responses to bullying. Answers with brief explanations are given on pages 43–44.

You might read the answers aloud, and/or have students come up with their own reasons why each response would or wouldn't work. Allow time for discussion. Make copies of the answers to give to students during or after the discussion.

Note: Answers are presented as "best answers" because each real-life situation is different. At the end of this activity and discussion, students should understand that: 1) there's more than one way to respond to bullying, 2) some responses can make things better, and 3) some responses can make things worse.

 Important: Tell students that in some situations—when they're being bullied by a gang, when they're in real danger of getting beat up or worse, when there's any chance that a weapon might be present—the best response is always to get away as fast as you can and tell an adult.

USE A NOTES-TO-THE-TEACHER BOX

Put a "Notes-to-the-Teacher Box" on the corner of your desk. It might be large or small, decorated or plain. (You might have your students decorate it.) It should have a lid with a slit in the top.

To explain the purpose of the box, you might say:

> "Here's another way for you to communicate with me. If there's anything you want to tell me about—a problem you're having at school, a classroom issue, an exciting event, or anything at all you'd like me to know—just write me a note and drop it in the box. I'm the *only* person who will open the box and read the notes inside, and I'll check the messages at the end of each day.
>
> "You don't have to sign your name if you don't want to, but I hope you

WHAT SHOULD YOU DO?

What should you do when someone bullies you?
Read each idea and decide if you think this is something you might do.
Check "Yes" if you would, "No" if you wouldn't, or "Not sure."

When someone bullies you, you should:	Yes	No	Not sure
1. cry			
2. tell a friend			
3. tell the bully's parents			
4. run away			
5. try to get even with the bully			
6. tell a teacher			
7. stay home from school			
8. hit, push, or kick the bully			
9. stand up straight, look the bully in the eye, and say in a firm, confident voice, "Leave me alone!"			
10. hunch over, hang your head, and try to look so small the bully will stop noticing you			
11. laugh and act like you just don't care			
12. stand up straight, look the bully in the eye, and say in a firm, confident voice, "Stop it! I don't like that."			
13. tell your parents			
14. threaten the bully			
15. stay calm and walk away			
16. call the bully a bad name			
17. shout, "Cut it out!" as loudly as you can			
18. ignore the bully			
19. tell a joke or say something silly			
20. if other people are nearby, join them so you're not alone			

Answers to
WHAT SHOULD YOU DO?

When someone bullies you, you should:

1. cry   Best answer: **NO.**

Bullies love having power over others. They enjoy making people cry. When you cry, you give them what they want. On the other hand, you might be so upset that you can't help crying. If this happens, get away as quickly as you can. Find a friend or an adult who will listen and support you.

2. tell a friend   Best answer: **YES.**

Make sure it's a friend who will listen, support you, and stand up for you. And don't just tell a friend. Tell an adult, too.

3. tell the bully's parents   Best answer: **NO.**

Some kids become bullies because their parents bully them. The bully's parents are more likely to believe their child, not you. They might even get defensive and blame you.

4. run away   Best answer: **NOT SURE.**

If you feel you're in real danger—for example, if you're facing a gang of bullies—then run as fast as you can to a safe place. At other times, it might be better to stand your ground and stick up for yourself. Follow your instincts!

5. try to get even with the bully   Best answer: **NO.**

The bully might get angry and come after you again. Plus getting even makes *you* a bully, too.

6. tell a teacher   Best answer: **YES.**

Especially if the bullying happens at school. Most bullying happens where adults aren't likely to see or hear it. Your teacher can't help you unless you tell (or someone else tells).

7. stay home from school   Best answer: **NO.**

Unless you feel you're in real danger, you should never stay home from school to avoid a bully. Remember, bullies love power. Imagine how powerful they feel when they can scare someone away from school! Plus staying home from school gets in the way of your learning and hurts you even more.

8. hit, push, or kick the bully   Best answer: **NO.**

Since bullies tend to be bigger and stronger than the people they pick on, chances are you'd get hurt. Plus you might get in trouble for fighting.

9. stand up straight, look the bully in the eye, and say in a firm, confident voice, "Leave me alone!"   Best answer: **YES.**

Bullies don't expect people to stand up to them. They usually pick on people who don't seem likely to defend themselves. So they're surprised when someone acts confident and strong instead of scared and weak. This might be enough to make them stop.

CONTINUED ⟶

10. **hunch over, hang your head, and try to look so small**
the bully will stop noticing you

Best answer: **NO.**

This gives bullies what they want—someone who appears even *more* scared and weak.

11. **laugh and act like you just don't care**

Best answer: **NOT SURE.**

Some bullies will give up if people don't react to their bullying. But others will bully harder to get the reaction they want.

12. **stand up straight, look the bully in the eye, and say**
in a firm, confident voice, "Stop it! I don't like that."

Best answer: **YES.**

See #9.

13. **tell your parents**

Best answer: **YES.**

Tell them what's happening and ask for their help.

14. **threaten the bully**

Best answer: **NO.**

The bully might get angry and come after you even harder.

15. **stay calm and walk away**

Best answer: **YES.**

Especially if you can walk toward a crowded place or a group of your friends.

16. **call the bully a bad name**

Best answer: **NO.**

This will only make the bully angry—bad news for you.

17. **shout, "Cut it out!" as loudly as you can**

Best answer: **YES.**

This may surprise the bully and give you a chance to get away. Plus, if other people hear you, they might turn and look, giving the bully an audience he or she doesn't want.

18. **ignore the bully**

Best answer: **NO.**

Bullies want a reaction from the people they're bullying. Ignoring them might lead to more and worse bullying.

19. **tell a joke or say something silly**

Best answer: **NOT SURE.**

Sometimes humor can defuse a tense situation. Be careful not to tell a joke *about* the bully or make fun of him or her.

20. **if other people are nearby, join them so you're not alone**

Best answer: **YES.**

Bullies generally don't pick on people in groups. They don't like being outnumbered.

will. I can only reply to you personally if you sign your name.

"You can also use the box to tell me about bullying in our classroom. You can write about bullying that happens to you, or bullying you witness personally. If you've been bullying someone else and you want to stop, you can write about that, too."

Then be sure to follow through. Check the box daily. Respond appropriately to the notes your students write. If students have special concerns, arrange to meet with them privately.

If notes reveal that some of your students are being bullied or are bullying others, try the suggestions in the "Helping Bullies" and "Helping Victims" sections of this book.

 Important: If a student uses the box to disclose abuse or another serious problem, follow your school's reporting procedures. Help your student to get the support and assistance he or she needs.

PROMOTE STRUCTURED ACTIVITIES

Much bullying takes place during unstructured activities, especially recess. Encourage your students to plan ahead for those times and tell you their plans. What will they do during recess? Will they play a game? What kind of game? Who will play? What about the students who won't take part in the game—what will they do? If you're one of the playground supervisors, you can watch to make sure students follow through with their plans. If you're not, you can ask them to report back to you after recess. Try to get them in the habit of deciding in advance how they will spend unstructured time. If they have difficulty making plans, offer suggestions.

Since bullies tend to be older, stronger, and more powerful than their victims, you might also explore the possibility of assigning older

and younger children to different playground areas. Talk with the principal and other teachers; work out an arrangement together.

PROVIDE SUPERVISION

It's believed that some children become bullies because the supervision they get at home is minimal or nonexistent. And bullies tend to do their bullying where adults can't observe and intervene. You can't supervise your students at home, but you can—and should—supervise them at school. This may be one of the most effective bully prevention strategies available to you.

1. Start by considering the level of supervision in your own classroom. Are you able to keep an eye on all (or most) of your students all (or most) of the time? If you're in charge of a large class, this may be difficult or impossible. How can you bring more adults into your classroom? Arrange for an aid or student teacher. Make parent helpers welcome. If local high schools have service learning requirements, find out if students can earn credits for helping out in your classroom.

2. Are you aware of bully problems on the playground, in the lunchroom, and/or in the hallways? Get together with other teachers and administrators and share what you've heard (or overheard). Increase the number of playground and lunchroom supervisors. Since lockers are common places for bullying, teachers should keep an eye on lockers during class changes.

It's true that spending more time supervising students will increase your workload. But the results are worth it. More supervision equals fewer bullying incidents, especially serious incidents. More positive supervision—where you interact with students, suggest ways they can interact with each other, and model kindness, acceptance, affirmation, and getting along—promotes more positive behavior. Before long, everyone feels safer and more secure, the school climate noticeably improves—and you're spending *less* time dealing with bully problems.

BUILD EMPATHY

Empathy is the ability to identify with and understand another person's feelings, situation, motives, and concerns—to put ourselves in someone else's place or, as the saying goes, "in someone else's shoes." This is one of the most important traits we develop—and the sooner, the better.

Empathy is basic to positive relationships with friends, peers, family members, and everyone else we encounter throughout our lives. Often, when children aren't liked by others, it's because they lack empathy. Research has shown that children are born with a predisposition toward empathy. However, if it isn't encouraged and supported, it doesn't grow.

It's not enough for students to empathize with people they have things in common with. That's easy. They also need to empathize with people who are very different from them—in their needs, experiences, points of view, life circumstances, beliefs, ethnic and cultural backgrounds, talents, abilities, accomplishments, etc. They need to be able to think about how other people feel—and, eventually, how other people *might* feel or *would* feel in response to specific events and circumstances.

There are many ways you can build empathy in your students. Here are four ideas you can try.*

ASK QUESTIONS

During lessons, group work, and other times, ask questions that draw students' attention away from themselves and toward the feelings, needs, and concerns of others. *Examples:*

How would you feel if . . .

- you were the new kid in school?

* See also "Build Understanding," pages 56–57.

- you were the most popular student? The least popular student?
- someone made fun of you or called you names?
- you came to school every day without eating breakfast?
- your parents were divorced?
- someone picked on you all the time?
- you didn't have a home or a safe place to live?
- walking down the street was dangerous?
- you were the smallest kid in class?
- you were the biggest kid in class?
- you couldn't speak English very well?
- you had a hard time reading?
- you used a wheelchair?
- you wore glasses?
- you couldn't hear well or at all?
- you had an illness and felt sick much of the time?

These and other questions might be topics for class discussions or journal writing (see "Weekly Journaling," pages 38–39).

 Go farther: Teaching Tolerance is a national education project dedicated to helping teachers foster equity, respect, and understanding in the classroom and beyond. Free and low-cost resources—including video-and-text teaching kits, posters, books, and *Teaching Tolerance* magazine—are available to educators at all levels. Write or call: Southern Poverty Law Center, 400 Washington Avenue, Montgomery, AL 36104; telephone (334) 264-0268. On the Web, go to: *http://www.splcenter.org/*

TAKE FIELD TRIPS

Expose students to people whose lives are different from their own. You might visit a juvenile home, a homeless shelter, a children's hospital, a senior citizens' home. When appropriate, you and your students might build relationships (with frequent visits) or start a pen-pal exchange. Or you might volunteer as a class to help at one of the places you visit. Plan volunteer experiences carefully. Check with your principal about procedures, and be sure to get permission from students' parents.

LEAD AN IMAGINATION EXERCISE

Have students sit comfortably and quietly in their chairs (or on the floor—you'll need cushions or a rug) with their eyes closed. Ask them to imagine that another person is sitting directly across from them. This should be someone they don't know very well, or someone they have neutral or negative feelings about. Then guide them with questions and suggestions like these:

- Picture the person in your mind. Is it a man or a woman? A boy or a girl? What color hair does the person have? What color eyes? What is he or she wearing? How is he or she looking at you?

- Say to yourself, "[The person's name] is a human being. So am I. This is something we have in common."

- Ask yourself [pause between each question to allow time for students to think about it]:

  - What do I really know about this person? Where does my knowledge come from? My own experience with him or her? Things other people have said? Rumors? Gossip? My own prejudices or biases?

  - What might be important to this person?

  - What is something this person might like? What is something this person might not like?

  - What are this person's needs? What does he or she want out of life?

  - What are some reasons this person acts the way he or she does?

  - What problems might this person have?

  - What might this person be struggling with?

  - What might this person be afraid of?

- What might this person wish he or she could do?

End by asking, "Were you able to see the world through the other person's eyes? How did that feel? What did you discover about the person—and about yourself?"

HELP STUDENTS DEVELOP A FEELINGS VOCABULARY

It's easier to empathize with feelings we can name. There are many ways you can help your students develop a feelings vocabulary. Here are some starter ideas:

- Invite students to name their feelings. When they enter your room, say, "Hello, [name]! How are you feeling today?"

- Make a large "pockets poster" for your room. Tape or staple several pockets to a piece of posterboard. Label each pocket with a feeling. (*Examples:* happy, sad, excited, worried, tired, wide awake, confused, anxious, contented.) Cut strips of paper (or construction paper) and write one student's name on each strip. When students arrive in your classroom, each puts his or her name strip in the pocket that best describes how he or she is feeling. (This also gives you a general idea of the "mood" your class is in.)

- Use books, videos, and posters to explore feelings and ways to express them.

- Play a "What Am I Feeling?" game. Pair students and have them sit across from each other. As one student imagines feeling a certain way and shows it in his or her body language and facial expression, the other student tries to identify and name the feeling.

- Distribute copies of the handout "50 Words That Describe Feelings" (page 48). Practice the words with your students. Make sure they understand what each one means. Invite them to use the words in class discussions, writing assignments, and reports. You might also include them in spelling lessons.

happy
excited
eager
joyful
"on top of
the world"

shy
bashful
helpless
lonely
unsure

sad
"down"
gloomy
miserable
tearful

confused
puzzled
mixed-up
distracted
tired

fidgety
anxious
tense
worried
restless

irritated
mad
angry
upset
furious

calm
content
satisfied
proud
relaxed

fearful
embarrassed
guilty
self-conscious
ashamed

surprised
startled
afraid
shocked
terrified

safe
secure
confident
hopeful
trusting

REWARD COOPERATION

Often, when we plan group activities for our students, we focus on the *product*—the paper, project, or other end result we expect them to accomplish. Another equally important (more important?) aspect of group activities is teaching students how to cooperate as they work toward a common goal.

Plan some group activities that stress this as the main purpose. *Examples:*

- a craft project designed so each student can make a contribution

- an anti-bullying classroom campaign, complete with posters, slogans, songs, and skits

- friendship role-plays

- kind-word crosswords or search-a-word puzzles

- new games for the rest of the class to play

Emphasize the value of effort over results. Establish checkpoints along the way during which students can report on how well they're working together, whether they're enjoying the process, and what they're learning from each other.

Sit in with each group, observe, and comment on what you see. Compliment students for their willingness to get along and value each other's unique abilities.

This type of group activity offers several rewards. It encourages unity and acceptance and discourages perfectionism. It invites students to take risks and explore new interests without fear of rejection. It gives them opportunities to acquire new skills and reveal hidden strengths, which boosts their standing among their peers. When students cooperate, everybody wins.

KEEP GRADES PRIVATE

Most students are concerned about their grades. Those with very high or very low grades are at increased risk of being bullied. For this reason (among others), you should keep grades and test scores private.

- If your students grade their own papers, collect them afterward and record the grades yourself. Don't ask them to call out their results.

- If you have students grade each other's homework assignments and quizzes, reconsider this practice. It probably saves you time, but is it good for your students? Have you noticed any who seem embarrassed or uncomfortable when their papers are being graded by their classmates? Have you noticed students making fun of someone else's papers? Even if you haven't witnessed these behaviors personally, it doesn't mean they're not happening.

- Never discuss a student's grades where other students might overhear.

- Don't post A papers or high test scores in your classroom. Celebrate students' achievements in other ways.

USE QUOTATIONS AS TEACHING TOOLS

Collect quotations about friendship, peace, peacemaking, self-esteem, assertiveness, tolerance, understanding, acceptance, kindness, respect, and other topics related to creating a positive classroom. Invite your students to bring in quotations they find.

Begin each day with a positive quotation, then ask your students to offer their thoughts on what it means—and what it means to them personally. Ask them to keep the quotation in mind throughout the day. *Tip:* Quotations also make good journal writing assignments. (See "Weekly Journaling," pages 38–39.)

Here are several quotations you may want to use to start your collection:

> • "If you judge people, you have no time to love them." *Mother Teresa*
>
> • "A friend is a present you give yourself." *Robert Louis Stevenson*
>
> • "Maturity begins to grow when you can sense your concern for others outweighing your concern for yourself." *John MacNaughton*
>
> • "What we see depends mainly on what we look for." *John Lubbock*
>
> • "Change your thoughts and you change your world." *Norman Vincent Peale*
>
> • "We each need to do what we can to help one another no matter how tiny it is. If we do something for peace—each of us—we can all make the difference." *Mairead Corrigan Maguire (1976 Nobel Peace Prize Laureate)*
>
> • "Friendship is the only cement that will ever hold the world together." *Woodrow Wilson*
>
> • "It is not enough simply to 'live and let live': genuine tolerance requires an active effort to try to understand the point of view of others." *Aung San Suu Kyi (1991 Nobel Peace Prize Laureate)*
>
> • "Blessed are we who can laugh at ourselves, for we shall never cease to be amused." *Anonymous*
>
> • "Never be bullied into silence. Never allow yourself to be made a victim. Accept no one's definition of your life, but define yourself." *Harvey Fierstein*
>
> • "Friendship with oneself is all-important, because without it one cannot be friends with anyone else." *Eleanor Roosevelt*

Random acts of kindness are proven, powerful ways to create a more positive environment anywhere—in the classroom, at home, and in the community. Here are five activities you can do with your students to promote kindness and help them form the habit of doing nice things for others "just because."

CLASS DISCUSSION

Talk about kindness as a class. You might ask questions like these:

• When was the last time someone did something really nice for you? What did the person do? How did it make you feel?

• Did the person have a reason for acting that way? Did he or she expect something from you in return? Or was the person kind "just because"?

• Have you ever done something nice for another person without being asked, and without expecting anything in return? What did you do? How did you feel? How do you think the other person felt?

• What if everyone in this class made the effort to be kind to each other? What would our class be like? Is this something we should try? How can we start?

Ask students to offer suggestions. List them on the chalkboard. Have them vote on one or more to try for the rest of the week.

 Go farther: Read aloud from *Kids' Random Acts of Kindness* (Emeryville, CA: Conari Press, 1994). In this wonderful book, kids from around the world tell their own stories of sudden, impetuous acts of kindness. Also available and just as inspiring: *Random Acts of Kindness* and *More Random Acts of Kindness* (Conari, 1993 and 1994).

KINDNESS BOX

Take a box with a lid (a large shoebox works well) and cut a slit in the top. Decorate it (or have students decorate it). Label it the "Kindness Box" and put it on a shelf or a corner of your desk.

Invite students to write brief notes about acts of kindness they do or witness and drop them in the box. Once a week, once a day, or whenever you choose, dip into the box, pull out a note, and read it aloud to the class. Thank your students for their kindness to each other.

KINDNESS PALS

Write your students' names on slips of paper, put the slips in a hat or box, and have students draw names. (Anyone who draws his or her own name should try again.) Explain that by the end of the week, everyone should do at least one act of kindness for the person whose name they drew. If you think your students might need ideas, brainstorm some as a class and write them on the chalkboard to serve as reminders.

At the end of the week, invite students to tell the class what they did. After each student reveals his or her act of kindness, lead the class in applause.

If your students are keeping journals (see pages 38–39), you might ask them to write about their acts of kindness. When you read their entries, be sure to leave a positive comment or two congratulating them on their efforts.

KINDNESS REPORTER

Select one student each week to serve as a "kindness reporter." He or she will watch for acts of kindness and briefly describe them in a notebook. (*Tip:* Kids might enjoy using a special notebook or steno pad provided for this purpose.) At the end of the week, have the reporter share the good news with the class.

BIG BOOK OF KINDNESS

Ask your students to watch for and collect stories about kindness. They might write brief descriptions of stories they see on television or in movies, or bring in stories from newspapers or magazines. They might write stories about kindness they experience in their own lives—at home, at school, in their neighborhoods, in clubs or organizations they belong to, and so on.

As students gather their stories, have them paste or write them on large sheets of paper. They can decorate them with drawings, photos, collages, or whatever they choose. Punch holes along the edges and bind the sheets together with pieces of string or yarn. Add cardboard covers with decorations and the title "Our Big Book of Kindness." Keep the book available so students can look through it and add to it often.

TEACH STUDENTS TO USE "I MESSAGES"

"I messages" are simple, powerful ways to communicate our wants, needs, and feelings. When you teach your students how to use them, you're giving them a tool that will help them in many different situations—including times when they're confronted by a bully.

You might introduce "I messages" by saying:

> "Sometimes we need to tell other people exactly how we feel and why. Maybe they're bothering us or bullying us and we want them to stop what they're doing and leave us alone.

> "An 'I message' is a good way to communicate what we want. When we use an 'I message,' we say what we need without blaming the other person. Blaming can make a problem worse. It puts the other person on the defensive."

Distribute copies of the handout "5 Steps to an 'I Message'" (page 52) and go over the steps with the students. Invite them to give other examples of messages they might use. Have them create and perform brief role-plays showing "I messages" in action.

5 STEPS TO AN "I MESSAGE"

1. Always start with "I," not "You." "I" puts the focus on your feelings, wants, and needs. "You" puts the other person on the defensive.

    "I _____"

2. Clearly and simply say HOW you feel.

    "I feel _____"   *Example:*   "I feel angry"

    "I'm _____"   *Example*:   "I'm upset"

3. Clearly and simply say WHAT the other person did (or is doing) that made you feel that way.

    "I feel _____ when you _____"   *Example:*   "I feel angry when you call me names"

    "I'm _____ because you _____"   *Example:*   "I'm upset because you tripped me"

4. Clearly and simply say WHY you feel the way you do.

    "I feel _____ when you _____ because _____"   *Example*:   "I feel angry when you call me names because I have a real name."

    "I'm _____ because you _____ and _____"   *Example:*   "I'm upset because you tripped me and I dropped my books all over the floor."

5. Clearly and simply say WHAT you want or need the other person to do.

    "I want you to _____"   *Example:*   "I feel angry when you call me names because I have a real name. I want you to start calling me by my real name."

    "I need you to _____"   *Example:*   "I'm upset because you tripped me and I dropped my books all over the floor. I need you to help me pick up my books."

TEACH ASSERTIVENESS SKILLS

Some students don't know what to do or how to react when they're bullied. Should they cry? Run away? Fight back? Get even? Do nothing? If your class did the "Explore Ways to Deal with Bullies" activity (page 41), you've discussed some effective and ineffective ways to respond. On the "What Should You Do?" handout (page 42), two of the ways listed (#9 and #12) are *assertive* responses to bullying.

In general, bullies tend to be *aggressive*—they behave as if their rights matter more than anyone else's rights. Victims tend to be *passive*—they behave as if other people's rights matter more than theirs. *Assertive* people respect their own rights *and* other people's rights.

Most of us could benefit from assertiveness training. Here are some tips and strategies for teaching your students to be more assertive. Practice them with your students and offer coaching where needed. Students who are naturally shy and withdrawn, and those who have been (or are) bullying victims, will need extra help learning and using assertiveness skills.

KNOW YOUR RIGHTS

Ask your students, "Do you have any rights? Do you know what they are?" As they offer ideas, write them on the chalkboard. Make sure that these rights appear somewhere on the list:

1. **We have the right to think for ourselves.**
2. **We have the right to have and express our opinions, views, and beliefs.**
3. **We have the right to make decisions about our lives.**
4. **We have the right to say no.**
5. **We have the right to say yes.**

6. **We have the right to stand up to people who tease us, criticize us, or put us down.**
7. **We have the right to have and express our feelings.**
8. **We have the right to respond when someone violates our rights.**

 Go farther: Have students create and illustrate a "Student Bill of Rights" poster for the classroom.

WATCH YOUR BODY LANGUAGE

Sometimes body language speaks more loudly than words. Kids who slouch, mumble, fidget, avoid looking people in the eye, back off, and appear frightened and worried are more likely to be victims than those whose body language expresses confidence and positive self-esteem. It's not right—those kids don't *deserve* to be bullied any more than other kids—but it's true.

Teach students how to look assertive. Practice with role-plays, skits, and face-to-face discussions. Here are the five basics of assertive body language:

1. Stand up straight. Stand with your feet slightly apart so you feel balanced and stable.

2. Keep your head up.

3. Keep your shoulders straight. Don't hunch.

4. Look people in the eye. Not over their heads, not at the ground—right in the eye.

5. Don't back off when you're talking to someone. Move closer—but not too close. Keep a comfortable distance between you.

When you *look* assertive, you're more likely to *feel* assertive. And other people are more likely to treat you with respect.

Pair assertive body language with assertive words, spoken in a firm, confident, determined voice. Don't mumble or whine—but don't shout, either. Then say what you mean and mean what you say. Use "I messages." (See page 51.)

USE THE ASSERT FORMULA

Distribute copies of the handout "The ASSERT Formula" (page 55) and lead students through it. Have them practice the formula in skits and role-plays.

 Go farther: Check out assertiveness training programs and opportunities at local community and youth organizations. Arrange for a trainer to visit your class and demonstrate ways to be assertive.

PROMOTE TEAMWORK

Students who participate in group activities are more likely to have positive feelings about other people. They develop fewer biases and prejudices—or rethink the biases or prejudices they already have.

Talk as a class about the attitudes, skills, and abilities people need to work well in groups. Ask your students to think about what makes a good team member and a good team. Write their ideas on the chalkboard. If they have difficulty coming up with ideas, you might start by offering one or more of these:

Good team members . . .

- accept each other as equals
- support the group's goals
- support the group's rules
- participate in discussions
- listen to each other during discussions

- disagree without being disagreeable
- express their needs and feelings honestly
- do their fair share of the work
- have a positive attitude
- suggest solutions to problems

Good teams . . .

- set clear goals and agree to reach them together
- set clear rules and agree to follow them
- resolve any disagreements fairly and peacefully
- identify the strengths of individual team members, then use those strengths to benefit the team as a whole
- compromise when there's a conflict
- share the responsibilities equally among the team members

You might ask your class:

- Do you think our class is a good team? Why or why not?
- What could we do to work better as a team? Who has specific ideas we can try?

WORK TOGETHER TO SOLVE A PROBLEM

When you and your students work together to solve a problem outside the classroom—when you face a common "enemy" as a group—you naturally grow closer to each other in the process. This builds unity, acceptance, and the satisfaction of joining forces for a good cause.

Ask your students to brainstorm specific problems they'd like to address. These might be problems in your school, your community, or the world. (*Examples:* pollution, smoking, drugs, cruelty to animals, homelessness, hunger.) Write their ideas on the chalkboard. Afterward, have students choose one to work on. You might ask

THE ASSERT FORMULA

A stands for **Attention.** Before you can talk about and try to solve a problem you're having with someone else, you need to get his or her attention. *Example:* "Sean, I need to talk to you about something. Is now a good time?"

S stands for **Soon, Simple, and Short.** Speak up as soon as you realize that your rights have been violated. Look the person in the eye and keep your comments brief and to the point. *Example:* "It's about something that happened in the hall today."

S stands for **Specific Behavior.** What did the person do to violate your rights? Focus on the behavior, not the person. Be as specific as you can. *Example:* "I didn't like it when you pushed me against my locker, I dropped my books, and you kicked them across the hall."

E stands for **Effect on Me.** Share the feelings you experienced as a result of the person's behavior. *Example:* "It was embarrassing, plus I was late for class. I had to wait for the hall to clear before I could pick up my books."

R stands for **Response.** Wait for a response from the other person. He or she might try to brush you off with "What's the big deal?" or "Don't be a baby" or "Can't you take a joke?" or "So what?" Don't let it bother you. At least it's a response. On the other hand, the person might apologize.

T stands for **Terms.** Suggest a solution to the problem. *Example:* "I want you to stop bothering me in the hall. If you don't, I'll report you to the teacher."

Tips: The ASSERT Formula may feel strange and awkward at first. It isn't foolproof, and it won't always work. In some situations—for example, bullying that involves physical violence—it might make things worse. And some bullies feed on getting *any* kind of response, even an assertive response. If your being assertive seems to anger or provoke the bully, walk away or run away.

Adapted from *Fighting Invisible Tigers: A Stress Management Guide for Teens,* copyright © 1995 by Earl Hipp, Free Spirit Publishing Inc., for *The Bully Free Classroom* by Allan L. Beane, Ph.D., copyright © 1999 Free Spirit Publishing Inc., Minneapolis, MN; 800/735-7323 *(www.freespirit.com).*
This page may be photocopied for individual, classroom, or group work only.

for a show of hands or prepare secret ballots so students can vote for their top choices.

Once you've identified a problem, find ways for your students to take action and make a difference. For ideas, see "Get Students Involved in Service" (pages 73–75).

BUILD UNDERSTANDING

Why do bullies bully? Why do victims put up with it? There are no easy answers to these questions, but experts have identified reasons why some kids become bullies and others become victims. Share this information with your students. It might help them understand why they and their classmates do some of the things they do, and it will also build empathy (see pages 46–47).

Some kids bully . . .

. . . because they love having power. Most bullying is about having power over other people.

. . . because their parents or other people bully them. They have learned by example that bullying is how bigger, stronger people relate to others and get their way.

. . . as a way to get attention.

. . . to make themselves look bigger or tougher than they really are—or they feel inside.

. . . because they are jealous of other people. They can't stand it when others are smarter, more popular, or more successful than they are.

. . . to protect themselves from being picked on or criticized. They're afraid of being hurt, and they take out their fear on other people.

. . . because they enjoy hurting other people and making them feel afraid.

. . . because they don't know any better. They haven't learned how to make friends and get along with others.

. . . because they like to win, no matter what. They can't stand losing at anything.

. . . because they have their own problems and don't know how to cope. Maybe they're miserable at home. Maybe they know they don't fit in and other kids don't like them. They take out their feelings on people who are weaker and unable to fight back.

Some kids are victims . . .

. . . because they are "different" in some way. They may be taller or shorter, heavier or thinner, wear braces, wear glasses, have a physical disability or a learning difference, "talk funny," "look funny," and on and on. Everyone is unique, so there are countless "differences" bullies can identify and pick on.

. . . because they seem vulnerable—like "easy marks." Maybe they're passive, sensitive, quiet, shy, or stand out in some other way. For whatever reason, they look as if they can't or won't stick up for themselves.

. . . because they don't know how to make friends and get along with others. They're isolated, alone, and lonely. They don't have people they can count on to come to their defense.

. . . because they're socially awkward. Maybe they say and do the "wrong" things. Maybe they wear the "wrong" clothes. For whatever reason, they don't fit in.

. . . as a way to get attention. They don't know how to seek positive attention, so they seek negative attention. They may act "strange" or annoying.

. . . because they're bullies. How does this work? Imagine that a 10-year-old bullies kids his (or her) age and younger. This person doesn't know how to make friends. He (or she) may be bossy, aggressive, and rude. Now put that 10-year-old in a group of older kids, and suddenly he (or she) isn't as big, strong, or scary. Instead, he (or she) is a kid who doesn't have friends, doesn't know how to act, and is suddenly very vulnerable.

Invite students to contribute their own reasons why some kids are bullies and some are victims. Listen for any reasons that indicate acceptance of bullying behaviors or scorn for victims. If necessary, remind students that no one has the "right" to be a bully, or a "good reason" to bully someone else. And no one "deserves" to be a victim.

SET AND REVIEW WEEKLY GOALS

Start each week with a brief discussion of how everyone can work together to create a positive classroom environment. Set specific goals everyone can agree on and work toward. For ideas, you might review your class rules (see "Set Rules," pages 31–32), acceptance statements (see "Build Acceptance," pages 16 and 19), and/or students' ideas for making the classroom bully free (see "Designate Your Classroom Bully Free," page 32). You might ask questions like these:

- What can we do this week so everyone feels safe, accepted, and appreciated?

- What can we do to prevent bullying?

- How will we treat each other?

- How will we expect to be treated?

- What specific actions can help us all have a great week?

As students offer ideas, write them on the chalkboard. Try to summarize the ideas into a single, simple statement of goals. Leave it on the chalkboard for the entire week.

On Wednesday, review the goals statement with the students. Ask questions like:

- Are we meeting our goals as a class?

- Is there anything we need to work harder on?

On Friday, look back on the week. Ask questions like:

- Did we meet our goals this week?

- In general, how did people treat each other during the week?

- Did we all have a good week? Why or why not?

- What can we do next week to improve?

Invite students' ideas about ways to make your classroom even friendlier, more peaceful, and more accepting. Use those ideas as starters for next week's goal-setting discussion.

Tip: For another approach, see "Assess the Week" (page 68).

ASSIGN RELATED READING

Have students read and report on books about bullying, friendship, conflict, and acceptance.* Discuss them as a class, or have students write original stories featuring characters they encountered in the books. How would these characters handle a fight on the playground? A shoving match in the hall? Teasing? Rejection? Hurt feelings? What else? Invite your students to come up with their own suggestions for situations they'd like to portray.

Reading and writing are reasonably nonthreatening ways to explore issues of friendship, rejection, prejudice, acceptance, conflict, bullying, and other topics.

---

* See "Books for Children" in "Resources" (pages 150–153) for suggestions. You might also ask your school librarian or the children's librarian at your local public library to point you toward appropriate books. Or check the latest issue of *The Bookfinder* or *The Best of Bookfinder: A Guide to Children's Literature About Interests and Concerns of Youth Ages 2–18.* Published by American Guidance Service, the *Bookfinders* group and describe books by topic. Ask for them at your library's reference desk.

TEACH CONFLICT RESOLUTION SKILLS

Conflict between people is normal and inevitable, and not all conflict is harmful or bad. *Destructive* conflict damages relationships, creates bad feelings, and leads to future problems. But *constructive* conflict helps us learn, grow, and change for the better. We see things from other perspectives. We become more open-minded, tolerant, and accepting. We build stronger relationships with the people in our lives.

What makes the difference? How we choose to *manage* the conflicts we experience. It takes (at least) two people to start and sustain a conflict. If both agree to seek a positive resolution, half the battle is won.

Everyone benefits from learning and practicing conflict resolution skills. Bullies discover the real power of solving problems without using force or intimidation. Victims are empowered to seek solutions instead of giving up and giving in. Your classroom becomes a place where people are willing to work together.

Conflict resolution isn't learned (or taught) in a day. For best results, you'll probably want to use a conflict resolution program. There are many good ones available; talk with your principal to find out if your school or district has a preference or has already chosen a program.

Note: Research shows that conflict resolution programs *work*. Students who are not trained in conflict resolution are more likely to withdraw from conflicts or use force in conflict situations. Students who are trained in conflict resolution are more likely to face conflicts, use problem solving to negotiate solutions—and have a more positive attitude toward school in general.*

If you don't yet have access to a conflict resolution program, there's a basic approach you can teach your students right away. Distribute copies of the handout "8 Steps to Conflict Resolution" (page 59). Lead students through it step-by-step. Reinforce it with practice, role-plays, skits, or whatever you think will reach your students most effectively.

SET UP A PEACE PLACE

Set aside a corner of your classroom as the "Peace Place." Tell students they can go there when they need to resolve a conflict, talk with another student about a problem they're having, or just spend some quiet time when they're feeling upset, frustrated, or overwhelmed.

Furnish your Peace Place with a small table or desk, two or three chairs (or cushions, or beanbags), peaceful posters (nature scenes, animals, people), a cassette player or two (with headphones), and cassettes of quiet music or nature sounds. Start and build a small library of appropriate books—on friendship, conflict resolution, peacefulness, and related topics—and keep them in a bookcase in your Peace Place.

As a class, develop a set of short, simple rules for the Peace Place. Have students make and decorate a poster listing the rules. *Examples:*

1. **If you're having a problem with another student, ask him or her to go to the Peace Place with you and talk it over.**
2. **If another student asks you to go to the Peace Place, say yes.**
3. **When you're in the Peace Place, use gentle, respectful words.**
4. **Take turns talking and listening.**
5. **Use "I messages" to communicate your wants, needs, and feelings.***
6. **Be a good listener. Pay attention to what the other person says. Don't interrupt.**
7. **If you can't solve the problem on your own, ask the teacher for help.**
8. **The Peace Place is special. Keep it neat and clean.**

---

* SOURCE: *Review of Educational Research* 66:4 (1996), pp. 459–506.

* See "Teach Students to Use 'I Messages,'" page 51.

8 STEPS TO CONFLICT RESOLUTION

1. **Cool down.** Don't try to resolve a conflict when you're angry (or the other person is angry). Take a time-out or agree to meet again in 24 hours.

2. **Describe the conflict.** Each person should tell about it in his or her own words. No put-downs allowed! *Important:* Although each person may have a different view of the conflict and use different words to describe it, neither account is "right" or "wrong."

3. **Describe what caused the conflict.** What specific events led up to the conflict? What happened first? Next? Did the conflict start out as a minor disagreement or difference of opinion? What happened to turn it into a conflict? *Important:* Don't label the conflict either person's "fault."

4. **Describe the feelings raised by the conflict.** Again, each person should use his or her own words. Honesty is important. No blaming allowed!

5. **Listen carefully and respectfully while the other person is talking.** Try to understand his or her point of view. Don't interrupt. It might help to "reflect" the other person's perceptions and feelings by repeating them back. *Examples:* "You didn't like it when I called you a name." "Your feelings are hurt." "You thought you should have first choice about what game to play at recess." "You're sad because you feel left out."

6. **Brainstorm solutions to the conflict.** Follow the three basic rules of brainstorming:
   • Everyone tries to come up with as many ideas as they can.
   • All ideas are okay.
   • Nobody makes fun of anyone else's ideas.

   Be creative. Affirm each other's ideas. Be open to new ideas. Make a list of brainstormed ideas so you're sure to remember them all. Then choose one solution to try. Be willing to negotiate and compromise.

7. **Try your solution.** See how it works. Give it your best efforts. Be patient.

8. **If one solution doesn't get results, try another.** Keep trying. Brainstorm more solutions if you need to.

If you can't resolve the conflict no matter how hard you try, agree to disagree. Sometimes that's the best you can do. Meanwhile, realize that the conflict doesn't have to end your relationship. People can get along even when they disagree.

EXPLORE THE LIVES OF FAMOUS PEACEMAKERS

Jane Addams. Amnesty International. Yasser Arafat. Menachem Begin. His Holiness the Dalai Lama of Tibet. Mikhail Gorbachev. The International Committee of the Red Cross. Martin Luther King Jr. Aung San Suu Kyi. Nelson Mandela. Mother Teresa. Linus Pauling. Yitzhak Rabin. Albert Schweitzer. Rigoberta Menchu Tum. Desmond Tutu. Lech Walesa. Elie Wiesel. Betty Williams. Jody Williams. What do these people and organizations have in common? All are winners of the Nobel Peace Prize, perhaps the world's most revered and prestigious award.

Have students research a Nobel Peace Prize winner or another peacemaker they admire. To share what they learn, they might write brief biographies, present skits, write songs, create collages, or do another activity they choose.

Encourage them to look for answers to this question: "What did this person do that I can do, too?" Help students "translate" their peacemakers' accomplishments into simple, inspiring statements. *Examples:*

- "1998 Nobel Peace Prize winners John Hume and David Trimble worked to find a peaceful solution to the conflict in Northern Ireland. I can be a peer mediator and help my classmates find solutions to their conflicts."

- "1992 Nobel Peace Prize winner Rigoberta Menchu Tum works for human rights. I can learn about the Universal Declaration of Human Rights and tell other people about it."

- "1984 Nobel Peace Prize winner Bishop Desmond Tutu worked against apartheid in South Africa. I can fight racism, bigotry, and prejudice in my school and community."

TEACH PEER MEDIATION SKILLS

Your students can learn to help each other resolve conflicts through peer mediation. Mediators don't offer solutions. Instead, they ask open-ended questions, encourage discussion, and guide people involved in a conflict to come up with and try their own solutions.

Identify students you believe would make good peer mediators. These will be students who can stay calm, listen carefully, remain objective, avoid taking sides, and be patient, plus they should be genuinely interested in serving as peer mediators. Make it clear that this isn't a "power position." Explain that mediators are "between" the people involved in a conflict, like the median strip in a road. Their job is to help the two sides come together, not to impose solutions or take credit for solutions that work.

Peer mediators start by asking themselves seven important questions:*

- Am I the right person?
- Can I assist without taking sides?
- Will both parties let me assist?
- Is this the right time to intervene?
- Are the parties relatively calm?
- Do we have enough time?
- Is this the right place?

If students can answer yes to these questions, they're ready to try mediating the conflict. The "Steps for Mediation" handout (page 61) can lead them through the process.

 Go farther: The questions above and the "Steps for Mediation" are both from the Resolving Conflict Creatively Program (RCCP), a nationwide initiative of Educators for Social Responsibility (ESR) that has taught thousands of teachers and students

---

* Reprinted with the permission of Educators for Social Responsibility Metropolitan Area © 1997 Educators for Social Responsibility.

STEPS FOR MEDIATION
from the Resolving Conflict Creatively Program

I. INTRODUCTION

1. Introduce yourself as a mediator.
2. Ask those in the conflict if they would like your help in solving the problem.
3. Find a quiet area to hold the mediation.
4. Ask for agreement to the following:
   —try to solve the problem
   —no name calling
   —let the other person finish talking
   —confidentiality

II. LISTENING

5. Ask the first person "What happened?" Paraphrase.
6. Ask the first person how she or he feels. Reflect the feelings.
7. Ask the second person "What happened?" Paraphrase.
8. Ask the second person how he or she feels. Reflect the feelings.

III. LOOKING FOR SOLUTIONS

9. Ask the first person what she or he could have done differently. Paraphrase.
10. Ask the second person what she or he could have done differently. Paraphrase.
11. Ask the first person what she or he can do here and now to help solve the problem. Paraphrase.
12. Ask the second person what she or he can do here and now to help solve the problem. Paraphrase.
13. Use creative questioning to bring disputants closer to a solution.

IV. FINDING SOLUTIONS

14. Help both disputants find a solution they feel good about.
15. Repeat the solution and all of its parts to both disputants and ask if each agrees.
16. Congratulate both people on a successful mediation.

how to respond nonviolently to conflict. To learn more about RCCP, write or call: Educators for Social Responsibility, Resolving Conflict Creatively Program, 23 Garden Street, Cambridge, MA 02138; telephone (617) 492-1764. On the Web, go to: *http://www.esrnational.org/*

Note: Peer mediation may not be the best approach to a bullying situation. Bullies have (and want) power over their victims. Victims may have low (or no) communication or assertiveness skills, especially in the bullies' presence. Victims might be intimidated and afraid because of past bullying incidents and worried about future retaliation, both of which can stand in the way of talking honestly, listening openly, and feeling free to suggest possible solutions. You may want to reserve peer mediation for other types of conflicts.

CHANGE SEATING ASSIGNMENTS

If you let students sit wherever they like, it may happen that the shy and lonely kids, bullying victims, or potential victims gravitate toward the outer edges of the class. It also may happen that the aggressive kids, bullies, or potential bullies sit toward the back, where their behavior is less likely to be noticed by you.

Take a look at where students are sitting. What do you see? Bring the shy and lonely "outsiders" into the center of the class, where they will have more opportunities to interact with other students. (Don't put them next to each other, or they'll mostly interact with each other.) Bring the aggressive kids up front, where you can keep a closer eye on them.

Change the seating assignments in your classroom periodically so students can get to know a variety of people.

SAY CHEESE!

Keep a camera close at hand. Routinely take pictures of your students working together, playing together, and interacting with each other in positive ways. Then:

- Post the pictures on your classroom bulletin board. Go ahead and fill it up with lots of pictures over the next several months; don't worry about overcrowding.

Or . . .

- Display the pictures in an oversized class photo album. Leave it out on a shelf or a corner of your desk so students can look through it often.

When students see themselves in pictures with each other, this gives them a sense of belonging to the group. (This is one reason why coaches take team pictures.) When you keep the pictures together in one place, this sends a message of unity and acceptance.

You'll probably notice that your students love looking at the pictures and discussing them with visitors. Don't be surprised if they're a special attraction on Parents' Night and at open houses.

 Go farther: Bring the camera with you on field trips and to school programs. Capture some action shots of students involved in projects, presentations, and sporting events. Schedule a "photo shoot" and encourage students to create their own scenes of classroom harmony and cooperation.

TEACH STUDENTS ABOUT GANGS, HATE GROUPS, AND CULTS

Young people who feel alienated at school, at home, and in their communities are often easy marks for gangs, hate groups, and cults—places where they can find acceptance and gain some sense of having power over other people and their own lives. Learn as much as you can about these groups and, as appropriate, share your knowledge with your students.*

Teach students how to respond if they are approached by a member of one of those groups. Very briefly, they should:

- stay calm and cool

- be confident (stand tall with head up and shoulders straight—try not to look scared)

- avoid arguing

- politely say "no thanks" to any offers (don't believe you'll be more popular or tougher if you say "yes" and decide to join)

- walk (don't run) to the nearest safe adult, group, or building

Your local police department can provide information about problems specific to your community. Invite an officer to speak to your students and answer any questions they might have about gangs, hate groups, and cults.

TRACK BULLYING ON TV

We already know that students are exposed to a great deal of violence on television. According to the American Psychological Association, research has shown that TV violence affects children negatively in three major ways:

- Children may become less sensitive to the pain and suffering of others.

- They may become more fearful of the world around them and perceive it as a mean and dangerous place.

- They may become more likely to behave aggressively toward others.

---

* See "Videos" in "Resources" (pages 153–157) for suggested videos.

Studies have shown that children's television shows contain about 20 violent acts each hour. It's likely that many of your students also watch programs aimed at adult audiences, where the violent content can be frequent, graphic, and realistic.

Bullying is a form of violence against others. Whether physical (hitting, kicking, pushing) or emotional (rejection, put-downs, threats), it can leave victims feeling powerless and abused.

Tell your students that you want them to track bullying on TV for one week. As they watch their regular programs, they should pay special attention to bullying behaviors. Give each student several copies of the handout "Bullying on TV" (page 64); have more copies available as needed throughout the week. Explain that students should use one handout per program to report on the bullying they see. They should bring each night's handouts to school the next day and give them to you. Review them as they come in to get an overall sense of your students' TV viewing habits and how much bullying they notice.

If you and your students did the "Define Bullying" activity (page 16) and the "Name Bullying Behaviors" activity (pages 21–22), everyone should have a general idea of what these behaviors include. If you didn't do these activities, take a few moments to introduce the main ideas. Make sure everyone understands that bullying encompasses a broad spectrum of behaviors.

At the end of the week, return each student's handouts and have a class discussion about bullying on TV. You might ask questions like these:

- How much bullying did you see on TV? None? A little? A lot?

- What kinds of bullying did you see?

- Which kinds seemed to be most common?

- Experts believe that watching violence on TV is bad for kids. Do you think that watching bullying on TV might be bad for kids, too? Why or why not?

BULLYING ON TV

Today's date: _____

Your name: _____

Name of the TV show you watched: _____

What channel was it on? _____ What network? _____

Did you notice any bullying?   yes ☐   no ☐

If *yes*, describe what happened: _____
_____
_____

How did the bullying affect the victim? _____
_____
_____

What did the victim do about the bullying? _____
_____
_____

What, if anything, happened to the bully? _____
_____
_____

Did it seem that:

    The victim deserved to be bullied?   yes ☐   no ☐

    The bullying was the victim's fault?   yes ☐   no ☐

- In general, when bullying happens on TV, do the bullies get away with it? Do the victims get hurt? Does it seem as if the bullying is the victims' fault?

- Now that you've watched for bullying on TV, how do you feel about it? What's your opinion?

 Go farther: If students are concerned about the amount of bullying they see on TV, have them write letters to the networks or local affiliates expressing their opinions about specific shows. Find addresses at the library or the networks' Web sites.

AFFIRM YOUR STUDENTS

Everyone appreciates a compliment. Students especially enjoy knowing that their teacher thinks well of them. Take every opportunity to say something positive to each of your students throughout the day. Your comments should be brief, honest, sincere, simple, and *specific*. *Examples:* "Christopher, I liked the way you helped Maria find her pencil." "Abby, I really appreciate your positive attitude today." "Kai, you did a great job on the reading assignment."

ICE CREAM CONE BULLETIN BOARD

This is a fun and colorful way to affirm and celebrate your students.

Provide construction paper in several colors (including brown for the cones). Have students create double-scoop ice cream cones, write their names on the cones, and give them to you. On each scoop, write a positive word or phrase that you think describes that student. Display the cones on a bulletin board or post them around the room.

Here's a list of starter words. You might also ask your students to come up with additional words they would use to describe each other or themselves.

- able to resolve conflicts
- alert
- ambitious
- analytical
- appreciative
- articulate
- assertive
- attentive
- aware
- calm
- careful
- caring
- cautious
- cheerful
- confident
- conscientious
- consistent
- cooperative
- courageous
- courteous
- creative
- dedicated
- dependable
- determined
- dynamic
- eager
- efficient
- empathetic
- energetic
- enthusiastic
- ethical
- fair
- faithful
- focused
- friendly
- fun
- generous
- gentle
- genuine
- giving
- goal setter
- good example
- good follower
- good listener
- good sport
- hard-working
- health conscious
- healthy
- helpful
- honest
- honorable
- hopeful
- humble
- humorous
- imaginative
- independent
- industrious
- ingenious
- innovative
- inspiring
- intelligent
- interesting
- intuitive
- inventive
- kind
- knowledgeable
- leader
- likable
- likes people
- lively
- logical
- loving
- loyal
- mature
- mediator
- merry
- motivated
- neat
- nice
- obedient
- open-minded
- optimistic
- organized
- patient
- peaceful
- people-oriented
- perceptive
- perseverant
- planner

- pleasant
- polite
- positive
- precise
- problem solver
- professional
- punctual
- quick
- reasonable
- relaxed
- reliable
- reputable
- resilient
- resourceful
- responsible
- safety conscious
- self-assured
- self-disciplined
- self-starter
- sensible
- sensitive
- service-minded
- sharing
- sincere
- spirited
- stable
- strong
- successful
- tactful
- tender-hearted
- thoughtful
- tolerant
- trusting
- trustworthy
- understanding
- unselfish
- upbeat
- versatile
- willing to compromise
- wise
- witty

 Go farther: Allow other people (students, teachers, other school personnel, visiting parents, aids, etc.) to add their own comments to students' books. To ensure that comments are positive, set two rules: 1) Everyone must sign his or her comment(s). 2) No one may write in another person's book without his or her permission.

Every so often, you might ask a student if it's okay to read aloud from his or her book. If it is, choose a few comments to share with the class. This encourages students to recognize and acknowledge each other's positive characteristics and notice similarities.

It's likely that these books will become cherished possessions—something your students will treasure for many years.

For more ways to help children learn to affirm themselves, see "Teach Positive Self-Talk" (pages 68 and 71).

TEACH STUDENTS TO AFFIRM THEMSELVES

Provide students with small blank books or notebooks (or put these on your list of school supplies to send home to parents at the start of the school year). Have them label their books "What's Good About Me" and use them to list and describe their positive characteristics. Get them started by asking questions like these:

- What do you like about yourself?

- What are you good at? Best at?

- What are your positive characteristics?

- What good things would you like other people to know about you?

- What makes you proud of yourself?

You might also refer to the list of starter words in "Affirm Your Students" (page 65 and above).

TEACH STUDENTS TO AFFIRM EACH OTHER

When students affirm each other, everyone feels accepted, appreciated, and valued. Here are six approaches you can try with your students.

AFFIRMATIONS BOX

Take a box with a lid (a large shoebox works well) and cut a slit in the top. Decorate it (or have students decorate it). Label it the "Affirmations Box" and put it on a shelf or a corner of your desk.

Invite students to write positive statements about each other whenever they like and drop them in the box. Once a week, once a day, or whenever you choose, dip into the box, pull out a statement or two, and read it aloud to the class.

This is a powerful way to encourage students to notice and appreciate each other's positive qualities. It helps them to see qualities they might have overlooked and discover similarities.

AFFIRMATIONS CARDS

Write each student's name on a 3" x 5" card. Hand out the cards randomly (just make sure that no one gets his or her own name). Then have each student write something positive about the student named on the card. *Examples:* "Sara is a terrific soccer player." "Ren is always willing to help." "Zach tells the best jokes." "Ashley has a great smile." Explain that you need them to take this seriously, because you (or they) will be reading their statements aloud. Ask students to sign their statements. (Anyone who's tempted to write something negative will think twice if his or her signature is on the card.)

Give the class a few minutes to write their statements. Collect them and review them quickly to make absolutely sure that all statements are positive. Then hand them back to the students and invite volunteers to read their statements aloud. If a student isn't comfortable doing this in front of the class, you can offer to read his or her statement. Either way, everyone should enjoy the experience.

Do this several times during the school year—once a week or once a month.

 Go farther: Take individual photos of your students and display them on a bulletin board along with their positive statements. Teachers who have done this report that students visit the bulletin board often, reading the statements and pointing out similar positive comments.

AFFIRMATIONS CIRCLES

Divide the class into two groups. (If you have an uneven number of students, join this activity yourself.) Have one group form a circle facing inward. Have the other group form a circle around the first group. Each student in the outer circle should stand directly behind a student in the inner circle.

On your cue, each student in the outer circle puts a hand on the shoulder of the student in front of him or her, then whispers a positive, encouraging statement in that student's ear. The statement should be brief, honest, sincere,

and simple. *Examples:* "I like the way you draw." "Thanks for helping me study for the math test." "I see you got your hair cut. It looks great." "I think you're the friendliest person in the class." "I'm glad you're my friend."

Next, have the students in the outer circle move one person to the left (or the right) and do it again (hand on the shoulder, positive statement). Keep going until the outer circle has moved all the way around the inner circle. Then have the circles switch places—the outer circle becomes the inner circle, and students who have been giving positive statements now have the chance to receive them.

Afterward, talk about the activity. Ask: "How did it feel to *say* something positive to another person?" "How did it feel to *hear* someone make a positive, encouraging statement about you?"

THUMBS UP

When one student makes a negative "thumbs down" comment about another, immediately ask him or her to make two positive "thumbs up" comments about that person. If the student has difficulty doing this (or won't do it), ask the class to make the positive comments. *Tip:* If you did the "Ice Cream Cone Bulletin Board" activity (pages 65–66), you can have one student read what you wrote about the student who was the target of the "thumbs down."

Encourage your students to use a "thumbs up" sign in class, on the playground, in the lunchroom, in the halls, and elsewhere to show their approval and support for each other.

APPLAUSE, APPLAUSE!

Invite your students to show their approval of a classmate's performance, good deed, or other positive action in a time-honored way: with applause. Encourage them to applaud vigorously and often.

You might say, "We applaud—or clap—for people to let them know we like something they're doing or something they've done. We enjoy it when people clap for us, and they enjoy it when we clap for them." Ask students to suggest times when they might applaud each other.

Have a brief practice session and set some ground rules so students don't get carried away with this. For example, they should stop clapping on a signal from you—perhaps when you raise your hand. You might create an "APPLAUSE!" sign or banner for your classroom. Point to the sign or banner to remind students to applaud when it's appropriate.

GOOD FOR YOU! CERTIFICATES

Once a week or twice a month, ask students to celebrate each other's achievements and accomplishments by completing "Good for You!" certificates (page 69). Explain that the achievements and accomplishments can be large or small, and they don't necessarily have to happen in the classroom or even be school-related.

Keep several copies of the certificate on hand. Post complete certificates around the classroom for a few days, then allow the honored students to take them down and bring them home to share with their families. *Tip:* Make sure that *all* students are recognized often, not just the same few students. Fill out certificates yourself for students whose achievements and accomplishments might otherwise go unnoticed.

ASSESS THE WEEK

According to an old saying, "Before we can decide where we're going, we have to know where we've been." End each week by inviting your students to reflect on the events of that week. Distribute copies of the handout "The Week in Review" (page 70). Tally the results (or have a volunteer do this) and report them on Monday morning. Use the results to set goals or objectives for the coming week.

Tip: For another approach, see "Set and Review Weekly Goals" (page 57).

WEAR "NO BULLYING" BUTTONS

Have students design and make buttons or badges with a "No Bullying!" message. They might say "No Bullying!" or "No Bullying Allowed!" or "Bully Free Classroom!" or whatever students prefer. If you want to make buttons with metal frames and pins, use a button machine. Check to see if your school has one; if it doesn't, contact a button company.* Inexpensive badge holders are available in bookstores or office supply stores.

TEACH POSITIVE SELF-TALK

It's no secret that positive thinking can be powerful—especially positive thinking about ourselves and our abilities to solve problems, reach goals, cope with hard times, and accomplish what we set out to do. Positive self-talk creates positive beliefs. Positive beliefs lead to positive attitudes and feelings about oneself and others. Positive attitudes and feelings promote positive behaviors.

Successful, capable, competent people tend to be self-affirmers. They don't get carried away ("I'm the greatest!"), but they do give themselves frequent pep talks ("I can do it!").

Many students who are bullied—and even those who aren't—have difficulty with this. It's easy for them to lapse into negative self-talk ("I can't do it," "Why even try?"), which can set the stage for negative beliefs, attitudes, feelings, and behaviors—and also for failure, which "proves" that their negative self-talk was right.

There are many ways to teach positive self-talk. Here are six you can explore with your students:

1. Have a class discussion about self-talk, both positive and negative. Make sure students know the difference. Give examples

---

* Badge-A-Minit can get you started with an easy-to-use hand press, sample designs, pinned backs, and instructions. Call 1-800-223-4103 for more information.

GOOD FOR YOU!

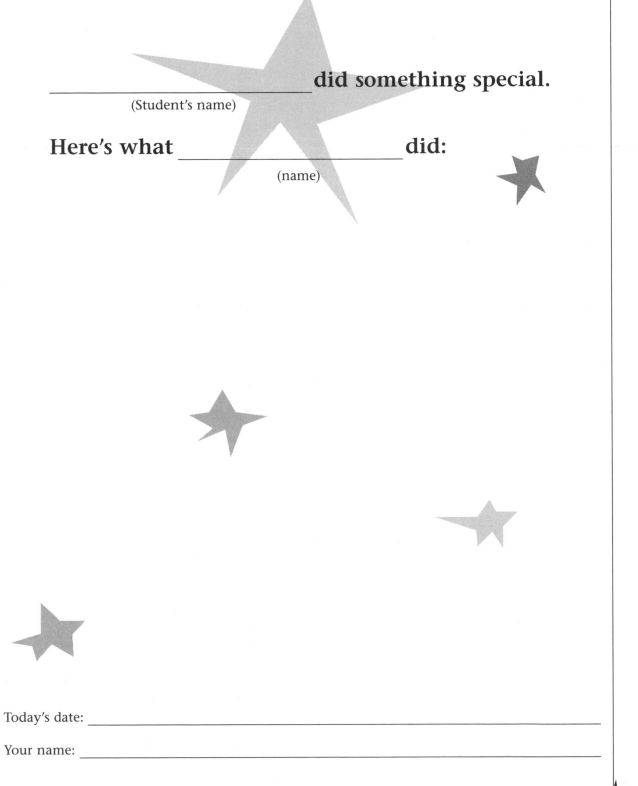

_____ **did something special.**
(Student's name)

Here's what _____ **did:**
(name)

Today's date: _____

Your name: _____

THE WEEK IN REVIEW

Today's date: _____

Your name (if you want to give it): _____

Think back on the past week in this classroom. Read each statement, then check the column that best describes how you feel about your week.

This week in school:	All of the time	Most of the time	Some of the time	Never
1. I was respected as a person.				
2. I treated others with respect.				
3. I was treated fairly.				
4. I treated others fairly.				
5. People helped me when I needed help.				
6. I helped others.				
7. We cared for each other.				
8. We worked hard to make our classroom a positive place to be.				
9. I felt like I belonged.				
10. I helped others feel like they belonged.				
11. I was encouraged to do my best.				
12. I encouraged others to do their best.				
13. We worked together to solve problems.				
14. We cooperated with each other.				
15. I felt accepted.				
16. I helped others feel accepted.				

or ask them for examples. Explain that positive self-talk *really works.*

2. Hand out copies of "Messages from Me to Me" (page 72), which lists several brief statements students can use in their positive self-talk. Read it aloud or invite students to read individual statements. Suggest that students keep the list and refer to it often.

 Go farther: Have students pick two or three statements from the list, write them on a 3" x 5" card, and carry the card with them in their pocket or backpack. Or they can write their own statements.

3. Have students write brief positive self-talk scripts to keep in their notebooks or at their desks. (*Example:* "I know I can do this. I have the ability. If I get stuck, I can ask for help. I can succeed.") When students catch themselves using negative self-talk (or when anyone else catches them), they can read their scripts. The briefer the better; after a few readings, many students will have their scripts memorized. Suggest that they close their eyes and take a few deep breaths before repeating their scripts to themselves.

4. Before starting a new class activity, ask students to close their eyes and silently say one or two positive statements to themselves. Or you might write statements on the chalkboard and say them aloud as a class.

5. Divide the class into small groups. Have each group come up with a list of negative self-talk statements, then brainstorm positive self-talk responses. Afterward, the groups can share their lists with the class.

6. Have students complete "Good for You!" certificates for themselves, describing their own achievements and accomplishments. See "Teach Students to Affirm Each Other," pages 66–68.

 Go farther: When you need more ideas, check out Douglas Bloch's *Positive Self-Talk for Children: Teaching Self-Esteem through*

Affirmations—A Guide for Parents, Teachers, and Counselors (New York: Bantam, 1993). This step-by-step guide helps adults instill positive messages and self-esteem in children right from the start.

USE HUMOR

Humor is a terrific tool for making everyone feel welcome, accepted, and appreciated. Laughter is good for us *physically* (increasing respiratory activity, oxygen exchange, muscular activity, and heart rate; stimulating the cardiovascular system and sympathetic nervous system; leading to an overall positive biochemical state) and *mentally* (decreasing stress, lifting spirits, improving moods). Here are six ways to bring humor and laughter into your classroom:

1. Start each day with a joke or two. You might have students bring in their favorite jokes to share.

2. For a special treat now and then, show a funny movie.

3. Start a class collection of joke books and cartoon books.

4. Have a "Humor Corner" in your classroom. Stock it with funny books, posters, audiotapes, and other resources.

5. Keep a "Joke Jar" in your classroom. Fill it with brief jokes written on small pieces of paper. Encourage students to contribute their own jokes. (Set a few ground rules first: No hurtful jokes. No biased jokes. No crude or tasteless jokes.) Once a day, you (or a student) can reach into the jar, pull out a joke, and share it with the class.

6. Read humorous stories aloud or give them as reading assignments.

Talk with your class about the difference between laughing *at* someone and laughing *with* someone. Ask questions like these:

"I'm a good person."

"I deserve to be treated with kindness and respect."

"I'm special and unique."

"I'm creative and talented."

"I can set goals and reach them."

"I can solve problems."

"I can ask other people for help."

"I have a right to be imperfect."

"I have a right to make mistakes."

"Everyone makes mistakes."

"I can learn from my mistakes."

"I'm valuable and worthwhile . . . just the way I am."

"I can get through this."

"I'm learning and growing."

"I'm not alone."

"I'm okay."

"I'm strong and capable."

"Even if I don't feel so great right now, I'll feel better soon."

"I can be patient with myself."

"I can manage."

"I can cope."

"I can do this."

"I can succeed."

"I can try again."

"I can expect the best of myself."

"I'm brave and courageous."

"I believe in myself."

"I'm not afraid."

- When is it okay to laugh?
- When is it not okay to laugh?
- Are there times when laughter can hurt? How can it hurt?
- Are there times when laughter can help? How can it help?

GET STUDENTS INVOLVED IN SERVICE

When students work together to reach a common goal—especially when that goal involves helping others—they experience a sense of unity, personal worth, and belonging. This has a bonding effect on the group as a whole. It also gives students an opportunity to observe and appreciate each other's knowledge and skills.

Of course, there are many more benefits of serving others. When Independent Sector surveyed youth who serve, the students reported 18 benefits of their volunteer experience. Here are the top 10:*

- **They learned to respect others.**
- **They learned to be helpful and kind.**
- **They learned how to get along with and relate to others.**
- **They gained satisfaction from helping others.**
- **They learned to understand people who are different from them.**
- **They learned how to relate to younger children.**
- **They became better people.**
- **They learned new skills.**
- **They developed leadership skills.**
- **They became more patient with others.**

---

* SOURCE: *Volunteering and Giving Among American Teenagers 12 to 17 Years of Age* (Washington, DC: Independent Sector, 1996).

There are countless ways you and your students can make a difference. Your biggest challenge might be getting your class to choose just one project from among so many possibilities available to you. Here are six suggestions to start with:

1. Find out if your school already offers service learning opportunities. Check with your principal or school counselor. If it does, ask your students what they would like to do. (Try the democratic approach and take a vote.)

 Go farther: On the Web, check out the Learn and Serve America National Service-Learning Clearinghouse *(http://umn. edu/~serve)*, an adjunct ERIC clearinghouse on service learning. This comprehensive information system focuses on all dimensions of service learning, covering kindergarten through higher education and community-based initiatives. You can also write or call: The Learn and Serve America National Service-Learning Clearinghouse, University of Minnesota, Department of Work, Community & Family Education, 1954 Buford Avenue, Room R-460, St. Paul, MN 55108; toll-free telephone 1-800-808-SERV (1-800-808-7378).

2. Start a service club in your classroom. Students can begin by identifying an issue they'd like to work on or a problem they'd like to address in your classroom, the whole school, or the school community. (What about a "Stop Bullying" club?)

 Go farther: You might want to start a Kids Care Club in your classroom or school. For a fee (at this writing, $95 for the first year), this national organization will provide you with a license to use the Kids Care Club name and logo and send you a Kids Care Start Up Kit including "all the materials you need to turn a group of kids into a force for kindness." For more information, write or call: Kids Care Club, PO Box 1083, New Canaan, CT 06840; telephone (203) 972-6601. Or visit their Web site *(http://www.kidscare.org/)*, where you can print out a membership application.

3. Ask other people in your school or community about ways to serve. Or make this a class assignment and have students gather information. They might contact one or more of the following:

- animal shelters
- arts centers
- children's shelters
- civic groups (*examples:* Elks, Rotary, Kiwanis, Lions clubs)
- community centers
- congregations
- conservation groups
- food pantries
- homeless shelters
- hospitals
- libraries
- the mayor's office
- residential facilities for people with disabilities
- other schools
- zoos

4. Check your phone book to see if any of these organizations have chapters near you, and ask how your students can serve:

- American National Red Cross
- Boy Scouts of America
- Boys & Girls Clubs of America
- Girl Scouts of the U.S.A.
- Girls, Inc.
- Habitat for Humanity International
- Kids Against Crime
- Kids Against Pollution
- Kids for Saving the Earth
- National 4-H Council
- United Way of America
- YMCA of the USA
- Youth Service America

5. Visit your local library or bookstore and look for books about kids and service. *Examples:*

- *The Kid's Guide to Service Projects* by Barbara A. Lewis (Minneapolis: Free Spirit Publishing, 1995). More than 500 service ideas for youth, from simple projects to large-scale initiatives. For ages 10 and up.
- *Teaching Your Kids to Care: How to Discover and Develop the Spirit of Charity in Your Children* by Deborah Spaide (Secaucus, NJ: Citadel Press, 1995). Spaide is the founder of the Kids Care Club. In this practical, inspiring book, she describes 105 projects that develop the charity instinct in children and youth from preschool through high school.

6. Explore the Internet's vast resources on volunteering and service. In addition to the Learn and Serve America National Service-Learning Clearinghouse and the Kids Care Club (both described on page 73), here are five more Web sites you can visit—and these are just the tip of the iceberg:

- **Nickelodeon's Web Site for Teachers** *(http://teachers.nick.com)*. Stop in to learn about ways to use The Big Help, Nickelodeon's ongoing, prosocial campaign to connect kids to their communities through volunteering. Or request Big Help print materials for your class by writing or calling: The Big Help, Box 929, New York, NY 10108; telephone (212) 259-7080.
- **Nickelodeon** *(http://nick.com)*. When your students are on the Web, they can go to this fun site, search for The Big Help, find out how other kids are helping, and download resources to help them begin their own volunteer projects. Or they can request The Big Help Kit by writing to the address given above.
- **The Points of Light Foundation** *(http://www.pointsoflight.org)*. Founded in May 1990, the Foundation is a nonpartisan nonprofit organization devoted to promoting volunteerism. It works in communities throughout the United States through a network of over 500 Volunteer Centers. The Web site features

profiles of "Daily Points of Light"—inspiring true stories about people and organizations helping their communities. Or write or call: The Points of Light Foundation, 1400 I Street, NW, Suite 800, Washington, DC 20005; telephone (202) 729-8000.

- **The Prudential Spirit of Community Initiative** *(http://www.prudential.com/ community)*. Find out about national honorees and finalists—young people actively involved in making their communities better places to live. Download a copy of "Catch the Spirit! A Student's Guide to Community Service." Or request this free 16-page booklet by writing to: The Consumer Information Center, Dept. 506E, Pueblo, CO 81009.

- **SERVEnet** *(http://www.servenet.org)*. Sponsored by Youth Service America, this big site brings thousands of volunteers and community organizations together online. Stop in to read stories about everyday service heroes, find out more about volunteering, learn the latest news and events in the service field, link to Youth Service America, and more. Or write or call: SERVEnet, 1101 15th Street, Suite 200, Washington, DC 20005; telephone (202) 296-2992.

MONITOR THE MESSAGES YOU SEND

Children—even very young children—are amazingly perceptive. They know when a student is the "teacher's pet." They can tell when a teacher dislikes a student or doubts the student's abilities to learn and get along with others.

How can you make sure you're sending the right "messages" to your students? Consider the following suggestions. Ask other teachers about what has and hasn't worked for them. When you share strategies, experiences, and insights, everyone benefits—you, your colleagues, and students in your school.

1. Greet each student by name as he or she enters your classroom.

2. Each day, let every student know you care about him or her—in your words, body language, and actions.

3. Make frequent eye contact with every student. Studies have shown that some teachers favor children they perceive as attractive. They make eye contact more often with those students, and they give them more positive attention, reinforcement, affirmations, and feedback. They may call on those students more frequently.

4. Children have a strong need to appear successful in front of their peers and a deep fear of looking foolish or being laughed at. Plan and arrange classroom activities so all of your students can show their strengths, not their weaknesses. *Examples:* Avoid asking poor readers to read aloud to the class. If you know that a particular student has weak math skills, don't insist that he or she work problems on the chalkboard.

5. Show interest in every student. This is a powerful motivator and helps all students feel welcome, appreciated, and accepted.

6. Be a good listener. Try to find time each day to really *listen* to each student. Lean forward, paraphrase their comments, and communicate your understanding of what they're saying and feeling.

7. As much as possible, individualize your teaching strategies and assignments. Research indicates that individualized instruction decreases antisocial behaviors in the classroom. It also increases the chances that your students will succeed.

8. Write personal, positive notes and letters to your students throughout the year. Students love getting letters from their teachers. Before the start of the school year, consider sending letters to each of your

future students, welcoming them to your class and hinting at some of what you'll be learning throughout the year. This can also help decrease some of their anxiety about the coming year.

9. Even though some students will be smarter, friendlier, better behaved, and more likable than others, make sure they don't become "teacher's pets." Children are sensitive to favoritism and may be jealous of "pets." Jealousy can lead to bullying.

10. Do your best to treat all of your students equally. Avoid giving special privileges to some students and not others. This can create envy and hostility, which in turn can lead to bullying. If a student requires special treatment (for example, because of a medical condition), make sure the rest of the class understands why. (Get the permission of the student and his or her parents first to avoid embarrassment and potential problems.)

11. Remind your students that "equal" doesn't mean "the same." Explain that you'll do your very best to give everyone equal opportunities to learn and grow, but they will learn and grow in different ways.

12. When students see you put your trust in someone, they tend to have more respect for that person—especially if they respect you. Is there someone who seems to be having a hard time in school? Someone who's being picked on, excluded, teased, or bullied? Plan an activity (in class or on a field trip) where you can demonstrate complete trust in that student. When other students see this, they may view the student in a more positive light.

13. It's a real challenge to like every student all the time. Do your best to be accepting, sensitive, and understanding even in difficult situations. Don't hide your feelings, but express them in positive, helpful ways. Give students a chance to respond. *Example:* "I'm disappointed that you didn't finish your math homework. What can we do to keep this from happening again?"

14. We all have biases and prejudices. Some are based on cultural or ethnic background, others on gender, religion, intelligence, or ability level. Examine your own prejudices. How did you come to learn or believe these things? Are they part of your daily life? Are they affecting your teaching? Are they having a negative effect on your students? Be honest with yourself. Make a conscious, deliberate, focused effort to check your prejudices, unlearn them, and get beyond them.

15. Smile, smile, smile. Show your students that you're glad to be their teacher. This may be the most obvious positive message you can send.

16. Think positive thoughts about all of your students. Wish them the best in everything they do. Have high hopes for them. If you're a religious person, you might consider praying for them. A former National Teacher of the Year used to go to school early each day (before the children arrived), sit at a student's desk, and pray for him or her. He believes this made a significant difference in his students' behavior and his own interactions with them.

HELPING
VICTIMS

I f you were bullied as a child, you can probably remember how you felt. You may recall the specifics of each incident—the people, places, words, insults, frustration, pain, anger, and powerlessness.

The good news is: Your students don't have to endure the bullying you put up with when you were their age. We know more about bullying now than we did ten or even five years ago, and we know more about how to prevent it and stop it. We know more about how to help the victims of bullying—and why we should and must.

The "Creating a Positive Classroom" section of this book includes many tips and strategies that can benefit victims and potential victims. *Examples:*

- "Teach Anger Management Skills" (page 32)

- "Teach Friendship Skills" (pages 34–36)

- "Explore Ways to Deal with Bullies" (page 41)

- "Use a Notes-to-the-Teacher Box" (pages 41 and 45)

- "Teach Students to Use 'I Messages'" (page 51)

- "Teach Assertiveness Skills" (pages 53–54)

- "Teach Conflict Resolution Skills" (page 58)

- "Teach Students to Affirm Themselves" (page 66)

- "Teach Positive Self-Talk" (pages 68 and 71)

Similarly, "Helping Victims" features suggestions that you can use with all of your students. But most focus on students who desperately need adults to notice them, see what they're going through, and do something about it.

As you try these ideas with your class, individual students, and small groups, and as you share them with other teachers and staff, here are some good things you can expect to happen:

Your students will learn how to:

- stick up for themselves and each other
- break the code of silence and report bullying incidents
- differentiate between reporting and "ratting"
- feel stronger, more confident, and better about themselves
- strengthen their bully resistance skills
- build their social skills
- plan ahead to avoid potential problems
- use humor and other "power skills" to disarm bullies.

You'll discover how to:

- identify victims or potential victims
- encourage students to report bullying
- act quickly and effectively when you learn of a bullying incident
- communicate with parents and get them involved in making your classroom bully free
- mobilize the masses—witnesses and bystanders—to become bully busters
- help students accept their differences
- equalize the power between victims and bullies
- protect yourself.

BE ALERT

Most bullying takes place where you (and other adults) can't see it or hear it. Bullies need an audience of their peers to establish their power over the victim, but the last thing they want is an audience of adults who have power over *them* and can make them stop.

Pay attention to interactions between your students. Are there some who seem fearful, withdrawn, lonely, and shy? Are there others who seem especially aggressive, need to "win" all the time, seek excessive attention, and are always pushing the boundaries of school or class rules? How do they get along with each other? What happens when they're seated beside each other, or are assigned to the same groups and expected to work together? Be watchful and alert.

Talk with lunchroom supervisors, hall monitors, playground supervisors, gym teachers, and other adults who spend time with your students. Ask for their insights and input into relationships between your students. What have they seen? What have they heard? Learn as much as you can. It may be that bullying has gone on behind your back (even under your nose) and you simply haven't noticed it. If so, you're not alone.

IDENTIFY VICTIMS OR POTENTIAL VICTIMS

You may know that some students in your classroom are victims of bullying—because you've witnessed bullying events personally, or other students have reported them to you, or the victims themselves have come forward.

But most bullying goes unnoticed and unreported. How can you identify victims or potential victims? You can watch for specific behaviors—and you can seek input from students' parents.

 Important: Experts have determined that there are *two* types of victims:

- *passive victims*—anxious, sensitive loners who give off "victim" signals, lack self-defense skills, don't think quickly on their feet, and have few friends to support them
- *provocative victims*—easily aroused, impulsive, annoying kids who tease or taunt bullies, egg them on, and make themselves targets but can't defend themselves

LOOK FOR WARNING SIGNS

For any student you suspect might be a victim or potential victim, complete the "Warning Signs" checklist (pages 79–80).

WARNING SIGNS

The following behaviors may indicate that a student is being bullied or is at risk of being bullied. For any student you're concerned about, check all that apply.

When any of these behaviors are evident and persistent over time, you should definitely investigate. There's no magic number of warning signs that indicate a student is definitely being victimized—but it's better to be wrong than to allow a student to suffer.

Some of these characteristics are obviously more serious than others. A child who talks about suicide or carries a weapon to school, for example, needs immediate *help. Don't wait for the child to come to you (this may never happen). Following the guidelines established by your school or district, contact a professional who is specially trained in dealing with high-risk behaviors.*

Today's date: _____

Student's name: _____

SCHOOL AND SCHOOL WORK

_____ **1.** Sudden change in school attendance/academic performance

_____ **2.** Erratic attendance

_____ **3.** Loss of interest in school work/academic performance/homework

_____ **4.** Decline in quality of school work/academic performance*

_____ **5.** Academic success; appears to be the teacher's pet*

_____ **6.** Difficulty concentrating in class, easily distracted

_____ **7.** Goes to recess late and comes back early

_____ **8.** Has a learning disability or difference

_____ **9.** Lack of interest in school-sponsored activities/events

_____ **10.** Drops out of school-sponsored activities he or she enjoys

SOCIAL

_____ **1.** Lonely, withdrawn, isolated

_____ **2.** Poor or no social/interpersonal skills

_____ **3.** No friends or fewer friends than other students, unpopular, often/always picked last for groups or teams

_____ **4.** Lacks a sense of humor, uses inappropriate humor

_____ **5.** Often made fun of, laughed at, picked on, teased, put down, and/or called names by other students, doesn't stand up for himself or herself

_____ **6.** Often pushed around, kicked, and/or hit by other students, doesn't defend himself or herself

_____ **7.** Uses "victim" body language—hunches shoulders, hangs head, won't look people in the eye, backs off from others

* True, #4 and #5 are opposites. They are also *extremes*. Watch for any extremes or sudden changes; these can be signs that something stressful is happening in a student's life.

CONTINUED →

_____ **8.** Has a noticeable difference that sets him or her apart from peers

_____ **9.** Comes from a racial, cultural, ethnic, and/or religious background that puts him or her in the minority

_____ **10.** Prefers the company of adults during lunch and other free times

_____ **11.** Teases, pesters, and irritates others, eggs them on, doesn't know when to stop

_____ **12.** Suddenly starts bullying other students

PHYSICAL

_____ **1.** Frequent illness*

_____ **2.** Frequent complaints of headache, stomachache, pains, etc.*

_____ **3.** Scratches, bruises, damage to clothes or belongings, etc. that don't have obvious explanations

_____ **4.** Sudden stammer or stutter

_____ **5.** Has a physical disability

_____ **6.** Has a physical difference that sets him/her apart from peers—wears glasses, is over-weight/underweight, taller/shorter than peers, "talks funny," "looks funny," "walks funny," etc.

_____ **7.** Change in eating patterns, sudden loss of appetite

_____ **8.** Clumsy, uncoordinated, poor at sports

_____ **9.** Smaller than peers

_____ **10.** Physically weaker than peers

EMOTIONAL/BEHAVIORAL

_____ **1.** Sudden change in mood or behavior

_____ **2.** Passive, timid, quiet, shy, sullen, withdrawn

_____ **3.** Low or no self-confidence/self-esteem

_____ **4.** Low or no assertiveness skills

_____ **5.** Overly sensitive, cautious, clingy

_____ **6.** Nervous, anxious, worried, fearful, insecure

_____ **7.** Cries easily and/or often, becomes emotionally distraught, has extreme mood swings

_____ **8.** Irritable, disruptive, aggressive, quick-tempered, fights back (but always loses)

_____ **9.** Blames himself or herself for problems/difficulties

_____ **10.** Overly concerned about personal safety; spends a lot of time and effort thinking/worrying about getting safely to and from lunch, the bathroom, lockers, through recess, etc.; avoids certain places at school

_____ **11.** Talks about running away

_____ **12.** Talks about suicide

* A school nurse can determine if these physical symptoms might have other causes. A nurse can also gently question a child to learn if he/she is being bullied.

Important: These forms should be kept confidential. You may want to share them with other adults—teachers, your principal, the school counselor, the student's parents—but they should never be accessible to students.

GET PARENTS' INPUT

If a student shows some or many of the warning signs, contact the parents. Arrange a face-to-face meeting at school.

No parent wants to hear that his or her child might be a victim or potential victim of bullying, so you'll need to offer a lot of reassurance along the way. You might start by emphasizing your commitment to making your classroom bully free. Share information about schoolwide efforts to reduce and eliminate bullying. Then tell the parents that you've noticed some behaviors at school which may indicate their child is being bullied or could be a potential victim of bullying. Give examples. Explain that there are other behaviors that don't show up at school, and you need their help identifying those behaviors.

Ask if they have noticed any of the following in their child:

- Frequent illness*
- Frequent complaints of headache, stomachache, pains, etc.*
- Sudden changes in behavior (bed-wetting, nail-biting, tics, problems sleeping, loss of appetite, depression, crying, nightmares, stammering, stuttering, etc.)*
- Seems anxious, fearful, moody, sad; refuses to say what's wrong
- Doesn't want to go to school, refuses to go to school, starts skipping school
- Changes walking route to school, wants to change buses, begs to be driven to school (refuses to walk or ride bus)

---

* Ask the parents if their child has been seen by a doctor recently; if not, suggest that they make an appointment. A doctor can determine if these symptoms and behaviors might have other causes. A doctor can also gently question a child to learn if he or she is being bullied.

- Comes home from school with scratches, bruises, damage to clothes or belongings, etc. that don't have obvious explanations; makes improbable excuses
- Comes home from school hungry (lunch money was "lost" or stolen)
- Possessions (books, money, clothing, etc.) are often "lost," damaged, or destroyed
- Frequently asks for extra money (for lunch, school supplies, etc.)
- Carries or wants to carry "protection" (guns, knives, forks, box openers, etc.) to school
- Sudden loss of interest in homework, school work, academic performance
- Has few or no friends; is rarely invited to parties or other social events
- Seems happy/normal on weekends but not during the week; seems preoccupied/tense on Sundays before school
- Obsesses about his or her height, weight, appearance, clothes, etc.
- Has started bullying other children/siblings; is aggressive, rebellious, unreasonable
- Talks about or attempts to run away from home
- Talks about or attempts suicide*

Keep a written record of your meeting and any relevant information the parents share with you. Thank the parents for coming in and talking with you. Tell them that you'll communicate with them often about their child's behavior and progress, and about your efforts to make sure the bullying stops (or never starts). Then be sure to follow through.

TALK WITH OTHER TEACHERS AND STAFF

If you think that a student is being bullied or might be at risk, share your concerns with other teachers or staff members.

---

* If parents report this behavior, urge them to seek professional help *immediately*. Follow the guidelines established by your school or district.

If the student spends part of the day in another classroom, talk with that teacher. How is the student treated by other kids in the class? Has the teacher noticed any sudden changes in the student's behavior? (See "Identify Victims or Potential Victims," pages 78–81.) Has the student said anything about feeling worried, anxious, or afraid to be in school?

Talk to a playground supervisor or hall monitor to find out how the student is treated at recess or during class breaks. If the student rides the bus to and from school, talk to the bus driver.

Other adults may be aware of events in the student's life that could indicate a bullying situation. You might also discover that problems you've noticed are not isolated incidents. If so, find out more and follow through.

EXAMINE YOUR OWN BELIEFS

To help victims gain the strength and skills to stop being victims, to help bullies change their behavior, and to reduce or eliminate bullying in your classroom, you need to believe that bullying is a problem that can be identified, addressed, and resolved.

Since you're reading this book, chances are you're already convinced. But many adults (including teachers) have lingering misconceptions about bullying. It's worth taking the time to do a reality check on your own beliefs. Following are four examples of erroneous thinking about victims, bullies, and bullying.*

"Bullying isn't a problem in my classroom or in our school."

Some teachers and administrators make this claim. In fact:

> Bullying in schools is a worldwide problem. . . . Although much of the

formal research on bullying has taken place in the Scandinavian countries, Great Britain, and Japan, the problems associated with bullying have been noted and discussed wherever formal schooling environments exist.*

- The National Association of School Psychologists estimates that 160,000 children miss school every day for fear of being bullied.

- According to the National Center for School Safety, three million bullying incidents are reported each year. Since most bullying goes unnoticed and unreported, this number probably represents the tip of the iceberg.

"It's best to let students solve their own problems, without adult interference. This is how they learn to get along in the world."

Many adults tell children not to "tattle" about bullying. In a normal peer conflict (sharing toys, deciding who goes first in a game, arguing about rules or privileges, etc.), kids should be allowed and encouraged to figure out and try their own solutions.

Bullying is not a normal peer conflict. Here are two reasons why:

1. In a normal peer conflict, both parties are emotionally involved. Both experience painful or uncomfortable emotions; they're hurt, upset, angry, frustrated, disappointed, outraged, etc. In a bullying situation, it's usually only the victim who feels emotional pain. In contrast, the bully might feel satisfied, excited, or nothing at all (flat affect).

2. In a normal peer conflict, both parties have some power—sometimes equal power, which is why arguments, disagreements, and differences of opinion can seem to last forever. In a bullying situation, there's always a power imbalance.

---

* See also "Expose the Myths" (page 16) and "Share Facts About Bullying" (pages 19 and 21).

* SOURCE: Ron Banks, "Bullying in Schools," ERIC Digest EDO-PS-97-17, March 1997.

The bully has all or most of the power; the victim has little or none.

For these reasons, adult intervention with bullying is necessary. This is not "interference." It's helping young people with a problem they aren't equipped to solve on their own.

"I've heard that bullying starts in the elementary school years, peaks in the middle school years, and declines during the high school years. That sounds almost like 'growing pains.' Maybe bullying is just a normal, unavoidable part of life."

Bullying does seem to follow this very general pattern . . . although many adults experience bullying in their relationships and in the workplace. We get over our "growing pains," but the effects of being bullied (and of being a bully) can last a lifetime.

For victims, feelings of low self-esteem, isolation, powerlessness, and depression can continue into adulthood. The psychological harm they suffer as children can interfere with their social, emotional, and academic development. They may develop health problems due to the prolonged stress of being bullied. Some victims drop out of school; some commit suicide.

What about bullies? A longitudinal study by psychologist E. Eron at the University of Michigan found that bullies remain bullies throughout their lives. As adults, they have more court convictions, more alcoholism, and more personality disorders than the general population. They use more mental health services and have difficulty maintaining relationships.

"I was bullied at school, and I survived. Bullying builds character."

If you were bullied at school, you probably have very clear memories of what happened and how you felt about it. Maybe you even have nightmares related to bullying you experienced as a child. Why would you wish this on any of your students? And what kind of "character" does bullying build? If bullying is allowed to continue, children learn that might is right, bullies

get their way, aggression is best—and adults can't be counted on to help.

BREAK THE CODE OF SILENCE

Research has shown that students are reluctant to tell adults about bullying. They don't believe it will help; they fear it will make things worse. Often, they're right.

Adults may not act on what they learn. They may not keep the confidence of young people who tell. And if they don't know much about bullying, they may give poor advice—such as "fight back" or "solve your own problems." A code of silence exists, especially as students move toward middle school, when the unspoken rule becomes "don't tell on other kids." Meanwhile, bullies make it known that anyone who reports their behavior will be their next target.

You can and should break this code of silence. The "Creating a Positive Classroom" section of this book describes several ways to do this. *Examples:*

- "Share Stories About Bullying" (page 22)
- "Take a Survey" (pages 22 and 24–30)
- "Respond Effectively to Reports of Bullying" (pages 32 and 34)
- "Learn More About Your Students" (pages 38–39)
- "Use a Notes-to-the-Teacher Box" (pages 41 and 45).

As you encourage students to come forward with their bullying stories, make sure they know the difference between "ratting" and "reporting." Ratting is when one student tells on another for the purpose of getting the other student in trouble. Reporting is when one student tells on another for the purpose of protecting someone else. When your students fully understand this, reporting will become less of a social taboo and more of a positive, acceptable action.

If a student comes to you to report bullying he or she has witnessed:

1. Listen carefully.* Ask questions to clarify the details. Who was involved? What happened? When? Where? Were there any other witnesses? Take notes.

2. If the student requests confidentiality, respect his or her wishes.

3. Thank the student for talking with you.

If a student comes to you to "just talk" and you suspect that he or she is a victim of bullying:

1. Be patient. Don't expect all the details to come pouring out immediately. The student may be reluctant to give specifics out of embarrassment or shame.

2. At first, don't question the student too closely. Avoid questions that imply he or she might have done something wrong or "deserved" the bullying in any way.

 Important: Some victims provoke bullies—by pestering, teasing, fighting back (even though they always lose), and coming back for more. But this doesn't mean they *deserve* to be bullied.

3. Approach the topic gently and indirectly. Give the student the option to talk about it or not.

4. If the student still skirts the issue, let him or her know that you're willing to listen anytime he or she wants to talk. Leave the door open for future conversations.

5. Once the student begins talking about the incident (or several incidents), don't be surprised if it's like a dam breaking. Let the student talk. Just listen. Try not to interrupt with suggestions or opinions. This might be the first time the student has told anyone about the bullying.

6. Be sympathetic, but don't overreact. The student will probably be emotional; it's your job to stay calm. On the other hand, don't trivialize what the student tells you. What sounds like simple teasing to you might be terrifying to him or her.

7. Let the student know that you believe what he or she is telling you.

8. Ask the student if he or she has any ideas for changing the situation.

 Important: This boosts self-confidence and self-esteem; you're letting the student know that you think he or she is capable of coming up with solutions to the problem. But even if the student has ideas, don't stop here. Bullying is *not* just another peer conflict. It's *always* a power imbalance. Adult intervention is required.

9. Ask the student if he or she wants your help. Chances are, the answer will be yes, otherwise the student wouldn't have come to you. But sometimes what a victim needs most at the moment is an adult who will listen respectfully and believe what he or she says.

10. Offer specific suggestions. (You'll find several throughout this section of the book. See also "Explore Ways to Deal with Bullies" on pages 41.)

Important: If you're not sure what to say or suggest, promise the student that you'll get back to him or her. Then seek advice from someone with experience in this area—another teacher, your principal, the school counselor.

11. Redouble your efforts to create a positive classroom where bullying is not tolerated.

12. If at any time the student mentions, threatens, or alludes to suicide, take this *very* seriously. *Get professional help immediately.*

Whether your reporter is a witness or a victim, be sure to follow through. Make it very clear that when someone tells you about a bullying

---

* See "Be a Good Listener" (pages 86–88).

incident, you *will* take action and you *won't* just "let it go."

ACT IMMEDIATELY

No matter how you're made aware of a bullying incident—whether you witness it personally, a student tells you about it, you receive a report in your "Notes-to-the-Teacher" box (see pages 41 and 45), you read about it in a student's journal (see pages 38–39), or you learn about it in some other way—take immediate action.

IF YOU WITNESS IT PERSONALLY . . .

Intervene then and there. Don't try to talk with anyone involved; don't solicit suggestions on how to resolve the problem. Just put a stop to it.

1. If the bullying is *physical,* say "(Student's name), stop (pushing, shoving, hitting, tripping, etc.) immediately" in a firm, authoritative voice. Instruct the bully to move away from the victim.

   If the behavior has attracted an audience, tell the onlookers to return to their seats, return to their classroom, or go somewhere else. When you remove the audience, you remove a large part of the bully's power.

   What if the bully and victim are fighting? Follow these suggestions from the Crisis Prevention Institute on how to break up a fight:*

- *Get assistance.* Intervening alone is dangerous.
- *Remove the audience.* Onlookers fuel the fire. The intensity of an altercation often parallels the intensity of the bystanders. Remove them as quickly as possible.

---

* Copyright © 1994 by the Crisis Prevention Institute, Inc. Used with permission.

- *Avoid stepping between the combatants.* This puts you in a vulnerable position and the combatants' aggression can quickly shift to you.
- *Always try verbal intervention first.* Often one or both combatants are waiting for someone to arrive and stop the fight. Avoid the temptation to immediately revert to physical intervention.
- *Use a distraction.* A distraction (loud noise, flickering of lights, etc.) can be enough to break the intensity of the aggression long enough to give you an edge.
- *Separate the combatants.* As soon as possible, break visual contact between the combatants. As long as they can see one another, their hostility will likely continue.

2. If the bullying is *verbal,* say "(Student's name), stop (teasing, name-calling, using racist or bigoted remarks, etc.) immediately. We don't use those words with each other." Refer to your class rules (see pages 31–32).

3. If the bullying is *emotional,* say "(Student's name), stop (intimidating, ignoring, excluding, etc.) immediately. In our classroom, everyone is welcome and accepted." Refer to your class acceptance statements (see page 16).

Once you've intervened with the bullying behavior, your work is just beginning.

WHETHER YOU WITNESS IT PERSONALLY OR LEARN ABOUT IT IN ANOTHER WAY . . .

Consult your school's or district's policies on handling bullying incidents. They should include some or all of the following general steps.

Important: Keep written records along the way of conversations, actions taken, follow-through, etc. You'll want these for reference and also to include in the students' files.

1. Talk to the victim and the bully *separately* and *soon.* Talk to witnesses one at a time.

   For tips on talking to victims, see "Break the Code of Silence" (page 83–85). Be sure to offer reassurance that you *will* take action, and you'll do everything in your power to prevent the bullying from happening again.

   When talking to bullies, don't ask for their account of what happened. (Bullies generally don't take responsibility for their actions; they deny or minimize their role.) Instead, explain simply and clearly why their behavior was unacceptable. Refer to school or district policies and/or your class rules. Tell them the behavior you do expect. Spell out the specific consequences of the bullying behavior, then apply the consequences right away. Let the bullies know that their parents will be informed.

   When talking to witnesses, ask for details. What did they see or hear? Who did what? When? What was the sequence of events? What, if anything, did they (the witnesses) do to stop the bullying? Seek their suggestions for ways to resolve the problem and prevent it from happening again in the future.

2. Talk with other teachers, administrators, and staff. Tell them about the bullying incident and also about your conversations with the bully, the victim, and any witnesses. Seek their advice and insights.

3. Contact the parents or guardians of both the bully and the victim. If possible, call them that day. Explain what happened, and arrange to meet with them at school as soon as schedules allow.

    Important: You'll want to meet *separately* with each set of parents or guardians.

When talking to the victim's parents, let them know what happened and what was done to stop it. Explain your school policies and class rules regarding the bullying behavior, and tell them the consequences. Reassure them that bullying is not tolerated, and that you and the school are taking specific steps to prevent future incidents. Tell them that you will stay in touch with them and let them know how the situation is resolved.

You can share essentially the same information with the bully's parents. Tell them that you'll be working with their child to change his or her behavior—and you'll need their help.

Depending on the nature and severity of the bullying incident, you may want to have follow-up meetings with the parents to report on the progress being made.

4. Continue to communicate with your colleagues and the parents until the situation is clearly resolved. Monitor the bully's behavior in your classroom; ask other teachers to do the same in the halls, in the lunchroom, on the playground, etc. and report back to you on what they see. Tell them that you also want to hear *good* news about the student's behavior, not just bad news. At the same time, monitor the victim's safety.

BE A GOOD LISTENER

If a student comes to you to report a bullying incident—as a witness or a victim—the first and most important thing you should do is *listen.*

It's estimated that we spend about 70 percent of our waking hours communicating (reading, writing, speaking, listening), and most of that time goes to listening. Yet we receive little or no training on how to listen. In school, we learn how to read, write, and speak . . . but not how to listen. We assume that listening "comes naturally."

There's an old saying: "We were born with one mouth and two ears because listening is twice as hard as talking." Here's how to be a good listener.

DO:

1. **Pay attention and be quiet.** Listening means not talking!

2. **Use attentive body language.** Face the speaker squarely, lean slightly toward him or her, and keep your arms and legs uncrossed.

3. **Make and maintain eye contact.** This allows you to pick up on the speaker's body language and facial expressions—important clues to how he or she is feeling.

4. **Be patient.** Allow time for the speaker to say what's on his or her mind. Especially if the speaker is embarrassed or uncomfortable, this might take a while. Also, people generally think faster than they speak. And students might not have the vocabulary or life experience needed to find precisely the right words.

5. **Ask for clarification if you need it.** Confirm the accuracy of what you're hearing. *Examples:* "I'm not sure I understand. Could you go over that again?" "Could you repeat that please?" "Can you tell me more about that?"

6. **Empathize.** Try to put yourself in the speaker's place and see his or her point of view.

7. **Ask questions to encourage the speaker and show that you're listening.** *Best:* Open-ended questions. *Worst:* Questions that require simple yes or no answers.

8. **Reflect the speaker's words and feelings from time to time.** *Examples:* "It sounds like you felt hurt when Marcy ignored you at recess." "I hear you saying you're angry because of how George treated you." Reflecting (also called mirroring) is simply paraphrasing what the speaker has said—objectively, without interpretation, emotion, or embellishment.

9. **Mirror the speaker's feelings in your own face.** If the speaker looks sad, hurt, or angry, you should, too.

10. **At points along the way, summarize what you're hearing the speaker say.** Check with the speaker to make sure you've got it right. *Example:* "You're saying that Zach pushed you against your locker, and you dropped your books and papers on the floor, and then Zach stepped on your math book."

11. **Use encouraging body language.** Nod your head, smile, lean a little closer to the speaker (but not too close).

12. **Use brief interjections to indicate that you're listening.** *Examples:* "I see." "Go on." "Tell me more." "Uh-huh." "Really." "Hmmmm." "What then?" "So. . . ."

13. **Really concentrate on what the speaker is saying.** Stay focused on his or her words.

14. **Invite the speaker to name his or her feelings.** *Examples:* "When Marcus called you a bad name, how did you feel?" "When Su-Lin made fun of you in front of the others, how did you feel?"

If you listen intently, you should feel somewhat tired afterward. That's because listening is *active,* not passive.

DON'T:

1. **Talk.** This is not the time to offer your advice or opinions. Wait until *after* the speaker has finished talking or asks for your input.

2. **Interrupt.** You don't like being interrupted when you're talking. Interruptions are rude and disrespectful.

3. **Doodle.** You'll probably want to take notes, however. Tell the speaker why—because

you want to keep the facts straight and have a written record of your conversation.

4. **Tap your pen or pencil, shuffle papers, wiggle your foot, look at your watch, yawn, etc.** These behaviors indicate boredom.

5. **Argue with, criticize, or blame the speaker.** This puts him or her on the defensive.

6. **Mentally argue with the speaker or judge what he or she is saying.** This takes your focus off the speaker's words.

7. **Evaluate or challenge what the speaker is saying.** Just listen.

8. **Interrogate the speaker.** Ask questions for clarification, or to encourage the speaker to tell you more. Make sure your questions don't imply that you doubt what the speaker is saying.

9. **Allow distractions.** Turn off the television, radio, etc. Don't answer the telephone. If someone else approaches you and the speaker, politely but firmly say, "I'm listening to (student's name) right now. I'll have time for you when we're finished here."

10. **Think ahead to what you're going to say when the speaker stops talking.** This is called "rehearsing," and it takes your focus off the speaker.

11. **Let your mind wander.** Sometimes a speaker's words can trigger our own thoughts, memories, and associations. If you feel this happening, change your body position and use one of the "Do's" listed on page 87. This should get you back on track.

12. **Mentally compare what the speaker is saying with what you've heard from other students.** If you're gathering information about a bullying incident or series of incidents, take notes and compare your notes later.

Tip: You might share some or all of these do's and don'ts with your students. Knowing how to listen is a social skill that builds friendships.

SEND A CLEAR MESSAGE

When you talk with a student who has been (or is being) bullied, you may find that the student blames himself or herself for being in the wrong place at the wrong time, provoking the bully, doing something to attract the bully's attention, or somehow "asking for it." Make it very clear that bullying is *never* caused by the victim. Tell the student:

- It's not your fault that you're being bullied.
- You didn't ask for it.
- You don't deserve it.
- You didn't do anything to cause it.
- Bullying isn't normal. It isn't okay.
- You don't have to face this on your own. I will help you. Other people will help you, too.

You might write these sentences on a card, sign it, and give it to the student. Or you might ask the student to repeat these sentences after you:

- "It's not my fault that I'm being bullied."
- "I didn't ask for it."
- "I don't deserve it."
- "I didn't do anything to cause it."
- "Bullying isn't normal. It isn't okay."
- "I don't have to face this on my own. My teacher will help me. Other people will help me, too."

Strong, positive statements like these can help students start feeling better about themselves— a bit more powerful and less like victims.*

---

* See also "Teach Students to Affirm Themselves" (page 66) and "Teach Positive Self-Talk" (pages 68 and 71).

PROVIDE COUNSELING

Being bullied is a very traumatic experience. If at all possible, victims should have access to some type of counseling—by a school psychologist, guidance counselor, or another trained adult. Peer counseling can also help.

See if your school can start a group for victimized students—a place where they can interact with others, build their social and friendship-making skills, and practice getting along. Group meetings can be structured and focus on specific topics (avoiding fights, avoiding bullies, coping with stress, being assertive, etc.), or they can be less structured (students can talk freely about issues that are important to them).

 Go farther: Learn how to organize groups (and find more than 100 complete 45-minute sessions) in *Child Support Through Small Group Counseling* by Lois Landy (Charlotte, NC: KIDSRIGHTS, 1996). Several states have added this book to their mandated lists for elementary and middle school counselors. See especially the "Peer Relations Group," "Self-Concept Group," and "Shyness Group" sections.

EMPOWER PARENTS

As you work to make your classroom bully free, get students' parents involved and keep them informed. Parents can be your allies—and can also clue you in to bullying situations you might not be aware of.

Tell parents about your efforts to prevent and intervene with bullying in your classroom. You might do this at parent-teacher conferences, on Parents' Night, during open houses, and in notes you send home with students.

As early as possible during the school year, give parents copies of "Keeping Kids Bully Free: Tips for Parents" (pages 90–92).

 Important: It's best to give this to parents in person. If this isn't possible, attach a brief cover letter introducing the handout and explaining why you're sending it home: because you believe *all* parents can benefit from this information. Otherwise you might alarm parents unnecessarily. If "Keeping Kids Bully Free" arrives out of the blue, a parent's first thought might be, "Oh no! This must mean that MY child is being bullied!" Preparation and explanation can prevent unnecessary worry and misunderstandings.

MOBILIZE WITNESSES

According to Denver psychologist (and bullying expert) Carla Garrity, "You can outnumber the bullies if you teach the silent majority to stand up."

Most students are neither bullies nor victims. They're witnesses or bystanders—kids who might not know what to do and might be afraid to get involved. In some cases, they're the bully's "lieutenants" or "henchmen," offering support for the bully and sharing a bit of the bully's power without actually doing the bullying.

In one Canadian study, 43 percent of students said that they try to help the victim, 33 percent said they should help but don't, and 24 percent said that bullying was none of their business.* If you can "mobilize the masses" to take action against bullying, you'll significantly reduce the bullying that occurs in your classroom and school.

OFFER SPECIFIC SUGGESTIONS

Students can make a difference simply by the way they react when they witness bullying incidents. Share these suggestions with your students, and ask if they have ideas of their own.

---

* SOURCE: A. Charach, D. Pepler, and S. Ziegler, "Bullying at school—a Canadian perspective: A survey of problems and suggestions for intervention," *Education Canada* 35:1 (1995), pp. 12–18.

1. If you think your child is being bullied, *ask your child.* Many children won't volunteer this information; they're ashamed, embarrassed, or afraid. Adults need to take the initiative. Ask for specifics and write them down.

    If you suspect that your child won't want to talk about being bullied, try approaching the topic indirectly. You might ask a series of questions like these:

    • "So, who's the bully in your classroom?"
    • "How do you know that person is a bully? What does he or she do?"
    • "What do you think about that?"
    • "Who does the bully pick on most of the time?"
    • "Does the bully ever pick on you?"
    • "What does the bully say or do to you? How does that make you feel?"

2. If your child tells you that he or she is being bullied, *believe your child.* Ask for specifics and write them down.

3. Please DON'T:

    • confront the bully or the bully's parents. This probably won't help and might make things worse.
    • tell your child to "get in there and fight." Bullies are always stronger and more powerful than their victims. Your child could get hurt.
    • blame your child. Bullying is *never* the victim's fault.
    • promise to keep the bullying secret. This gives the bully permission to keep bullying. Instead, tell your child you're glad that he or she told you about the bullying. Explain that you're going to help, and you're also going to ask the teacher to help.

4. Contact the teacher as soon as possible. Request a private meeting (no students should be around, and ideally no students except for your child should know that you're meeting with the teacher). Bring your written record of what your child has told you about the bullying, and share this information with the teacher. Ask for the teacher's perspective; he or she probably knows things about the bullying you don't. Ask to see a copy of the school's anti-bullying policy. Stay calm and be respectful; your child's teacher wants to help.

    Ask what the teacher will do about the bullying. Get specifics. You want the teacher to:

    • put a stop to the bullying
    • have specific consequences for bullying in place, and apply them toward the bully

CONTINUED

- help the bully change his or her behavior
- help your child develop bully resistance and assertiveness skills
- monitor your child's safety in the future
- keep you informed of actions taken and progress made

 Important: It takes time to resolve bullying problems. Try to be patient. The teacher will need to talk with your child, talk with the bully, talk with other children who might have witnessed the bullying, and then decide what's best to do for everyone involved.

5. Make a real effort to spend more positive time with your child than you already do. Encourage your child to talk about his or her feelings. Ask your child how the day went. Praise your child as often as possible. Give your child opportunities to do well—by helping you with a chore, taking on new responsibilities, or showing off a talent or skill.

6. Help your child develop bully resistance skills. Role-play with your child what to say and do when confronted by a bully. Here are a few starter ideas:

- Stand up straight, look the bully in the eye, and say in a firm, confident voice, "Leave me alone!" or "Stop that! I don't like that!"
- Tell a joke or say something silly. (Don't make fun of the bully.)
- Stay calm and walk away. If possible, walk toward a crowded place or a group of your friends.
- If you feel you're in real danger, run away as fast as you can.
- Tell an adult.

Ask your child's teacher or the school counselor for more suggestions. Also ask your child for suggestions. It's great if your child comes up with an idea, tries it, and it works!

7. Consider enrolling your child in a class on assertiveness skills, friendship skills, or self-defense. Check with your child's teacher or community resources—your local public library, YMCA or YWCA, community education, etc.

 Important: Self-defense classes aren't about being aggressive. They're about avoiding conflict through self-discipline, self-control, and improved self-confidence. Most martial arts teach that the first line of defense is nonviolence.

8. If your child seems to lack friends, arrange for him or her to join social groups, clubs, or organizations that meet his or her interests. This will boost your child's self-confidence and develop his or her social skills. Confident children with social skills are much less likely to be bullied.

→

CONTINUED

9. Consider whether your child might be doing something that encourages bullies to pick on him or her. Is there a behavior your child needs to change? Does your child dress or act in ways that might provoke teasing? No one ever *deserves* to be bullied, but sometimes kids don't help themselves. Watch how your child interacts with others. Ask your child's teachers for their insights and suggestions.

10. Label everything that belongs to your child with his or her name. Things are less likely to be "lost" or stolen if they're labeled. Use sew-in labels or permanent marker.

11. Make sure your child knows that his or her safety is always more important than possessions (books, school supplies, toys, money, etc.). If your child is threatened by a bully, your child should give up what the bully wants—and tell an adult (you or the teacher) right away.

12. Encourage your child to express his or her feelings around you. Give your child permission to blow off steam, argue, and state opinions and beliefs that are different from yours. If you allow your child to stand up to you now and then, it's more likely that he or she will be able to stand up to a bully.

13. Check with your child often about how things are going. Once your child says that things are better or okay at school—the bullying has slowed down or stopped—you don't have to keep asking every day. Ask once every few days, or once a week. Meanwhile, watch for any changes in behavior that might indicate the bullying has started again.

14. If you're not already involved with your child's school, get involved. Attend parent-teacher conferences and school board meetings. Join the Parent-Teacher Association or Organization (PTA or PTO). Learn about school rules and discipline policies. Serve on a school safety committee. If you have the time, volunteer to help in your child's classroom.

15. Remember that *you* are your child's most important teacher. Discipline at home should be fair, consistent, age-appropriate, and respectful. Parents who can't control their temper are teaching their children that it's okay to yell, scream, and use physical violence to get their way. *Tip:* Many children who bully others come from homes where their parents bully *them*.

> *If you want to stop bullying, you can:*
> - refuse to join in
> - refuse to watch
> - speak out ("Don't treat him that way. It's not nice." "Stop hitting her." "Don't use those words." "Don't call him that name." "I'm going to tell the teacher right now.")
> - report any bullying you know about or see
> - stand up for the person being bullied and gather around him or her, or invite the person to join your group (there's safety in numbers)
> - be a friend to the person being bullied
> - make an effort to include students who are normally left out or rejected
> - distract the bully so he or she stops the bullying behavior

Role-play various ways to react to bullying incidents.

PRAISE BULLY BUSTERS

Encourage students to tell you about times when they intervened with bullying incidents or helped put a stop to bullying. Praise them for their courage—because it definitely takes courage to stand up to a bully, especially if you're one of the first to do it.

You might create a "Bully Busters" bulletin board with photographs of students who have taken action against bullying in your classroom or school. Make sure there's room to display everyone's picture eventually; that should be your goal.

HAVE STUDENTS SIGN A CLASS PLEDGE

Make a copy of the "Class Pledge" (page 94). Introduce it by saying that *everyone* can help

your classroom become and stay bully free. Read the pledge aloud, then pass it around for everyone to sign. Post it in a prominent place in your classroom. Or turn the pledge into a large poster and invite students to decorate it as well as sign it.

ENCOURAGE A POSITIVE ATTITUDE

All students—especially those who have been or are being bullied—can benefit from facing life with a positive attitude. Encourage your students to look for what's good in their lives. This might be as simple as a sunrise, warm gloves on a cold day, or a puppy's wagging tail. Help them to see that no matter how bad things might seem at the moment, something good is waiting just around the corner.

Use stories of hope and courage to inspire students to feel optimistic and reach for the stars. *Examples:**

- *Champions: Stories of Ten Remarkable Athletes* by Bill Littlefield (Boston: Little, Brown, 1993). Grades 5–8.
- *Kids with Courage: True Stories About Young People Making a Difference* by Barbara A. Lewis (Minneapolis: Free Spirit Publishing, 1992). Grades 6 and up.
- *Mirette on the High Wire* by Emily Arnold McCully (New York: The Putnam Publishing Group, 1992). Grades K–3.
- *Ruth Law Thrills a Nation* by Don Brown (New York: Ticknor & Fields, 1993). Grades K–3.
- *Worth the Risk: True Stories About Risk Takers Plus How You Can Be One, Too* by Arlene Erlbach (Minneapolis: Free Spirit Publishing, 1998). Grades 4–8.

* Ask your school librarian or the children's librarian at your local public library to point you toward other appropriate books. Or check the latest issue of *The Bookfinder* or *The Best of Bookfinder: A Guide to Children's Literature About Interests and Concerns of Youth Ages 2–18.* Published by American Guidance Service, the *Bookfinders* group and describe books by topic. Ask for them at your library's reference desk.

CLASS PLEDGE

1. We won't bully others.

2. We will help students who are being bullied.

3. We will include students who are left out.

4. We will report any bullying we know about or see.

SIGNED:

BUILD STUDENTS' SELF-ESTEEM

Most bullying victims have low self-esteem. Here are six ways you can build self-esteem in *all* of your students.*

STAR CHARTS

Create a separate chart for each student. Whenever he or she does something positive or helpful, write it on the chart and decorate it with a star. Or create charts listing specific positive/helpful behaviors you want to encourage in your classroom.

FEEL-GOOD POSTERS

Create a poster for each student (or have students create their own posters). Put a photograph of the student at the center. Surround it with positive comments about the student. Display the posters in the classroom; they'll be especially noticed and appreciated on Parents' Night and at open houses.

FEEL-GOOD LISTS

Make copies of the handout "My Feel-Good List" (page 96). Complete the first column for each student, then invite students to complete the second column. They can share their lists or keep them private—whatever they prefer.

Tip: If any students have difficulty completing their columns, offer help. Make simple suggestions. *Examples:* "Everyone has talents, and so do you. What are some of your talents? What are you good at? What do you do best?" They can also take their handouts home and ask their parents and siblings for help.

Tell students that whenever they feel down or sad, they can look at their lists and feel better about themselves.

---

* See also "Affirm Your Students" (pages 65–66), "Teach Students to Affirm Themselves" (page 66), "Teach Students to Affirm Each Other" (pages 66–68), and "Teach Positive Self-Talk" (pages 68 and 71). There are many books and resources available on helping students build self-esteem, develop self-confidence, and form a positive self-concept. Several are listed in "Resources" at the end of this book.

SELF-ESTEEM BOOSTERS

Ask students, "What are specific things you can do to feel good about yourself?" Write students' ideas on the chalkboard. If they have difficulty getting started or run out of ideas too soon, you might suggest some of the following:

- use positive self-talk (see "Teach Positive Self-Talk," pages 68 and 71)

- learn a new skill

- develop/strengthen a skill you already have

- start a new hobby

- join a club or group that interests you

- earn money from doing a job or chore

- volunteer to help someone (see "Get Students Involved in Service," pages 73–75)

- read a book

- get involved in a cause you care about

- take a class in self-defense

- exercise every day

- make a new friend

- be more assertive (see "Teach Assertiveness Skills," pages 53–54)

- get more sleep

Once you've written a list of ideas on the board, have students read it over (or read it aloud to the class) and choose 3–5 ideas they might like to try. Have them write the ideas in a notebook or on a sheet of paper. Encourage them to try the ideas as soon as possible; offer to help them find resources, get in touch with groups or organizations, etc. Wait a few days (or a week), then ask students to report on their progress.

CHOICES

Whenever possible, give students opportunities to make choices—all kinds of choices. They might decide where to sit, how to arrange their

MY FEEL-GOOD LIST

**10 things my teacher
likes about me:**

1. _____

2. _____

3. _____

4. _____

5. _____

6. _____

7. _____

8. _____

9. _____

10. _____

**10 things I like
about myself:**

1. _____

2. _____

3. _____

4. _____

5. _____

6. _____

7. _____

8. _____

9. _____

10. _____

desks, what types of projects to work on (written reports, oral reports, art projects, etc.). Even if their choices aren't always successful, find something positive about them to recognize. If you must comment on a poor choice (with the goal of helping students make better choices next time), do it privately, not publicly.

THEY'RE THE TEACHERS

Set aside time to learn with and from your students. Let them tell you about their interests, demonstrate their skills, talents, and abilities, and show off a little. Give them opportunities to do things better than you; students delight in this, and it gives them a major self-esteem boost.

TEACH POSITIVE VISUALIZATION

Let your students in on the secret of "mind over matter." Arnold Schwarzenegger once said, "As long as you can envision the fact that you can do something, you can do it—as long as you really believe it 100 percent."

It's a fact that many successful athletes have improved their performance with positive visualization—mentally "seeing" themselves succeed. *Examples:* golfer Jack Nicklaus, champion boxer Muhammad Ali, skier Jean-Claude Killy, and tennis stars Billie Jean King and Virginia Wade.

In a famous experiment, an Australian basketball team divided into three groups. All three wanted to be able to shoot more baskets.

- Group 1 practiced taking foul shots for 30 minutes every day. After 20 days, they noticed a 24 percent improvement.

- Group 2 did nothing. They noticed a 0 percent improvement.

- Group 3 practiced mentally. These players didn't actually shoot baskets. Instead, they imagined themselves shooting baskets. They noticed a 23 percent improvement—

nearly as great as Group 1, who practiced for 30 minutes every day.

Learn about positive visualization and mental imagery. Teach your students how to use it—especially those who are or have been victims of bullying, or who lack friends, social skills, and self-esteem.

Example: Teach students to see/imagine themselves getting along with others. With practice, they'll project an attitude of confidence and acceptance, which will improve their chances of fitting in. *Tip:* The more details they can imagine, the better. Can they picture themselves walking into a room? Smiling at people? Saying hello? Can they see people smiling back at them? What do they look like? What are they wearing? What are they saying? How does it feel to be in a group of smiling, welcoming people?

 Go farther: Read *Self-Esteem* (revised edition) by Matthew McKay, Ph.D., and Patrick Fanning (New York: St. Martin's, 1994). This step-by-step program for building self-esteem includes a detailed description of how to use visualization for self-acceptance.

PLAY A "POSITIVE SELF-TALK" GAME

Write a series of put-downs or nasty names on individual slips of paper. Or invite your students to do this, but be sure to read the names before you use them to make sure they're not *too* nasty (or obscene, personal, specific, racist, etc.).

Drop the slips into a hat. Invite one student to draw a slip out of the hat and give it to you. Write the put-down or name on the chalkboard.

Tell the class that they have your permission to call the student that name (or use the put-down) *just for now* because you're going to play a game.

Have the class form two lines with enough space between them for you and the student to walk comfortably. As you and the student walk through the group, the other students call him or her the name (or use the put-down). Meanwhile, you whisper positive comments in the student's ear. *Examples:* "You're not like that." "You can stay calm." "Don't believe what they say." "You're more mature than they are."

Next, the student walks back through the group alone, using positive self-talk ("I'm not like that," "I can stay calm," etc.).

Repeat this game with the other students. Afterward, talk about how they felt when you whispered positive comments to them, and when they used positive self-talk.

For more tips on helping students develop this powerful skill, see "Teach Positive Self-Talk" (pages 68 and 71).

HELP STUDENTS ACCEPT THEIR DIFFERENCES

If you and your students did the "Build Acceptance" activity (pages 16 and 19), students learned ways to accept each other. Victims and potential victims also need to know how to accept themselves.

Most bullying victims are "different" from the majority in one or more ways. Bullies zero in on differences and make them the focus of their attacks. Kids are bullied for being too tall, too short, too thin, or too heavy; for having a physical disability or learning difference; for belonging to ethnic, racial, cultural, or religious groups that aren't the "norm"; for having special needs . . . for almost any reason that sets them apart.

How can you help students accept themselves? Here are several ideas to try. Ask other teachers and experts (your school counselor, local spokespersons, etc.) for more suggestions.

- Model acceptance and affirmation by learning as much as you can about your students' differences. Invite them to educate you.

- When assigning projects and reports, allow students to research their differences. A student who wears glasses might report on the history of eyeglasses . . . and identify famous people in history who have worn them. A student with a chronic illness might contact a national organization, learn about other people who have his or her illness, and share their stories. Encourage students to identify reasons to be proud of their differences, and/or positive ways to cope with their differences.

- Help students identify role models who share their differences. (*Examples:* Tom Cruise, Whoopi Goldberg, Albert Einstein, Thomas Edison, former U.S. president George Bush, and race car driver Jackie Stewart all have something in common: dyslexia.)

- Ask your librarian or media specialist to recommend books and other resources related to your students' differences. Incorporate them into lessons and displays. *Example:* Look for *Succeeding with LD (Learning Differences)* by Jill Lauren, M.A. (Minneapolis: Free Spirit Publishing, 1997). Read 20 inspiring true stories about people with LD.

- On the Web, check out the People with Disabilities Resource, the Institute for Global Communications' gateway site to hundreds of resources for people with all kinds of disabilities. Go to: *http://www.igc.org/pwd/*

- Overweight students are often picked on and rejected, especially if they lack social skills. You might want to contact the National Association to Advance Fat Acceptance (NAAFA) for information about its Kids' Project. A nonprofit human rights organization, NAAFA has been working since 1969 to eliminate discrimination based on body size. Write or call: NAAFA, PO Box 188620, Sacramento, CA

95818; toll-free telephone 1-800-442-1214. On the Web, go to: *http://naafa.org/*

- Are there local support groups for people with disabilities and other differences? Find out and get in touch with them. You might invite a speaker to visit your class or school.

- Make it a privilege for students to help those with special needs.

- As a class or a school, raise funds to buy a piece of equipment or other resources to help students with special needs.

- Help students talk more openly about their differences. A willingness to talk indicates a positive attitude and acceptance, which serves as an example for others. Students who are embarrassed or ashamed of their differences can become targets for bullies.

- Help students develop a sense of humor. Kids who can laugh at themselves are better able to cope with teasing. Humor can also defuse potentially volatile situations.

SEE YOUR CLASSROOM THROUGH YOUR STUDENTS' EYES

Students who are bullied often say that adults "never noticed" the way they were treated. Try seeing your classroom (and yourself) through your students' eyes.

Watch how students interact. Listen to how they talk to each other. If you were a child, would you be comfortable in your classroom? Would you feel safe, welcome, accepted, and free to learn? Is this a place where you could be and do your best without feeling threatened, intimidated, or excluded? Would you feel as if the teacher were approachable—as if the teacher would really listen if you reported a problem or asked for help?

Try being a student for an hour (or a day). Have your students teach the lessons and manage the class. You might learn a great deal about how they see you.

SHARE TIPS FOR STAYING BULLY FREE

Make several copies of "Ways to Stay Bully Free" (page 100). Cut along the dotted lines and give one card to each student. (*Tips:* Make copies on heavy paper or thin cardboard. Laminate them for durability.) Spend class time discussing the ideas listed on the cards. Students can keep the cards in their pockets or backpacks and review them whenever they need ideas or reminders.

 Go farther: Get a classroom copy of *Bullies Are a Pain in the Brain,* written and illustrated by Trevor Romain (Minneapolis: Free Spirit Publishing, 1997). With wit and humor, this little book teaches children ages 8–13 ways to become bully-proof.

TRY THE METHOD OF SHARED CONCERN

The Method of Shared Concern is a nonpunitive, counseling-based intervention model that was developed by Swedish psychologist Anatol Pikas in the 1980s. It has since been used successfully in many parts of the world.

It involves conducting structured interviews with individual bullies, during which they are asked to take responsibility for their actions and commit to more responsible behavior. Interviews are also done with victims and then with groups of bullies and victims together.

This method is not designed to teach children how to make friends, or to reveal detailed facts about the bullying situation. It is designed to

WAYS TO STAY BULLY FREE

**WAYS TO STAY
BULLY FREE**

Avoid bullies
Act confident
Look confident
Be observant
Tell a friend
Tell an adult
Be assertive
Stay calm
Keep a safe distance
Walk away
Say "Stop it!"
Say "Leave me alone!"
Say "Whatever!"
Use humor
Use "I messages"
Travel in a group
Join a group
If you're in danger, RUN

**WAYS TO STAY
BULLY FREE**

Avoid bullies
Act confident
Look confident
Be observant
Tell a friend
Tell an adult
Be assertive
Stay calm
Keep a safe distance
Walk away
Say "Stop it!"
Say "Leave me alone!"
Say "Whatever!"
Use humor
Use "I messages"
Travel in a group
Join a group
If you're in danger, RUN

**WAYS TO STAY
BULLY FREE**

Avoid bullies
Act confident
Look confident
Be observant
Tell a friend
Tell an adult
Be assertive
Stay calm
Keep a safe distance
Walk away
Say "Stop it!"
Say "Leave me alone!"
Say "Whatever!"
Use humor
Use "I messages"
Travel in a group
Join a group
If you're in danger, RUN

**WAYS TO STAY
BULLY FREE**

Avoid bullies
Act confident
Look confident
Be observant
Tell a friend
Tell an adult
Be assertive
Stay calm
Keep a safe distance
Walk away
Say "Stop it!"
Say "Leave me alone!"
Say "Whatever!"
Use humor
Use "I messages"
Travel in a group
Join a group
If you're in danger, RUN

**WAYS TO STAY
BULLY FREE**

Avoid bullies
Act confident
Look confident
Be observant
Tell a friend
Tell an adult
Be assertive
Stay calm
Keep a safe distance
Walk away
Say "Stop it!"
Say "Leave me alone!"
Say "Whatever!"
Use humor
Use "I messages"
Travel in a group
Join a group
If you're in danger, RUN

**WAYS TO STAY
BULLY FREE**

Avoid bullies
Act confident
Look confident
Be observant
Tell a friend
Tell an adult
Be assertive
Stay calm
Keep a safe distance
Walk away
Say "Stop it!"
Say "Leave me alone!"
Say "Whatever!"
Use humor
Use "I messages"
Travel in a group
Join a group
If you're in danger, RUN

change the situation by getting children to change their behavior.

Shared Concern seems to be most effective with children age 9 and older, but it has also been used with younger children. It involves a three-stage interviewing and meeting process:*

1. individual interviews with each child
2. follow-up interviews with each child
3. a group meeting

PRELIMINARIES

1. Determine that a bullying situation exists—that one or more children are being bullied by another child or group, and that this has been going on for a period of time.

2. Get reliable information about who is involved, and identify the ringleader of the bullies.

3. Talk to the teachers of the bullies and the victims. Schedule interviews with the children. Ask the teachers not to alert the children that they will be interviewed. They should simply send the children to the interviews as scheduled.

 Important: Plan to conduct all of the interviews in sequence, without a break, so the children involved don't have the opportunity to talk to each other between interviews.

4. Arrange to do the interviews in a room where you'll have privacy and won't be interrupted. It's best if there are no windows. If windows can't be avoided, the child being interviewed should sit with his or her back to the window.

5. Know and understand your role. Throughout the interviews, you will be a nonjudgmental facilitator who encourages children to consider their own behav-

iors and the consequences of their behaviors, then suggest alternate behaviors. *Notes:* Young children may find it difficult to come up with ideas; you may need to offer suggestions. Girls seem to have a hard time finding a middle ground between "friends" and "enemies." You may need to explain that they're not being asked to make the other children their "best friends."

**INITIAL INTERVIEWS
(7–10 minutes each)**

Interview the ringleader first, then the rest of the bullies (if a group is involved), then the children who are being bullied. See the guidelines and sample scripts on pages 102–103.

 Important: The interviews must be non-confrontational. Students should appear relaxed when they return to class.

Each interview should end with the child agreeing to try his or her own suggestion(s) during the following week.

**FOLLOW-UP INTERVIEWS
(3 minutes each)**

The purpose of the follow-up meetings is to determine whether the children did what they agreed to during the initial interviews. If they did, congratulate them and invite them to the group meeting.

Sometimes bullies don't try the suggestions they agreed to try—but they do leave the victims alone. If this is the case, congratulate them and invite them to the group meeting. Leaving the victims alone is an important change in behavior.

**GROUP MEETING
(30 minutes)**

The purpose of the group meeting is to maintain the changes made since the initial interviews.

1. Meet with the bullies first. Ask them to think of something positive they can say to the victims.

---

* The procedure and guidelines described here are adapted from *Tackling Bullying in Your School,* edited by Sonia Sharp and Peter K. Smith (London: Routledge, 1994), pp. 79–88. Used with permission.

INTERVIEWING A BULLY: GUIDELINES AND SAMPLE SCRIPT

Start by saying:

> I hear you have been nasty to (student's name). Tell me about it.

The bully will probably deny this. Follow up immediately with:

> Yes, but nasty things have been happening to (student's name). Tell me about it.

Listen to what the bully tells you. Be patient; give him or her time to think, and don't worry about lengthy silences. If the child doesn't respond after a significant period of time has elapsed, say:

> It seems that you don't want to talk today. You'd better go back to class now.

He or she might start talking at this point. If so, just listen. Don't accuse or blame. Avoid asking questions. Try to determine if the child feels justified in his or her behavior toward the victim. The child might feel quite angry toward the victim. Work toward an understanding that the victim is having a bad time, whoever is to blame. Say with force and emphasis:

> So, it sounds like (student's name) is having a bad time in school.

By now, the child should assent to this. Move on quickly to say:

> Okay. I was wondering what you could do to help (student's name) in this situation.

See what solution the child can come up with. Be encouraging. If the child never offers a solution, ask:

> Would you like me to make a suggestion?

If the child offers a solution that depends on someone else's efforts (yours or the victim's), say:

> I was thinking about what *you* could do. What could you do?

If the child makes an impractical suggestion, don't reject it. Instead, ask:

> So, if this happened, the bullying would stop?

When the child proposes a practical and relevant solution, say:

> Excellent. You try that out for a week, and we'll meet again and see how you've done. Good-bye for now.

NONPROVOCATIVE VICTIM

Teacher: Hello, Matthew. Sit down. I want to talk with you because I hear some nasty things have been happening to you.

Child: Yes. It's the others in my class. They just keep on picking on me. They won't leave me alone. They mess around with my bag . . . putting stuff in it.

Teacher: You sound as if you're fed up with it.

Child: It just doesn't stop. The rest of the class joins in now.

Teacher: Is there anything you can think of that might help the situation?

Child: I could change schools.

Teacher: Mmm. So you feel it would be better to get out of the situation altogether.

Child: Well, sometimes. But I don't suppose my mother would let me. They're not so bad when I hang around with Simon.

Teacher: So being with someone else helps the situation?

Child: Yes. He backs me up when I tell them to stop it.

Teacher: So he supports you?

Child: Yes. I could sit next to him.

Teacher: Okay. You do that over the next week and then we'll have another chat to see how things have been going. Okay? Good-bye.

PROVOCATIVE VICTIM

Teacher: Hello, Matthew. Sit down. I want to talk with you because I hear some nasty things have been happening to you.

Child: Yes. It's the others in my class. They just keep on picking on me. They won't leave me alone. They mess around with my bag . . . putting stuff in it.

Teacher: You sound as if you're fed up with it.

Child: It just doesn't stop. The rest of the class joins in now.

Teacher: Tell me more about what happens. How does it all start?

Child: It's usually when I go over and sit by them. They just can't take a joke.

Teacher: So you play jokes on them?

Child: Yes, just messing around. I go on really good vacations and they never do so I ask them where they are going . . . it makes them really mad. They're just jealous.

Teacher: Then they get angry with you. What happens when they get angry with you?

Child: Well, that's when they started messing around with my bag.

Teacher: Is there anything you can think of that might help the situation?

Child: I guess I could leave them alone.

Teacher: Okay. You do that over the next week and then we'll have another chat to see how things have been going. Okay? Good-bye.

2. Ask the victims to enter the room. Place their chairs where they won't have to walk past the bullies to reach their seats.

3. Have the bullies say their positive statements.

4. Congratulate everyone on their success—they have made the bullying situation better than it was.

5. Ask everyone how they can maintain this new and improved situation.

6. Ask them what they will do if the bullying starts again.

7. Introduce the idea of tolerance—being in the same school and classroom without quarreling, accepting each other's differences, coexisting peaceably (but without necessarily being friends).

It might not be necessary to meet again for several weeks. Monitor the situation and call an interim meeting if needed.

TRY THE NO BLAME APPROACH

Developed by Barbara Maines and George Robinson, the No Blame Approach encourages children to take responsibility for their actions and the consequences of their actions. Like the Method of Shared Concern (see pages 99 and 101–104), this is a nonpunitive intervention model that involves children directly in resolving a bullying situation.*

Step 1: Interview the bullied child

Talk with the child about his or her feelings. Do not question the child directly about the bully-

ing incident(s), but do try to establish who is involved.

Step 2: Arrange a meeting for all the children who are involved

Set up a meeting for all the children who are directly involved. Include children who joined in but did not directly bully the victim.

Step 3: Explain the problem

Tell the children how the bullied child is feeling. You may want to use a drawing, poem, or other piece of writing by the child to illustrate his or her feelings. Do not discuss the details of the incident or blame any of the bullying students.

Step 4: Share responsibility

State clearly that you know the group is responsible and can do something about it. Focus on resolving the problem rather than blaming the children.

Step 5: Identify solutions

Ask each child in turn to suggest a way in which he or she could help the bullied child feel happier in school. Show approval of the suggestions, but don't ask the children to promise to implement them or go into detail about how they will implement them.

Step 6: The students take action themselves

End the meeting by giving responsibility to the group to solve the problem. Arrange a time and place to meet again and find out how successful they have been.

Step 7: Meet with them again

After about a week, see each student and ask how things have been going. It is usually better to see them individually in order to avoid any new group accusations about who helped and who didn't. The important thing is to ascertain that the bullying has stopped and the bullied student is feeling better.

---

* This description is adapted from *School Bullying: Insights and Perspectives*, edited by Peter K. Smith and Sonia Sharp (London: Routledge, 1994), pp. 88–89. Used with permission.

ENCOURAGE STRONG FAMILY RELATIONSHIPS

Do as much as you can to support closeness and togetherness in your students' families. *Examples:*

- Work with other teachers and staff to schedule open houses, family nights, and other events that welcome parents and students.

- Bring in speakers who talk about family life and issues.

- Invite students to attend parent-teacher conferences with their parents.

- Regularly call or write to parents. Let them know about their children's progress. Report on something special their children did—something that deserves praise and recognition.

- Have students interview their parents for homework assignments.

ENCOURAGE RELATIONSHIPS WITH OTHER ADULTS

When students develop close relationships with adults—not only their parents, but also other family and community members—they learn important social skills and build their self-confidence and self-esteem. This is important for *all* students, and can be especially beneficial to those who lack social skills and are victims or potential victims of bullying.

SCHOOL STAFF

Do teachers, administrators, and other staff members make the effort to get to know students? Do they sponsor clubs, coach teams, supervise before-school and after-school activities, and/or lead discussion groups for kids? Do they take time to listen to students' concerns and offer support and advice? Talk with your coworkers. What can you do individually and together to form positive, meaningful relationships with students?

Enlist the help of all school employees in making students feel welcome, accepted, and appreciated. Custodians, cafeteria workers, librarians, office personnel, and others can greet students by name, share a kind word with them, and intervene if they see a student being mistreated.

Encourage school staff to find ways for students with low self-esteem or poor social skills to shine. *Examples:* A student could deliver the principal's telephone messages or help younger children do library research.

GRANDPARENTS

Encourage students to spend time with their grandparents, sharing their problems and concerns as well as their achievements.

Because many of your students might not be in regular contact with their grandparents, consider establishing an Adopt-a-Grandparent program in cooperation with a local nursing home or retirement center.

Arrange for your class to visit their adopted grandparents regularly. Bring class plays, presentations, and musical performances to them. Make artwork for the grandparents' rooms and send them cards on special occasions. Invite all grandparents to visit your students at school and volunteer in your classroom and on field trips.

CLUBS, GROUPS, TROOPS, AND TEAMS

Gather information about local and national clubs, groups, troops, teams, and organizations led by caring adults. *Examples:*

Boy Scouts of America
Contact your local council or visit the Web site: *http://www.bsa.scouting.org*

Boys & Girls Clubs of America
Contact your local club or visit the Web site: *http://www.bgca.org/*

Camp Fire Boys and Girls
Contact your local council or visit the Web site: *http://www.campfire.org/*

4-H
Contact your local program or visit the Web site: *http://www.4h-usa.org/*

Girl Scouts of the U.S.A.
Contact your local council or visit the Web site: *http://www.girlscouts.org/*

Girls Incorporated
Contact your local affiliate or visit the Web site: *http://www.girlsinc.org/*

You might also invite representatives to visit your class, tell about their organizations, and talk with your students.

 Go farther: Check out the *Directory of American Youth Organizations* by Judith B. Erickson, Ph.D. (Minneapolis: Free Spirit Publishing, updated often). This guide lists and describes more than 500 hobby groups, academic and sports clubs, character-building and service groups, organizations for peace and global understanding, conservation and humane education groups, and more for young people—all adult-sponsored and national in scope.

COMMUNITY MEMBERS

Start a card file or computer database of people in your community who are willing to spend time with students—exploring shared interests, helping kids develop their talents, and making a difference in their lives. Pair interested students with caring adults.

 Important: You'll want to get parents' permission and take all safety precautions. Check with your principal about how to proceed.

MENTORS

Kids of all ages have formed strong relationships with mentors—caring adults who make active, positive contributions to their lives. You might find out if teachers, administrators, and other school staff are willing to serve as mentors; match them up with students who share their interests and arrange for them to spend time together. Parents might be available to mentor other students in your class.

To learn more about mentoring and mentorships, contact these organizations:

Big Brothers Big Sisters of America
The oldest mentoring organization serving youth in the country, BBBSA has provided one-to-one mentoring relationships between adult volunteers and children at risk since 1904. BBBSA currently serves over 100,000 children and youth in more than 500 agencies throughout all of the United States. Contact your local office or visit the Web site: *http://www.bbbsa.org/*

The National Mentoring Partnership
A resource for mentors and mentoring initiatives nationwide, the National Mentoring Partnership forges partnerships with communities and organizations to promote mentoring. It also educates youth and adults about how to find and become mentors. Write or call: The National Mentoring Partnership, 1400 I Street, NW, Suite 850, Washington, DC 20005; telephone (202) 729-4345. Or visit the Web site: *http://www.mentoring.org/*

PROVIDE SAFE HAVENS

Students who are bullied at school need places to go where they feel safe and accepted. Work with other teachers, your principal, and staff to set aside a special room or place where all students are welcome. Provide adequate supervision. Older students can help run a quiet activities room.

If space in your school is tight, you might identify a corner of the media center or cafeteria as a safe haven. Or use your classroom Peace Place (see page 58).

 Go farther: Find out about McGruff houses or block parent programs in the neighborhoods where your students live, then let students know that these havens exist. A McGruff House is a safe place especially for kids who are bullied, followed, or hurt while walking in a neighborhood. It has a picture of McGruff the Crime Dog and the words "McGruff House" in a window or on a door. For neighborhoods that don't have McGruff houses or programs, talk with parents and encourage them to work with their neighbors or police department to start them. For more information about McGruff, write or call: National Crime Prevention Council, 1700 K Street, NW, Second Floor, Washington, DC 20006-3817; telephone (202) 466-6272. On the Web, go to: *http://www.ncpc.org/*

PLAY "WHAT IF?"

Lead class discussions, small group discussions, or role-plays around "What If?" questions. *Examples:*

- What if you're walking down the hall and someone calls you a bad name?

- What if someone tries to make you give him (or her) your lunch money?

- What if someone picks a fight with you?

- What if someone pushes you down on the playground?

- What if someone spreads a nasty rumor about you?

Invite students to contribute their own "What If?" questions to talk about or act out. Don't be surprised if this takes an interesting twist. The questions students offer might relate to real bullying incidents they have experienced or witnessed—and you haven't heard about until now.

As students come up with suggestions or role-play possible ways of coping with problem situations, remind them that bullies enjoy having control over their victims. They target individuals who are physically weaker and lack confidence. Guide students to come up with answers that are assertive, confident, and strong—and, at the same time, aren't likely to make things worse.

Tip: If you and your students haven't done the "Explore Ways to Deal with Bullies" activity (page 41), you might want to do this before playing "What If?"

EQUALIZE THE POWER

Bully-victim relationships always involve the unequal distribution of power. Bullies have it, victims don't—or bullies have most of it and victims have very little.

Look for opportunities to boost the power of students who are bullied or at risk for being bullied. *Examples:*

- Praise them sincerely, appropriately, and publicly.

- Learn their skills and areas of expertise, then suggest that other students consult them as "experts" on a topic.

- Show that you trust them and have confidence in their abilities. From time to time, give them special tasks to do. Make sure these are tasks that other students would find desirable and enjoyable. Assigning "busy work" or "grunt jobs" further stigmatizes victims and potential victims.

Equalizing the power can be a delicate balance. You'll want to offer victims chances to succeed—but without making them "teacher's pets." (See also "Give Them Opportunities to Shine," page 108.) Be careful not to pit victims and bullies against each other as you're handing out praise and special tasks. This might make the bully even more determined to show the victim who's in charge.

GET STUDENTS INVOLVED IN GROUPS

Students who are bullied have plenty of experience feeling isolated, excluded, rejected, and afraid. They need experience feeling welcome, safe, and accepted.

You might start a counseling group (see "Provide Counseling," page 89) for *any* students who need help making friends and practicing social skills—not just bullying victims. Other types of groups to consider are:

- a peer support group
- a new student orientation group
- a cooperative learning group
- a special interest group or club

For students who aren't ready to integrate with their peers during unstructured times (such as recess), you might start a club that meets at those times. This approach has been used effectively in England. Meetings can be structured around specific topics (how to make friends, how to stand up to bullies, etc.), or students can learn and practice social skills. Some of the meetings should be set aside for fun and play.

This club also provides an alternative for students who are new to the school and not yet comfortable or confident on the playground. The club should provide a well-supervised environment that allows and encourages friendships to form. Once they do, students may be less reluctant to go outside and play.

You can also suggest that students get involved with groups, clubs, and youth-serving organizations in your community. For starter ideas, see pages 105–106. Parents can also arrange these opportunities for their children; you might raise the topic during a parent-teacher conference. The goals of any group involvement should be to develop the student's peer support network, self-confidence, and social skills.

GIVE THEM OPPORTUNITIES TO SHINE

Increase students' social contacts by giving them specific responsibilities that are social in nature. *Examples:* tutoring other students on the computer, working in the school office, mentoring younger students, reading aloud to younger students, being in charge of group projects. This offers them opportunities to interact with others, help their peers, and demonstrate their skills. Plus assigning students these responsibilities shows that you trust and accept them. (See also "Equalize the Power," page 107.)

Help students discover and develop their talents and skills. This boosts their self-confidence and increases their standing among their peers. *Example:* If one of your students enjoys making kites, he or she could bring some examples for show-and-tell, teach other students what he or she knows, and lead a project on kite-making related to a science or geography lesson.

HAVE STUDENTS KEEP JOURNALS

Writing is a way to get in touch with our feelings, record events in our lives, formalize our plans and goals, and explore what's important to us. For students who are bullied, writing is a way to regain some of the power they've lost— and keep track of important details (what happened when, who did or said what) that you and other adults can use to stop the bullying and prevent future bullying. Written records make bullying easier to prove.

If possible, give students spiral-bound notebooks or small blank journaling books.* In one-on-one or small group meetings, explain or demonstrate some of the ways they might use

_____
* See also "Weekly Journaling" (pages 38–39).

their journals. Or give them a topic to write about each week. *Examples:*

- a time when I was bullied (what happened, who was there, how I felt about it, what I did about it)

- a list of people I can talk to about my problems—people I trust

- a list of people I can count on to help me

- a list of things I can say when a bully teases me or calls me names

- a list of funny things I can say to a bully

- ways to build my self-esteem

- good things I can tell myself (positive self-talk)

Students might use their journals to tell you about things that are happening in their lives—things they don't feel comfortable talking about.

TEACH PLANNING SKILLS

Students can learn to dodge potential bullying situations by planning ahead. With the whole class or in small groups, work with students to brainstorm ways to avoid bullies, ways to stay safe in their everyday lives, and ways to be more observant. *Examples:*

- When you're walking down the hall and you see a bully, don't make eye contact. Stay as far away from the bully as you can. Try to keep other people between you. If possible, turn and go in a different direction.

- Travel in groups. When you're on the playground, stay close to a friend or two. When you're in the lunchroom, sit with kids who are friendly to you.

- Make a list of places where you feel unsafe. Plan to stay away from those places. If

that's not possible, make sure you never go to those places alone. This might mean changing your route to school, avoiding parts of the playground, or only using common rooms or bathrooms when other people are around.

- If you notice a bully coming toward you, walk calmly but quickly in the opposite direction.

- Stay away from anyone who makes you feel uncomfortable, anxious, scared, worried, or nervous.

- When you're walking in a public place, don't look at the ground. Look around you and notice who else is there.

- Always let a trusted friend or caring adult know where you're going.

- Stick with a group, even if they aren't your friends.

Distribute copies of "Planning Ahead" (page 110). Students can complete them on their own, or work in pairs or small groups. Afterward, share and discuss responses. Praise students for coming up with good ideas.

TEACH POWER SKILLS

Teach these skills to students you believe are ready to go beyond the basics (stay calm, walk away, join a group, tell an adult). Use demonstration, discussion, role-playing, and plenty of guided practice. *Note:* Some students may be too timid to try these approaches. If that's the case, don't force it.

1. **Agree with everything the bully says**

Examples: "Yes, that's true." "You're right." "I see what you mean." "You are absolutely 100 percent correct! I am a wimp!"

PLANNING AHEAD

Ways to avoid bullies:

Ways to stay safe:

Ways to be observant:

2. Disarm the bully with humor

Laugh and walk away. Or laugh and don't walk away. Act as if the two of you are sharing a good joke. Play along. When the bully starts laughing, you can say something like, "Wow, that was fun! See you later. Gotta go!"

Turn a put-down into a joke. *Example:* "You called me a wimp. You're right; I need to lift weights more often."

When a bully mocked her stutter, one student replied, "If you can't st-st-stutter better than that, I'll have t-t-to g-g-give you l-l-lessons."

3. Bore the bully with questions

Examples: "I'm a wimp? What do you mean by that? How do you know I'm a wimp? Do you know any other wimps? Have you compared me to them? Am I more or less wimpy than they are? What exactly is a wimp, anyway?"

4. Be a broken record

Whatever the bully says, say the same thing in response . . . over and over and over again. *Examples:*

Bully: "You're a wimp."
You: "That's your opinion."
Bully: "Yeah, and I'm right."
You: "That's your opinion."
Bully: "So what are you going to do about it?"
You: "That's your opinion."
Bully: "You'd better shut up."
You: "That's your opinion."
Bully: "I'm getting sick of you."
You: "That's your opinion."
Bully: "I mean it! Shut up!"
You: "That's your opinion."
Bully: "Oh, forget it!"

Bully: "You want to fight?"
You: "I don't do that."
Bully: "That's because you're a wimp."
You: "I don't do that."
Bully: "You're too scared to fight. You're chicken."
You: "I don't do that."
Bully: "I'll bet I can make you fight."
You: "I don't do that."

Bully: "What's with you? Is that all you can say?"
You: "I don't do that."
Bully: "Oh, forget it!"

5. Just say no

Examples: "You can't have this toy. I'm playing with it now." "You can't have my lunch. I'm eating it." "You can't have my money. I need it to buy lunch later." "You can't have my pencil. I need it. Give it back."

6. Use "fogging"

If being assertive and telling a bully to stop calling you names doesn't work, try responding with short, bland words and phrases that neutralize the situation. *Examples:* "Possibly." "You might be right." "It might look that way to you." "Maybe." "That's your opinion."

7. Use "Nonreward Retort Strategies"

These strategies were developed by Dorothea M. Ross, Ph.D., to empower children to combat teasing on their own.*

- **Exhaust the topic.** Stay calm and confident. Respond to the bully by asking questions after each put-down that require the bully to explain or expand on his or her comments. *Example:* "You called me 'fatso.' What do you mean by 'fatso'? Can you explain how big a person has to be in order to be fat? How many students in our school are fat?" The bully may get tired of the questioning and walk away.

- **Make an asset of the topic.** If a bully targets a difference and uses it as a topic for put-downs, turn the difference into an asset. *Example:* A student lost his hair after a series of medical treatments. A bully started teasing him about it. The student explained that a lot of famous people are bald, and he hoped he'd stay bald at least

* Reprinted from *Childhood Bullying and Teasing* by Dorothea M. Ross, Ph.D. (Alexandria, VA: American Counseling Association, 1996), © ACA. Reprinted with permission. No further reproduction authorized without written permission of the American Counseling Association.

until Halloween. This took the bully by surprise, and he stopped the teasing.

- **Give the teaser permission to tease.** *Example:* "It's okay to say whatever you want. It doesn't bother me."

8. **Use "Punishment Retort Strategies"**

Here are more strategies developed by Dorothea M. Ross, Ph.D., to empower children to combat teasing on their own.*

- Act like you can't remember the bully's name.

- Respond with a comment like, "It takes one to know one." Then turn and walk away, saying, "I'll leave and let you think about that."

- Reverse the teasing. Give the bully the same put-down.

- Call the bully by name and ask, "What did you say?" and "Could you say that again?" The bully may repeat what he or she said two or three times. Then you, in a condescending manner, say something like "Good boy, Sam! You said that three times."

- Make the bully look foolish when he or she says the obvious. *Example:* "He noticed that I don't have any hair. Wow!"

- Make the bully look ignorant about medical conditions. Correct the bully by giving accurate information about your medical condition. Then say something like, "You must not read much, or you'd know that."

- Make fun of the bully for repeating taunts. Nod when the bully says something, then wait for the bully to repeat himself or herself. Then say something like, "You keep saying the same thing over and over. Can you say it in a different way, or even sing it?"

---

* Ibid.

- Anticipate the bully's put-downs. Move closer to the bully before he or she has said anything, and ask, "What do you have to say today?" Then reel off several put-downs the bully has used before.

Tip: Tell the student that the bully might have comebacks for any of these strategies. Ask the student to report back to you on what the bully says. Then work with the student to improve his or her efforts.

PROTECT YOURSELF

Teachers can be bullied, too. Maybe you have an intimidating or aggressive student—someone who makes you feel uneasy or threatened. Or maybe the problem is a coworker, a group of your coworkers, or a superior.

Check your school or district policies on how to handle student bullies. There should be guidelines in place. If none exist, talk with your principal and other teachers about this issue.

 Go farther: Contact the Crisis Prevention Institute (CPI) and ask about their Nonviolent Crisis Intervention program, which teaches the safe management of disruptive or assaultive behavior. Many schools and districts have benefited from this training. Write or call: Crisis Prevention Institute, Inc., 3315-K North 124th Street, Brookfield, WI 53005; toll-free telephone 1-800-558-8976. On the Web, go to: *http://www.crisisprevention.com/*

What if you're being bullied by your coworkers or superiors? (Workplace bullying is on the rise, and schools are workplaces, just like businesses or factories.) Talk to your principal. Talk to your union representative. You don't have to put up with rude, hostile behavior or put-downs. Learn about the laws that protect you.

 Go farther: Contact the Campaign Against Workplace Bullying (CAWB). Founded by Gary Namie, Ph.D., and

Ruth F. Namie, Ph.D., this nonprofit organization acts as a resource for employee and employer solutions. Write or call: The Campaign Against Workplace Bullying, PO Box 1886, Benicia, CA 94510; telephone (707) 747-9000. CAWB's Web site offers information, research results, surveys, and news articles about workplace bullying. Go to: *http://www.bullybusters.org/*

Meanwhile, here are some commonsense tips you can follow to safeguard yourself:

- Vary your routine. If you walk to and from school, don't always walk the same route at the same time. If you drive, change your route frequently (and try stopping for coffee at a different place now and then).

- Pay attention to your intuition; act on it. It's better to be safe and risk a little embarrassment than stay in an uncomfortable situation that may turn out to be dangerous.

- Don't label keys with your name or any identification.

- Try not to overload yourself with books and other materials when walking down the hall or walking to and from the school building.

- Before or after school hours, check your surroundings before getting out of your car.

- Have your keys ready before you leave the school building. Look inside and under your car before getting in, and always lock your car.

- If your school has an elevator, stay close to the controls and locate the emergency button.

- Get to know your coworkers and look out for each other.

- Walk with confidence. Be assertive. Watch your body language. (See pages 53–54.)

- Be extra watchful when you're walking between buildings, in poorly lighted areas, etc. Try to have another adult with you.

- If you feel that you're in serious, immediate danger from a bully, don't try to defuse the situation on your own. Get help from school security or law enforcement personnel.

HELPING BULLIES

Bullies need help—the sooner the better. Bullying among primary school-age children is recognized as an antecedent to more violent behavior in later grades. If children don't learn to change their behaviors, bullying becomes a habit that carries forward into their teens and their lives as adults.

Although bullies may be popular in the early grades (because they're powerful, others look up to them), their popularity wanes during late adolescence; by the time they reach senior high, their peer group may be limited to other bullies or gangs. They may get in trouble with the law; studies show that one in four bullies will have a criminal record before age 30. They may bully their spouses, children, and coworkers and have difficulty forming and sustaining healthy, positive relationships.

The "Creating a Positive Classroom" section of this book includes many tips and strategies that can help all students—including bullies—learn better ways of relating to others. Some of the strategies in "Helping Victims" can be adapted for use with bullies and potential bullies. *Examples:*

- "Encourage a Positive Attitude" (page 93)

- "Build Students' Self-Esteem" (pages 95–97); although it's a myth that all bullies have low self-esteem, some do

- "Teach Positive Visualization" (page 97)

- "Give Them Opportunities to Shine" (page 108)

One of the strategies in "Helping Victims" is meant to be used with both victims and bullies:

- "Try the Method of Shared Concern" (pages 99 and 100–104)

Some of the strategies in "Helping Victims" will benefit all of your students. *Examples:*

- "Encourage Strong Family Relationships" (page 105)

- "Encourage Relationships with Other Adults" (pages 105–106)

"Helping Bullies" focuses mainly on suggestions for working with bullies or potential bullies. As you try these ideas in your classroom, here are some good things you can expect to happen:

Your students will learn how to:

- change their thinking
- know what to expect when they use inappropriate behavior
- accept responsibility for their behavior
- manage their anger
- explore positive ways to feel powerful
- understand why they bully others
- stop bullying.

You'll discover how to:

- identify bullies or potential bullies
- have clear consequences in place
- work to change bullies' behavior—without being a bully yourself
- communicate with parents
- teach students positive ways to feel powerful
- change bullies' thinking, not just their behavior.

 Important: Most children can change their behavior with guidance and help from caring adults. Sometimes, however, you might encounter a student who resists your efforts and simply won't change. Find out ahead of time what your school and district are prepared to do in these extreme circumstances. When you truly run out of options—when strategies don't work, the parents can't or won't support your efforts, and the student's behavior gets progressively worse—you may have no choice but to take the problem to your principal or other administrators and leave it in their hands. The ideas in this book are not intended to help incorrigible bullies or children with severe behavioral and personality problems.

CATCH THEM IN THE ACT

The first and most important thing you can do to help bullies is notice their behavior and respond appropriately.

Obviously, you want to catch them "being bad"—teasing, using hurtful words, intimidating other students, hitting, shoving, kicking, and so on—and put a stop to that behavior as soon as you become aware of it. See "Act Immediately" (pages 85–86) for specific suggestions on intervening with bullying you witness personally or learn about in another way; see also "Have Clear Consequences in Place" (pages 126–128).

 Go farther: Contact the Crisis Prevention Institute (CPI) and ask about their Nonviolent Crisis Intervention program, which teaches the safe management of disruptive or assaultive behavior. Many schools and districts have benefited from this training. Write or call: Crisis Prevention Institute, Inc., 3315-K North 124th Street, Brookfield, WI 53005; toll-free telephone 1-800-558-8976. On the Web, go to: *http://www.crisisprevention.com/*

Not as obviously (and sometimes not as easily), you also want to *catch them being good*. No one can be a bully 24 hours a day; even the worst bully takes an occasional break. Bullies need "strokes" as much as other students—probably more.

- Recognize and reward positive and accepting behaviors whenever you observe them. This will increase the likelihood that such behaviors will be repeated.

- Go the extra distance and praise behaviors you might take for granted in other students—waiting one's turn, sharing, saying please or thank you.

- Create situations that give bullies the opportunity to shine. *Examples:* Ask a problem student to help you with an important project. Or send an older bully to a younger class to help a student practice spelling words or do math problems. Then recognize your student's positive behavior.

Of course, you'll want to notice and praise positive, prosocial behaviors in *all* of your students. You can do this verbally each day ("Thanks for helping, Evan." "Nice job, class. You're making our new student feel welcome."). You might also award special certificates recognizing specific behaviors. Students will appreciate "You Were Caught Being Good!" certificates (page 118)—and parents will treasure them.

Tip: In one school, students who are seen or reported as displaying positive social interactions (sticking up for a friend, making a new friend, welcoming or accepting a new student, being a good role model, cooperating, showing empathy, etc.) are given a "Gotcha!" card to sign. The cards are entered in a prize drawing at the end of each week.

 Go farther: Work with other teachers and administrators to arrange a special awards ceremony to be held once a month or several times a year. Try to schedule it for a time when parents and grandparents can attend. Instead of handing out the usual awards—for athletic or academic achievement—reserve this ceremony for students whose prosocial behaviors have made a positive difference in your classroom and school.

Finally: Monitor your own interactions with your students. Are they mostly negative, mostly positive, or a mixture of both? Make an effort to increase the number of positives—smiles, acknowledgments, words of praise and approval, thank-yous, nods. The National Association of School Psychologists (NASP) recommends that teachers give approximately *five positives* for each negative. Keep track of your behavior for a day or two. How close do you come to the five-to-one ratio? Is there room for improvement?

HAVE COMPASSION

Bullies can be distracting, disruptive, annoying, frustrating, and even scary at times. But they need as much help, understanding, and compassion as you can give them. Food for thought:

- Many bullies have family problems—parents, siblings, or other bigger, stronger people who bully them. They don't know other ways to behave. And even if they learn and observe other ways in your classroom, they experience a sort of "dissonance" when they return home. Like children of divorced parents who alternate between their parents' homes, they must fit into both environments, and it's not easy.

- Many bullies are angry all or most of the time. Being angry is no fun—especially if you're not really sure *why* you're angry, you don't have anyone to talk to about your anger (or think you don't, and even if you do, you might not know *how* to talk about it), and your peers avoid and fear you. For some bullies, being angry is a vicious circle, and they're caught in the middle with no way out.

- It's hard to be the meanest, toughest kid in the classroom or on the playground. You're always having to prove yourself and fend off other kids who want to take over as meanest and toughest.

- It's hard to feel that you always have to win and can't ever lose. No one likes to lose, but bullies can't afford to lose—it's too risky. So they cheat, play dirty, and intimidate anyone who stands in their way. And eventually no one wants to play with them or against them.

- Many bullies are jealous of other people's success. Jealousy is a nasty, uncomfortable feeling. It's so overpowering that it can prevent you from enjoying your own successes—or distract you so much that you don't achieve your true potential.

- Some bullies never wanted to hurt or harass anyone else. They were bullied by someone else into joining a bully gang and are going along just to stay on the bully's good side.

You Were Caught Being
GOOD!!!

Today's date: _____

Your name: _____

Teacher's comment:

Teacher's signature: _____

- Bullies lack social skills. When you don't know how to get along with others, and when you see groups of friends hanging out, laughing, telling jokes, and enjoying each other's company, you know you're missing out on something important . . . but you don't know how to get it for yourself. Which may be another reason why bullies are so angry.

- Bullies have hangers-on, "henchmen," or "lieutenants," but they seldom have real friends. Life without friends is lonely.

The bullies in your classroom may be some of the most unpleasant, least appealing kids you know. The good news is, they're still kids . . . for now. As kids, they have the potential to learn, grow, and change.

IDENTIFY BULLIES OR POTENTIAL BULLIES

You may know that some students in your classroom are bullies; either you've seen them in action yourself, or you've heard reports from other students and teachers. But what about the bullies whose actions aren't noticed by adults, whose victims are too intimidated or ashamed to come forward, and whose witnesses either don't want to get involved or fear reprisals if they do? And what about those students who haven't started bullying others but may be heading in that direction?

"Identify Victims or Potential Victims" (pages 78–81) explains how to look for warning signs and seek input from students' parents. You can use similar approaches to identify bullies or potential bullies.

LOOK FOR WARNING SIGNS

For any student you suspect might be a bully or potential bully, complete the "Warning Signs" checklist (pages 120–121).

 Important: These forms should be kept confidential. You may want to share them

with other adults—teachers, your principal, the school counselor, the student's parents—but they should never be accessible to students.

GET PARENTS' INPUT

If a student shows some or many of the warning signs, contact the parents. Arrange a face-to-face meeting at school. You may want to include the school counselor or psychologist in the meeting.

No parent wants to hear that his or her child might be a bully or potential bully, so you'll need to handle this *very* carefully. You might start by emphasizing your commitment to creating a positive classroom environment where every student is valued, accepted, safe, and free to learn. Share information about what's being done at your school to reduce and eliminate bullying.

Next, tell the parents about the *positive* behaviors you've observed in their child. (See "Catch Them in the Act," pages 116–117.) Parents love hearing good things about their children, and this sets the stage for a productive meeting.

Then tell the parents that you've noticed some behaviors at school which may indicate their child is bullying others or might be headed in that direction. Give examples. Explain that there are other behaviors that don't show up at school, and you need their help identifying those behaviors.

Ask if they have noticed any of the following in their child:

- having more money than he or she can explain

- buying things he or she normally can't afford

- having new possessions (games, clothing, CDs, etc.) and claiming that "my friends gave them to me"

WARNING SIGNS

The following behaviors and traits may indicate that a student is bullying others or, if bullying isn't yet evident or hasn't been reported, has the potential to become a bully. For any student you're concerned about, check all that apply.

Today's date: _____

Student's name: _____

_____ **1.** Enjoys feeling powerful and in control.

_____ **2.** Seeks to dominate and/or manipulate peers.

_____ **3.** May be popular with other students, who envy his or her power.

_____ **4.** Is physically larger and stronger than his or her peers.

_____ **5.** Is impulsive.

_____ **6.** Loves to win at everything; hates to lose at anything. Is both a poor winner (boastful, arrogant) and a poor loser.

_____ **7.** Seems to derive satisfaction or pleasure from others' fear, discomfort, or pain.

_____ **8.** Seems overly concerned with others "disrespecting" him or her; equates "respect" with fear.

_____ **9.** Seems to have little or no empathy for others.

_____ **10.** Seems to have little or no compassion for others.

_____ **11.** Seems unable or unwilling to see things from another person's perspective or "walk in someone else's shoes."

_____ **12.** Seems willing to use and abuse other people to get what he or she wants.

_____ **13.** Defends his or her negative actions by insisting that others "deserved it," "asked for it," or "provoked" him or her; a conflict is always someone else's "fault."

_____ **14.** Is good at hiding negative behaviors or doing them where adults can't notice.

_____ **15.** Gets excited when conflicts arise between others.

_____ **16.** Stays cool during conflicts in which he or she is directly involved.

CONTINUED

_____ **17.** Exhibits little or no emotion (flat affect) when talking about his or her part in a conflict.

_____ **18.** Blames other people for his or her problems.

_____ **19.** Refuses to accept responsibility for his or her negative behaviors.

_____ **20.** Shows little or no remorse for his or her negative behaviors.

_____ **21.** Lies in an attempt to stay out of trouble.

_____ **22.** Expects to be "misunderstood," "disrespected," and picked on; attacks before he or she can be attacked.

_____ **23.** Interprets ambiguous or innocent acts as purposeful and hostile; uses these as excuses to strike out at others verbally or physically.

_____ **24.** "Tests" your authority by committing minor infractions, then waits to see what you'll do about it.

_____ **25.** Disregards or breaks school and/or class rules.

_____ **26.** Is generally defiant or oppositional toward adults.

_____ **27.** Seeks/craves attention; seems just as satisfied with negative attention as positive attention.

_____ **28.** Attracts more than the usual amount of negative attention from others; is yelled at or disciplined more often than other students.

_____ **29.** Is street-smart.

_____ **30.** Has a strong sense of self-esteem. _Tip:_ This is contrary to the prevailing myth that bullies have low self-esteem. In fact, there's little evidence to support the belief that bullies victimize others because they feel bad about themselves.

_____ **31.** Seems mainly concerned with his or her own pleasure and well-being.

_____ **32.** Seems antisocial or lacks social skills.

_____ **33.** Has difficulty fitting into groups.

_____ **34.** Has a close network of a few friends (actually "henchmen" or "lieutenants"), who follow along with whatever he or she wants to do.

_____ **35.** May have problems at school or at home; lacks coping skills.

- defying parental authority; ignoring or breaking rules; pushing parental boundaries harder than ever

- behaving aggressively toward siblings

- exhibiting a sense of superiority—of being "right" all the time

- being determined to win at everything; being a poor loser

- blaming others for his or her problems

- refusing to take responsibility for his or her negative behaviors

What else can the parents tell you? What else have they noticed that you should know—that might help you help their child?

 Important: Studies show that bullies often come from homes where physical punishment is used, where children are taught to handle problems by striking back physically, and where parental involvement and warmth are minimal or lacking. But never *assume* that this is true for every child. In my experience, parents of bullies are deeply concerned about their children. They want their children to be accepted by others; they want them to develop social skills, friendships, and positive character traits including tolerance, compassion, and empathy. So instead of expecting the worst, hope for the best. Project a sense of optimism; communicate your belief that you and the parents can work together to turn the child around.

You'll also want to talk with the parents about how bullying violates your school and classroom policies and rules. Mention the consequences of such behavior, but don't dwell on these too long. Rather, the purpose of this meeting should be to identify warning signs and reach an agreement that everyone involved—you, the parents, and the counselor (if present)—will work together to help the student. Make it clear that you have high expectations that the problem can and will be

resolved successfully. You want the parents to leave your meeting with a desire to work with you on their child's behalf, not the feeling that you and the school are united "against" them and their child.

Toward the end of the meeting, give parents a copy of "Bringing Out the Best in Kids: Tips for Parents" (pages 123–124). Explain that this is a list of suggestions they can try at home. Answer any questions they may have. *Tip:* You may want to find out ahead of time about parenting courses and resources available in your community, so you can give this information to parents who want it.

Thank the parents for coming in and talking with you. Tell them that you'll communicate with them often about their child's behavior and progress, and ask them to do the same for you. Then be sure to follow through.

Make a written record of your meeting. Note any relevant information the parents shared with you, any conclusions you came to, and any agreements you reached.

NEVER BULLY THE BULLY

When faced with a bully and frustrated or angered by his or her behavior, it's easy for adults to "lose their cool." Shouting, spanking, and threats aren't uncommon.

Severe punishment may suppress the current behavior, but it doesn't teach alternate behaviors, including positive ways to act. Here are eight more reasons why "bullying the bully" is always a bad idea:

1. Adults who respond to bullies with violence, force, or intimidation are modeling and reinforcing the same behaviors they're trying to change. Children imitate what they see adults do.

2. Severe punishment reinforces the power imbalance and shows kids that bullying is acceptable.

1. Have regular home meetings with your child. Show interest in what he or she is doing. Ask questions and be a good listener. Who are your child's friends? What are your child's likes and dislikes? How does your child spend his or her time at school, and away from school when he or she isn't with the family? *Tip:* Some of the best family discussions happen around the dinner table.

2. Make a real effort to spend more positive time with your child than you already do. Try to do things together that your child enjoys. Encourage your child to talk about his or her feelings. Ask how the day went. Praise your child as often as possible. Give your child opportunities to do well—by helping you with a chore, taking on new responsibilities, or showing off a talent or skill.

3. Monitor the television shows your child watches, and reduce the amount of TV violence he or she is exposed to. Experts have found that TV violence has a negative effect on children. Also limit the amount of violence your child encounters in video and computer games.

4. Supervise your child's whereabouts and activities even more closely than you already do. Set reasonable rules and limits for activities and curfews. Make it a point to always know where your child is and who he or she is with.

5. Consider enrolling your child in a class on conflict resolution, stress management, anger management, friendship skills, or self-defense. Check with your child's teacher or community resources—your local public library, YMCA or YWCA, community education, etc.

   ⚠ *Important:* Self-defense classes aren't about being aggressive. They're about avoiding conflict through self-discipline, self-control, and improved self-confidence. Most martial arts teach that the first line of defense is nonviolence.

6. If your child's teacher has told you that your child is bullying others, take it seriously. Kids who bully often have serious problems later in life.

   • Talk with your child. Be aware that your child might deny or minimize his or her behavior; this is normal. Don't blame; don't ask "why" something happened or "why" your child acted in a certain way, because this may lead to lies and excuses. Stay calm and make it clear that bullying is NOT okay with you.

   • Reassure your child that you still love him or her. It's the bullying *behavior* you don't like. Tell your child that you'll work together to help change the behavior—and you won't give up on him or her.

⟶

CONTINUED

- Talk with your child's teacher(s) and other adults at the school—in private, when no other students are around. Get the facts on your child's behavior. Ask them to keep you informed.

- Work with the school to modify your child's behavior. Stay in touch with teachers, administrators, and playground supervisors so you know how your child is progressing. Let them know about your efforts at home.

- Apply reasonable, age appropriate, developmentally appropriate consequences (withdrawing privileges, giving time-outs, assigning extra chores around the house) for bullying behavior. Avoid corporal punishment, which sends your child the message that "might is right."

- Talk with your child about how bullying affects the victim. If you remember times from your own childhood when you were bullied, you know how much it hurts.

- Help your child learn and practice positive ways to handle anger, frustration, and disappointment. (How do you handle those feelings at home? Remember: you're an important role model for your child.) Try role-playing new behaviors with your child.

- Praise your child's efforts to change. Praise your child for following home and school rules. The more positives you can give your child, the better. *Tip:* Try giving your child five positive comments for every negative comment.

7. If you think you might need a refresher course on parenting skills, you're not alone. Many parents today seek advice and insights from other parents and trained professionals. Check your local bookstore or library for parenting books. See if your child's school sponsors parenting discussions, programs, or workshops; find out what's available in your community. The more you learn, the more you know!

8. If you think you might need more help than you can get from a book, program, or workshop on parenting, and especially if you feel that your child is developing problem behaviors, get professional help. Ask the school counselor, psychologist, or social worker for recommendations. Check with the children's mental health center in your community. There's no shame in this; it takes wisdom and courage to acknowledge that you can't do it all.

3. Severe punishment may stop one behavior temporarily but stimulate other aggressive behaviors.

4. The child may stop the punished behavior only when adults are around and increase it in other settings.

5. The child may strike back at the adult who's doing the punishing, or strike out at someone else because of displaced anger.

6. Angry children who don't fear authority may become even angrier and focus on getting revenge.

7. Frequent punishment may cause some children to withdraw, regress, and give up. Others may feel a strong sense of shame and low self-esteem.

8. Severe punishment is a short-term "solution" that may cause more problems down the road. ("If adults can hit, why can't I? Maybe I just have to wait until I'm bigger.")

If you feel that you sometimes overreact and would like to learn ways to control your emotions, check with your school psychologist or counselor. Or visit your local library or bookstore and look for books on managing stress and handling challenging kids. Ask other teachers what they do when they feel like they're about to blow up. Meanwhile:

- Remember that you're the adult, then behave like one.

- Tell yourself that you'll stay calm no matter what.

- Learn and practice simple relaxation techniques you can use when students push you to the edge of your patience.

- Make an agreement with another teacher whose classroom is near yours. Whenever one of you reaches the end of your rope, you can ask the other to take over your class for a few minutes while you go to a quiet place and regain control of your emotions. Or you can send a student who's driving you crazy to the other teacher's room for a short period of time.

- Never spank a child—even if your school permits corporal punishment. Why model a behavior you're trying to teach your students never to use? When you swat or paddle a student, you're saying, "It's okay for bigger, stronger people to hit smaller, weaker people."

Go farther: Many states still permit corporal punishment in schools. Corporal punishment of children is unsupported by educational research, sometimes leads to serious injury, and contributes to a pro-violence attitude. If your state still permits corporal punishment in schools and you'd like to do something to change that, the Center for Effective Discipline (CED) can help. This national organization provides educational information to the public on the effects of corporal punishment and alternatives to its use. It is headquarters for and coordinates two other organizations: the National Coalition to Abolish Corporal Punishment in Schools (NCACPS) and End Physical Punishment of Children (EPOCH-USA). Write or call: The Center for Effective Discipline, 155 W. Main Street, Suite 1603, Columbus, OH 43215; (614) 221-8829. On the Web, go to: *http://www.stophitting.com/*

What if a bully threatens you? Try not to look angry, upset, or afraid. Don't grab the student. Don't raise your voice. Don't set up a power struggle by challenging him or her. Don't cross your arms and shout across the room. Don't verbally attack the student and back him or her into a corner by demanding immediate compliance.

Instead, remain calm, confident, assertive, and under control. Keep your body language and facial expression neutral. Speak clearly in your normal tone of voice as you move closer to the student (no closer than arm's length), state your expectations, and give the student a choice: stop the behavior and accept the consequences, or continue the behavior and bring on worse consequences. If the student wants to argue, simply restate the choice.

Tip: If you feel that you might be in real danger, get reinforcements—another teacher, an administrator, the school security officer, or local law enforcement.*

HAVE CLEAR CONSEQUENCES IN PLACE

If your school or district already has consequences in place for bullying behaviors, familiarize yourself with them. Communicate them to students and parents so everyone knows what they are.

• You might summarize the consequences simply and clearly on a poster for your classroom.

• Create a handout for students; send copies home or give them to parents during conferences, open houses, or Parents' Night.

• If your school publishes a student or parent handbook, the consequences should be included there.

Consequences are essential because they tell you exactly how to follow through when a student behaves inappropriately. You know which behaviors are grounds for a reprimand, timeout, in-school detention, dismissal, suspension, and (a last resort) expulsion. You don't have to decide what to do each time a bullying situation arises; uncertainty is replaced by consistency, and there are no surprises for anyone.

What if your school or district hasn't spelled out specific consequences for bullying behaviors? Form a team of other teachers and administrators and work together to determine consequences that are:

• *practical* (doable where you are and with the resources available to you)

• *logical* (they make sense and are related to specific bullying behaviors)

• *reasonable and fair* (excessively punitive consequences "bully the bully")

• *inevitable* (if a student does A, then B happens—no exceptions)

• *predictable* (everyone in the school community knows that A leads to B)

• *immediate* (consequences are applied at the earliest possible opportunity)

• *escalating* (continuing the behavior leads to more serious consequences)

• *consistently enforced* (if two students do A, then B happens for both)

• *developmentally appropriate and age appropriate* (the consequences for name-calling in first grade will be different from the consequences for name-calling in sixth grade)

Tip: Consider including students on your team. Since bullying affects them directly, they'll have a personal interest and commitment to the process, and they'll bring their unique perspective to the table.

At your team's first meeting, you might want to share the following advice from the National Association of School Psychologists (NASP).* Use it as a starting point for determining consequences for bullying behaviors:

---

* SOURCE: "Bullying Fact Sheet" by George Batsche and Benjamin Moore, in *Helping Children Grow Up in the '90s: A Resource Book for Parents and Teachers* (Bethesda, MD: National Association of School Psychologists, 1992).

---

* See also "Protect Yourself" (pages 112–113).

Discipline practices should empha-size restitution and positive practice rather than expulsion, paddlings, and humiliation. That is, when students are caught bullying they should apologize, demonstrate the correct behavior, and then have to spend a specified period of time help-ing (public service) younger, less able children. . . . Although it is very dif-ficult to justify, bullies should not be removed from the school setting unless absolutely necessary.

ONE SCHOOL'S STORY

The staff at one Maine elementary school per-ceived that informal student interactions on the playground and the bus included too much teasing and too many put-downs. After lengthy discussions about the negative effects of hurtful comments, they developed a Zero Tolerance standard to eliminate name-calling and insults.

Students who called others "dork," "moron," or other names were sent to the school office to call home and tell their parents what they had done. Consequences were spelled out for infrac-tions that continued or escalated. Teachers vol-unteered extra-duty periods to implement the new standard and establish the expectation: no name-calling.

Some people thought the standard seemed extreme. During the first month or so, the office saw a virtual parade of students for noon-time detention. But it didn't take long for stu-dents to adjust, and today the change in school climate is noteworthy; only a few students each week get into trouble. When students were sur-veyed about the program, one wrote, "I don't have to worry about Zero Tolerance because I don't use those words."*

APOLOGIES AND AMENDS

Although opinions differ on whether bullies should apologize to their victims, saying "I'm sorry" is the first step toward recognizing that a behavior is inappropriate and taking respon-

* SOURCE: "Respect among peers is a goal of Wayne pol-icy" by Janet Adelberg, *The Chalkboard*, December 1998.

sibility for that behavior. Many bullies blame the victim ("he/she made me do it," "he/she deserved it") and see no need to apologize. Don't listen to excuses; simply insist that the bully apologize—verbally or in writing. If he or she refuses, apply appropriate consequences for his or her lack of cooperation.

Beyond apologizing to the victim, the student should also make amends for his or her behav-ior. *Examples:*

- For every "put-down" comment the stu-dent makes about another, he or she should make one or more "build-up" comment.

- If the student extorted money, he or she should pay it back as soon as possible. Also consider having the student do work around the school (in the media center, office, etc.) for a half hour every day for one week.

- If the student damaged or destroyed something belonging to another, he or she should repair or replace it as soon as possible.

TIME-OUTS

The time-out is a time-honored way to modify students' behavior—or at least put a stop to inappropriate behavior and give tempers a chance to cool.

Tell students when time-outs will be used, and describe the specific behaviors that will lead to a time-out. Establish a time-out place in your classroom—a special area away from the group where students can be seen and supervised. In contrast to the rest of your classroom, try to keep the time-out place relatively dull and bor-ing—no fun posters, no books or toys.

As you use time-outs with your students, keep these general guidelines in mind:

- A time-out is not a detention. Rather, it's time spent away from the group and its activities, social feedback, and rewards.

- A time-out is not a punishment. It's an opportunity for a student to calm down and ponder his or her behavior.

- A time-out is brief. A few minutes is usually sufficient—longer for more serious or disruptive behaviors, but no more than 10–15 minutes.

- A time-out is not to be used for classwork or homework. (Nor should it be used by the student as an opportunity to get out of an assignment or classwork he or she doesn't want to do.)

- A time-out is not a battleground. Don't argue with the student. Don't engage in any kind of conversation with the student. Simply say, "You (broke a particular class rule, or violated a guideline), and that's a time-out. Please go to the time-out place right now."

- What if a student refuses to go to the time-out place? Try adding one or two minutes to the time-out for each minute the student delays going. Or you might say, "For every minute you put off going to time-out, that's five minutes you'll have to stay in from recess."

- When a time-out is over, it's over. The student returns to the group without criticism, comments, or conditions.

Tip: Consider giving students the option to put *themselves* on a time-out when they feel they are about to behave inappropriately. This empowers students to make good choices on their own behalf and teaches them to remove themselves from a potentially volatile situation.

CHANGE THEIR THINKING

As you work to help bullies, it's as important to change their *thinking* as it is to change their behavior. Bullies often deny that they've done anything wrong and refuse to take responsibility for their behavior. They believe that their actions are someone else's "fault." Or they dismiss them as "no big deal" or insist that they were "misinterpreted."* You'll need to challenge their thinking without preaching.

1. Ask them to consider this question and respond verbally or in writing:

   If you think you're not *bullying another person, but that person thinks you* are, *who's right?*

   Lead students to understand that bullying is in the "eye of the beholder"—that the other person's feelings and fears are real to him or her.

2. Suggest that there are three ways to look at any situation involving two people:

   - my interpretation—what I think happened and why
   - your interpretation—what you think happened and why
   - the facts—what really happened

   Sometimes it helps if there's a third person present (a bystander or witness) who's objective and can give his or her view of the facts.

3. Have students keep a daily journal of events that upset, frustrate, or anger them.** For each event, they should write a brief, factual description, followed by their own interpretation of what happened.

   Review and discuss their journal entries one-on-one or in small group discussions. Encourage students to look for possible errors in their interpretations. *Example:* Maybe what happened was an accident. Maybe they misinterpreted something that wasn't meant to upset them. Maybe *they* caused the problem.

4. When dealing with specific bullying situations, use the Method of Shared Concern (pages 99 and 100–104) or the No Blame

---

* See "Warning Signs" (pages 120–121).

** See also "Weekly Journaling" (pages 38–39).

Approach (page 104), both of which encourage children to take responsibility for their actions.

 Go farther: For a list of thinking errors and the correct social thinking, see *Bully-Proofing Your School: A Comprehensive Approach for Elementary Schools* by Carla Garrity, Kathryn Jens, William Porter, Nancy Sager, and Cam Short-Camilli (Longmont, CO: Sopris West, 1996).

5. Help students self-identify. The "Are You a Bully?" handout (page 130) will start them thinking about their own behavior. You might give these only to students you know or suspect are bullying others. Or make this a whole-class exercise, followed by discussion. Even students who don't bully can benefit from examining some of their own attitudes and behaviors.

Important: Collect the completed handouts and keep them confidential.

COMMUNICATE WITH PARENTS

Once you've informed a student's parents that their child is or may be bullying others, it's essential to follow through with regular communication and updates on their child's progress. It's normal for parents to be defensive at first, perhaps even angry that their child has been identified as a "problem" student. You can help to allay their fears, calm their worries, lower their defenses, build trust, and increase their willingness to cooperate by promising to stay in touch and keeping your promise.

You probably already communicate with your students' parents—in conferences, at open houses and parents' nights, with notes home, and in other ways. Here are a few more ideas to consider:

- Pick up the phone and call parents, or let them know the best times to call you.

Offer alternatives—before school, after school, during lunch or break times.

- Each day, write comments on a note card about the child's behavior in school and send it home with the child. (For privacy, put the card in a sealed envelope.) Make sure to write at least as many positive comments as negative comments (if possible, write *more* positives than negatives). You might put a star by each positive comment. Suggest to parents that when a child has earned a certain number of stars for the week, they might offer the child a reward—doing something special with mom or dad, choosing a video to watch, having a friend spend the night. *Tip:* For the first few days, you might follow through with a phone call to make sure your notes are getting into parents' hands and not being "lost" on the way home from school.

- If both you and the parents have access to email, this is a fast and easy way to stay in touch.

Depending on the situation, you can also have the student communicate directly with his or her own parents. *Example:* If Kevin calls Marcus a name, have Kevin write a note describing what he said and what happened afterward. Kevin might write, "I called Marcus a bad name in school. First Ms. Sellick said to apologize to Marcus. I said I was sorry. Then she put me on a time-out. I thought about how Marcus felt when I called him the bad name. I won't do it again." Read the note before it goes home; check to make sure that the student has taken responsibility for his or her behavior (as opposed to "Marcus is a !@#$%" or "I got in trouble because Stefan ratted on me"). Follow through with a phone call to make sure parents receive the note.

As the student progresses, daily communication can eventually become weekly communication, then twice monthly, and so on until the problem behaviors have greatly improved or stopped altogether.

ARE YOU A BULLY?

Have you ever wondered if you're a bully? Here's a quick way to tell if you are or might be. Read each question and circle "Y" (for yes) or "N" (for no). When you're through, give this handout to the teacher.

Be honest! Your answers will be kept private.

1. Do you pick on people who are smaller than you, or on animals?   Y   N

2. Do you like to tease and taunt other people?   Y   N

3. If you tease people, do you like to see them get upset?   Y   N

4. Do you think it's funny when other people make mistakes?   Y   N

5. Do you like to take or destroy other people's belongings?   Y   N

6. Do you want other students to think you're the toughest kid in school?   Y   N

7. Do you get angry a lot and stay angry for a long time?   Y   N

8. Do you blame other people for things that go wrong in your life?   Y   N

9. Do you like to get revenge on people who hurt you?   Y   N

10. When you play a game or sport, do you always have to be the winner?   Y   N

11. If you lose at something, do you worry about what other people will think of you?   Y   N

12. Do you get angry or jealous when someone else succeeds?   Y   N

Read this AFTER you answer all of the questions!

If you answered "Yes" to one or two of these questions, you may be on your way to becoming a bully. If you answered "Yes" to three or more, you probably *are* a bully, and you need to find ways to change your behavior. Good news: Bullies can get help dealing with their feelings, getting along with other people, and making friends. Parents, teachers, school counselors, and other adults can all give this kind of help. JUST ASK!!!

GET PARENTS TOGETHER

When you first inform parents that their children are bullying others or being bullied, you'll want to meet *separately* with each set of parents (or guardians). It's hard enough for parents to hear this kind of news without having to face the parents of the child who is hurting their son or daughter (or being hurt by him or her). It's tempting to go on the offensive or become defensive, and suddenly you have another set of problems on your hands.

In time, however, and especially if you're making progress helping both students, you might want to consider getting the parents together for a face-to-face meeting. You might want to include the school counselor or psychologist.

 Important: Use your judgment, follow your instincts, and ask the parents (separately) how they feel about this. Are they ready to sit down and talk to each other? Can they set aside their negative feelings—anger, disappointment, fear, hostility—and keep an open mind? Can they agree to hear both sides? Can they present a united front of caring adults who all want the best for their children?

When parents are willing to communicate and work together, this brings a special energy to the situation. Students who are having difficulty getting along see a good example: adults on opposite sides of a problem who are willing to talk and work together. This gives both sets of parents the opportunity to serve as positive role models.

KEEP THE FOCUS ON BEHAVIOR

In your interactions with a student who bullies others, be sure to emphasize that the problem is the *behavior,* not the student himself or herself.

Never label the student a "bully." Instead of saying, "I've noticed that you're a bully," or "People tell me you're a bully," or "You must stop being a bully," say something like "Hitting (or kicking, teasing, excluding, name-calling, etc.) are bullying behaviors, and they are not allowed in our classroom." Or "There are lots of good things I like about you—your smile, your talent for drawing, and your sense of humor. But I don't like it when you tease other students, and we need to work on that behavior." For every negative statement you make to point out an undesirable behavior, try to include one or more positives.

When you need to remove a student from a situation, be specific about your reasons for doing so. *Example:* "Jon, I'm putting you on time-out because you shoved Tracy, and shoving isn't allowed." Make sure the student knows why he or she is being removed. Ask, "Why am I putting you on time-out?" If the student offers excuses ("Tracy shoved me first" or "I didn't mean to shove her" or "It was an accident"), calmly restate your reason ("I'm putting you on time-out because you shoved Tracy, and shoving isn't allowed"). Ask the student to reflect on his or her reasons for being removed. You might even use an old-fashioned technique and have the student write the reason on paper—25 times? 50 times? ("I'm on time-out because I shoved Tracy, and shoving isn't allowed.")

Take every opportunity to show your approval and acceptance of the student as a *person.* Separate the student from the behavior. *Example:* "Shawna, you know I like you a lot. But I don't like it when you pick on kids who are smaller than you. Let's talk about ways you can change that behavior."

TEACH STUDENTS TO MONITOR THEIR OWN BEHAVIOR

Have students who bully others monitor their own behavior. Work with each student to identify and list inappropriate behaviors he or she needs to change. The student then keeps a tally of how often he or she engages in each behavior. Or, to cast this in a more positive light, the student can record the amount of time (in 15-minute intervals or number of class periods) during which he or she *doesn't* engage in the behavior. Either way, this deliberate, conscientious record-keeping usually leads to greater control over one's behavior. *Tip:* The student must *want* to change the behaviors, or self-monitoring won't work.

For more on self-monitoring, see:

- *Teaching Self-Management Strategies to Adolescents* by K. Richard Young, Richard P. West, Deborah J. Smith, and Daniel P. Morgan (Longmont, CO: Sopris West, 1991). This program for students in grades 6–12 helps children develop new, productive habits to help them succeed in school and in life.

- *It's Up to Me: A Self-Monitoring Behavior Program* developed by Janie Haugen (San Antonio, TX: PCI, 1995). Choose behavioral objectives from 150 reproducible Monthly Charting Sheets. Students carry their own notebooks and chart their own behavior. Write or call: PCI, PO Box 34270, San Antonio, TX 78265-4270; toll-free telephone 1-800-594-4263.

PROVIDE COUNSELING

Students who bully others need help learning how to relate to their peers in more positive, productive ways. If at all possible, they should have access to some type of counseling—by a school psychologist, guidance counselor, or another trained adult. In some cases, peer counseling can also be useful. Some experts feel that counseling or discussion with students involved in bullying should occur *before* consequences are applied.

Counseling groups have a big advantage over punishment or other disciplinary tactics, although they shouldn't take the place of reasonable and consistent consequences for specific behaviors. Rather than driving the problem underground, groups bring it out in the open where students can discuss it and adults can offer their input and advice. Rather than making bullies feel even more excluded and socially inept, groups offer opportunities for students to talk about what's bothering them, explore reasons for their behavior, and learn alternatives to bullying others.

In general, bullies don't "outgrow" their problem without some type of professional help. Often, it's not enough to counsel only the bully—especially if his or her inappropriate behaviors were learned at home. During your discussions with the student's parents, you might suggest they consider family counseling. Have a list of local and community resources available for parents who seem willing to give it a try.

GET OTHER STUDENTS INVOLVED

Never underestimate the power of peer pressure! As you're helping bullies change their behavior, get the whole class involved.*

In some schools, students have formed "good gangs" to defend victims of bullies. When they see someone being mistreated (perhaps when the teacher's back is turned), they shout in unison at the student who's doing the bullying: "Leave (victim's name) alone!" You might role-play this with your class to see how it works.

Have students practice things they might say to friends who bully others. *Examples:* "If you want me to keep being your friend, you have to stop teasing Paul." "I don't like it when my friends hurt other people." "When you hit Raisa, that makes *me* feel bad and I don't want to be around you."

---

* See also "Mobilize Witnesses" (pages 89 and 93).

When you notice bullying behavior, call students' attention to it. You might say, "Look at what Ben just did to Alex. He threw his notebook on the floor. That's not fair, is it? What can we do to help?" Then encourage students to act on a valid suggestion (helping Alex pick up his notebook; telling Ben to cut it out).

Give students permission to point out when someone is breaking a class rule (see "Set Rules," pages 31–32). *Example:* A student might say, "Class Rule Number Two! We don't tease people."

 Go farther: Have students brainstorm ways to express their intolerance for bullying behavior. Write their ideas on the chalkboard and invite class discussion. They might vote for their top 5 ideas, then create a poster titled "Ways to Be a Bully Buster."

SET UP A BULLY COURT

Some schools have set up "bully courts"—forums in which bullies are tried and sentenced by their peers. Half of the court's members are elected by the bully's classmates, and half are appointed by the teacher. The teacher serves as chairperson to ensure fair play. "Sentences" have included banning bullies from school trips and playgrounds, and having bullies perform service-related tasks such as tidying classrooms.

Bully courts might be more appropriate for older students than younger students. But if you want to explore the possibility for your classroom, check out these resources on teen, youth, and student courts:

American Bar Association
Division for Public Education
541 North Fairbanks Court
Chicago, IL 60611-3314
(312) 988-5735
http://www.abanet.org/

Request a free packet of information about teen/youth/student courts.

Juvenile Justice Clearinghouse and Office of Juvenile Justice and Delinquency Prevention
1-800-638-8736
http://ojjdp.ncjrs.org/

Request a copy of "Peer Justice and Youth Empowerment: An Implementation Guide for Teen Court Program." Or read it online at: *http://www.ncjrs.org/peerhome.htm*

HELP STUDENTS IDENTIFY AND PURSUE THEIR INTERESTS

It's often true that students who bully others don't have special interests or hobbies. They spend much of their time picking on others, planning ways to pick on others, or responding to imagined slights or offenses. Because they tend to be very competitive and are poor losers, they may choose not to get involved in activities where there's a chance they won't excel or win.

Identify students who are bullies or potential bullies (see pages 119–122), then make time to talk with them one-on-one. Explain that you'd like to get to know them better. Ask them what they like to do in their free time; don't be surprised if they can't (or won't) answer right away. They may be suspicious or defensive. Be patient, friendly, welcoming, and warm; back off if you sense that a student feels uncomfortable.

You might guide them with questions like the following.* *Tip:* Along the way, share information about your own interests and hobbies, as appropriate. The discussion shouldn't be about *you,* but if you're willing to reveal a little about your life, students might follow your example and let you in on theirs.

1. Do you like to read books or magazines? What are your favorites? Do you have a favorite time to read? A special place where you like to curl up or sprawl out and read?

---

* See also "Learn More About Your Students" (pages 38–39).

2. What do you like to watch on TV?

3. Have you seen any good movies lately? What are your favorite movies or videos? What do you like about them?

4. What's your favorite kind of music? Who are your favorite groups or bands?

5. What's your favorite way to let off steam? Do you run? Bike? Skate? Shoot hoops?

6. When you have free time at home, what do you like to do best? Do you have a hobby? Tell me about it.

7. How much time to you spend on your hobby? What do you like most about it?

8. Imagine that you have all the money and all the freedom in the world. What's *one* thing you'd really like to do?

9. What do you think you might want to be when you grow up?

10. Imagine that you could go anywhere in the world. Where would you like to go? Why? What would you do there?

11. Imagine that you could be anyone in the world—past, present, or future. Who would you be? Why would you want to be that person? What would you do if you were that person?

12. Is there something you've always wanted to try? What about (acting in a play, starting a collection, singing in a band, playing on a team, joining a club, playing a musical instrument, dancing, working with animals, etc.)?

If you learn that the student has a hobby, encourage him or her to tell you more about it. If it's a collection, maybe the student can bring all or part of it to school and share it with the class.

If you learn that the student has a special interest (or the potential to develop a special interest), offer to help him or her pursue it. Put the stu-

dent in touch with people or organizations in your school and community.* Offer encouragement and follow through by asking questions about his or her progress and experiences as the year goes on.

TEACH LEADERSHIP SKILLS

Bullies are skilled at getting and using power over others. They do it for the wrong reasons (to intimidate and control), in the wrong ways (with physical force, verbal abuse, or emotional manipulation), and to the wrong ends (victimizing others and making them miserable), but clearly they possess real ability. Why not channel all that talent into something worthwhile?

Consider offering leadership training especially for students who have been identified as bullies or potential bullies. Check to see what's available in your community through Family and Children's Services and other organizations that serve children and youth.**

Good leadership training promotes and strengthens many positive character traits and skills. *Examples:*

- activism
- admitting mistakes
- assertiveness
- being a good sport
- caring
- citizenship
- coaching
- communication
- compromise
- concern
- confidence
- conflict resolution
- cooperation
- courage
- creativity
- credibility
- decision-making
- dedication
- delegating
- dependability
- endurance
- enthusiasm
- fairness
- follow-through
- goal-setting
- honesty
- imagination

* See also "Encourage Relationships with Other Adults" (pages 105–106).

** See "Clubs, Groups, Troops, and Teams" (pages 105–106).

- independence
- influencing others
- ingenuity
- initiative
- inspiring others
- integrity
- judgment
- justice
- learning
- listening
- loyalty
- motivating others
- patience
- perseverance
- planning
- positive attitudes
- positive risk-taking
- pride
- purpose
- resiliency
- resourcefulness
- respect for others
- responsibility
- self-awareness
- self-esteem
- self-improvement
- self-respect
- service to others
- setting a good example
- tact
- team-building
- thoughtfulness
- trustworthiness
- unselfishness

Imagine what might happen if we could turn bullies into leaders! It's worth a try . . . and it could turn troublemaking students into contributing assets to our schools and communities.

HELP STUDENTS FIND MENTORS

Students who bully others are students at risk for serious problems now and in the future. It's a proven fact that students at risk can be helped to improve their behavior and stay out of trouble by being matched with mentors—adults or teens who care about them and spend time with them.

In 1992 and 1993, Public/Private Ventures (P/PV), a national research organization based in Philadelphia, studied the effects of mentoring during an 18-month experiment involving nearly 1,000 boys and girls ages 10–16 in eight states.* Half of the children were matched with mentors through Big Brothers Big Sisters of America (BBBSA) agencies; half were assigned to a waiting list, or control group. The children in the first group met with their Big Brothers/Sisters about three times a month for at least a year.

At the end of the study, P/PV found that the mentored students were:

- **46% less likely than the students in the control groups to start using illegal drugs**
- **27% less likely to start using alcohol**
- **53% less likely to skip school**
- **37% less likely to skip a class**
- **almost 33% less likely to hit someone**
- **getting along better with their peers**
- **getting along better with their parents**

You can make a big difference in the life of any student by matching him or her with a mentor. For more information about BBBSA, contact your local office or visit the Web site *(http://www.bbbsa.org/)*. Ask about the "High School Bigs" program, which pairs younger kids with local high school students.

You can also ask other teachers in your school if they would be willing to mentor students in your classroom who need more positive interaction with adults. (At the same time, *you* might offer to mentor a student in another teacher's classroom.)

For more about mentoring, see page 106.

---

* SOURCE: "Mentoring—A Proven Delinquency Prevention Strategy" by Jean Baldwin Grossman and Eileen M. Garry (Washington, DC: U.S. Department of Justice, Office of Juvenile Justice and Delinquency Prevention), April 1997.

LEARN MORE ABOUT YOUR STUDENTS

Learn as much as you can about the bullies or potential bullies in your classroom.* Show interest in them as individuals—as people worth knowing. Make it clear that even though you don't like some of their behaviors,** you still value them as human beings. You want them to succeed, and you care about their future.

LEARN ABOUT THEM

- Meet with them individually or in small groups as often as you can. You might start by meeting weekly, then twice a month, then monthly.

- Show interest in their lives and be a good listener (see pages 86–88).

- Communicate your high expectations for them—and your confidence that they can meet your expectations.

- Point out and praise the positive behaviors you've noticed, and encourage them to keep up the good work. Let them know that you're keeping an eye on them—and you want to "catch them being good."***

- You might also mention the negative behaviors you've noticed and remind them of why these behaviors are not acceptable, but don't dwell on these. This isn't the time. "Learn More" meetings should focus on positive qualities, characteristics, and behaviors as much as possible.

LEARN ABOUT THEIR FAMILIES

- Ask students about their families. You might have them write essays, poems, stories, songs, or skits about their families. If your students are keeping journals (see pages 38–39), you might ask them to write about their families in their journals.

---

* See also "Learn More About Your Students" (pages 38–39) and "Help Students Identify and Pursue Their Interests" (pages 133–134).

** See also "Keep the Focus on Behavior" (page 131).

*** See also "Catch Them in the Act" (pages 116–117).

- Hold regular conferences with their parents; you might include the students, too. Observe the interactions between parents and children. If you sense that the parents don't like you or trust you—perhaps because they see you as part of the problem—try to find out if there's another teacher or administrator they do like and trust. Ask if they're willing to meet with that person instead.

- Ask the parents if it's okay to visit them at home. This will give you a better understanding of how the students' family experiences might be affecting their behavior at school.

CAMPAIGN AGAINST BULLYING

One way to help bullies change their behavior is to make it clear that bullying won't be tolerated in your classroom. When you and the majority of your students present a united front against bullying, bullies find it harder to behave in ways that are obviously unwanted, undesirable, and unpopular.

The "Creating a Positive Classroom" section of this book includes many tips and strategies that can discourage bullies from bullying—and encourage them to explore more positive ways of relating to others. You might also conduct an all-out campaign against bullying. Have your students work together (as a class or in small groups) to create posters, banners, jingles, skits, raps, songs, etc. around one or more anti-bullying themes. *Examples:*

- **Bullying isn't cool.**
- **Kindness is cool.**
- **Acceptance is cool.**
- **Tolerance is cool.**
- **We stand up for ourselves and each other.**

- In our classroom, no one is an outsider.
- In our classroom, everyone is welcome.
- We treat others the way we want to be treated.
- Spreading rumors isn't cool.
- Gossip isn't cool.
- Name-calling isn't cool.
- New students are welcome here.
- No one ever deserves to be bullied.
- Everyone is unique.
- Hurray for differences!
- No teasing allowed.
- If we see someone being bullied, we're telling!
- Telling isn't tattling.
- Reporting isn't ratting.
- Bullying? No way! There's always a better way.

Or have students brainstorm anti-bullying themes, then choose one they'd like to work on.

 Go farther: Have groups of students research successful advertising campaigns, then try to determine what made them successful. Did the campaigns have catchy slogans? Appealing graphics? Popular spokespersons? Songs or jingles that were easy to remember? Ask students to create anti-bullying campaigns based on what they learned from their research. You might even have a schoolwide competition, with the winning campaign adopted by the whole school. Keep your local media (newspapers, magazines, radio stations, TV stations) informed about the competition and the winner.

HELP STUDENTS MANAGE THEIR ANGER

Students who bully others have a hard time managing their anger. That's one reason they bully. They need help learning how to control their temper, curb violent or aggressive impulses, and resist taking out their anger on others.

Have one-on-one conversations with students who bully others—or who might not be bullies but seem to have difficulty managing their anger. Or you might have a class discussion on this topic.

Ask questions like the following. If you prefer, you might adapt these questions for a worksheet. Have students complete it in class or as a homework assignment. Then review their responses and meet individually or in small groups with students who seem to need help.

1. How can you tell when you're angry? What do you do?

2. How do you feel when you're angry? Hurt? Misunderstood? Frustrated? Sad? Hot all over? Like you're about to explode? Like you want to strike out at someone else?

3. Describe a time when you were very angry. How did you feel? What did you do? What happened next? How did you feel afterward?

4. How do you feel when someone gets angry at you? Are you scared? Upset? Do you wish you could just disappear?

5. Do you think it's fair when someone else takes out his or her anger on you?

6. How does your anger affect the people around you? What about your family? Friends? The person or people you're angry at? How do you think they feel when you take out your anger on them?

7. Is there anything you'd like to change about the way you feel and act when you get angry?

8. Would you like to learn different ways to act when you get angry?

With your students, brainstorm ideas for managing anger. Write their ideas on the chalkboard. Afterward, have students choose one idea to work on for the next few days, then report back to you on whether it works for them. Here are some starter ideas:*

- Learn to recognize the signs that you're about to explode. Do something *before* you explode.

- Walk away from the person or situation that's making you angry. You're not running away. You're doing something positive to make sure things don't get worse or out of control.

- Take five deep breaths. Take five more.

- Count to ten s-l-o-w-l-y. Do it again if you need to.

- Let off steam in a safe, positive way. Go for a run. Shoot some hoops. Take a bike ride. Jump up and down.

- Make yourself relax and cool down. Think calm, peaceful thoughts. Try tensing, then relaxing every muscle in your body, from your head to your toes.

- Pretend that you're not angry. You may do such a good acting job that you convince yourself.

- Ask yourself, "Why am I angry?" Maybe the person didn't mean to make you angry. Maybe it was an accident or a misunderstanding.

- Try not to take things so personally. Understand that the whole world isn't against you.

_____
* See also "Teach Anger Management Skills" (page 32).

 Go farther: Talk with your school psychologist or counselor about starting an anger management group for students. The group might meet during recess or lunch—times that are otherwise unstructured.

GET OLDER STUDENTS INVOLVED

Often, students who bully others find it easier to talk and work with older students than adults. See if your local high school trains students to serve as peer mediators and peer counselors. If the answer is yes, ask if one or more students might be available to work with bullies at your school.

USE "STOP AND THINK"

Most teachers have developed a "sixth sense" when it comes to student behavior. They can detect a problem before it occurs and act quickly to prevent it. Sometimes all it takes is a look or a word from the teacher to get students back on track.

"Stop and Think" takes this a step further. Not only does it interrupt inappropriate behavior, it also invites students to consider what they're doing (or about to do) and make a better choice.

Here are three ways to use "Stop and Think" in your classroom:

1. Tell your students, "You have the power to *stop and think* before you speak or act. This is a way to keep yourself from saying or doing something that might get you in trouble or hurt someone else. Whenever I say 'Stop and Think,' I want the person or people I'm addressing to do just that. STOP whatever you're saying or doing. Then THINK about what you're about to say or do. Decide if you should say or do something else instead."

Once you've introduced "Stop and Think," use this short, simple phrase whenever necessary. Keep your voice calm and your expression positive or neutral. (This is a great alternative to yelling or other emotional responses.)

2. Distribute copies of the handout on page 140. Have students color in the stop sign and thought bubble, then cut along the dark solid line, fold along the dotted line, and tape or staple the top together.

   Younger students might want to wear their "Stop/Think" signs as necklaces (punch two holes in the top corners, then weave a length of yarn or string through the holes). Older students can carry their signs in their pockets.

   Tell your students, "You have the power to *stop and think* before you speak or act. Your 'Stop/Think' sign can remind you to do this."

3. Give students permission to use "Stop and Think" with each other. Enlist their help in interrupting impulsive or negative behaviors.

GIVE STUDENTS MEANINGFUL RESPONSIBILITIES

As you're planning special class projects and events, try giving some of the most meaningful and desirable tasks to students who might otherwise use their time and energy bullying others.* Make sure these are tasks that really matter, and let students know you're counting on them to do their best.

Tip: If you know that a younger student is being bullied on the playground, consider assigning one of your class "bullies" as that child's protector. Talk this over with your student ahead of time; emphasize that he or she is not to bully

---
* See also "Give Them Opportunities to Shine" (page 108).

the child's bully. Your student's presence might be enough to dissuade the child's bully from picking on him or her.

TEACH THEM TO "TALK SENSE TO THEMSELVES"

Schools can have rules and anti-bullying programs, adults can determine and apply consequences, but ultimately each student must learn to control his or her own inappropriate and/or impulsive behaviors.

Just as students can learn positive self-talk (see pages 68 and 71), they can also learn to "talk sense to themselves"—to talk themselves *out of* behaviors that are likely to hurt someone else and/or get them into trouble, and *into* behaviors that are more desirable and acceptable.

Work with your students one-on-one or in small groups to come up with brief, powerful, easy-to-remember words and phrases they can use to "talk sense to themselves." *Examples:*

- I don't have to do this.
- I can make a better choice.
- I can keep my hands to myself.
- I can walk away.
- I can control myself.
- There's a better way.
- I'm better than this.
- I'm in charge of me.
- I can stop and think.
- I can put on the brakes.

Have students choose their favorite word or phrase, then write it on a 3" x 5" card and carry it in their pocket. Tell them to think (or whisper) their phrase whenever they feel they might say or do something to hurt another person.

1. Cut along
the dark line

→

2. Fold on the
dotted line

→

COMPILE BEHAVIOR PROFILES

For each student who exhibits bullying behaviors, create a Behavior Profile in a special folder.

Throughout the day and/or at the end of the day, jot down detailed notes about the student's behavior.

 Important: Be sure to include positive as well as negative behaviors.

Use the folder to collect and store notes and reports you receive from other students, teachers, and staff about the student's behavior; notes taken during meetings and conversations with the student's parents; and anything else you feel is meaningful and relevant.

Toward the end of each week, review and summarize the Behavior Profile. Has the student's behavior improved during the week? Are there areas that still need work? What strategies and techniques did you try to help the student? Which ones were most effective? If the student behaved inappropriately, what consequences were applied? Did the consequences have the desired effect?

Share pertinent information from your Behavior Profile with the student, his or her parents (through a phone call or a note home), and other staff members involved in helping the student improve his or her behavior.

Tip: Careful notes can be very useful during parent-teacher conferences and meetings with school officials.

TEACH POSITIVE WAYS TO FEEL POWERFUL

Offer bullies positive ways to channel their need for power. Here are ten examples and ideas to try:

1. In one school, officials learned that an older student was harassing younger students. The school counselor took the bully aside, told him that someone was picking on the little kids in the school, and asked him to help. The bully became a guardian.

2. In another school, bullies were sent to clean up the kindergarten classroom as a subtle form of punishment. The kindergartners then wrote thank-you notes to the bullies—a not-so-subtle form of praise that made the bullies feel good about themselves.

3. Consider having bullies hand out awards to students who have done good deeds, taken part in social service projects, helped other students, or otherwise set positive examples for others to emulate.

4. There's power in correcting mistakes and righting wrongs. Emphasize that mistakes are for learning and wrongs are opportunities to step forward, be a leader, and win well-deserved admiration from peers and adults.

5. Assign bullies to watch out for and help students who are especially timid or shy. Encourage them to feel good about protecting their new friends.

6. Some experts suggest holding bullies responsible for the safety and well-being of their victims. If something happens to their victims, the bullies suffer the consequences—even if someone else did the deed.

7. Encourage (even require) bullies to get involved in school activities—plays, sports, clubs, etc. Do everything in your power to ensure that their experiences are positive and successful. If they aren't interested in any of the activities currently available, offer to help them start a club or group of their choosing. Participating gives students a sense of belonging, which helps them feel valued—and powerful.

8. Ask your school counselor or psychologist to assess bullies' self-esteem. It's a myth that all bullies have low self-esteem (in fact, some have *high* self-esteem), but it's worth checking into. If bullies are found to have low self-esteem, start a group or program to help them.

9. Doing good by helping others is a powerful feeling. See "Get Students Involved in Service" (pages 73–75).

10. Invite bullies to brainstorm their own ideas for being powerful without hurting or intimidating others. Express confidence in their ability to come up with good strategies.

TRY CRITICAL QUESTIONING

Immediately after intervening with a bullying incident (removing the audience, removing the bully, and giving the bully a few moments to calm down), ask the bully a series of questions that require him or her to reflect on the incident. *Examples:*

1. What just happened? (Insist on "just the facts"—no excuses, no rationalizations, no blaming the victim.)

2. What exactly did you do? (Not *why,* just *what.*)

3. What will happen next for you? (Remind the student of the consequences of his or her behavior.)

4. How do you feel right now?

5. How do you think the other person feels?

6. Is this really what you wanted to happen?

7. What could you do next time instead of (hitting, kicking, name-calling, teasing, or whatever occurred)?

8. How can you make sure something like this doesn't happen again? What can you do?

PROVIDE A PLACE FOR STUDENTS TO GO

If at all possible, set aside a room in your school where students who bully others can be sent to calm down and consider their behavior.

You might call this the Resource Room, the Learning Room, the Quiet Room, the Thinking Room, or anything else that sets it apart from a regular classroom (and doesn't obviously label it "the place where bullies go"). Staff it with a full-time, trained professional who can work with students, talk with them, provide structured activities, listen to their concerns, and help them learn and practice positive ways of relating to others.

Going to this special room might be a consequence for bullying behavior, or a choice students can make for themselves when they feel they're losing control.

START A CLUB

Once you've identified the bullies or potential bullies in your classroom (see pages 119–122), start a club exclusively for them. Have it meet during recess or lunch—times when students' activities usually aren't structured and bullying can be a problem.

You might run the club yourself or train someone else to run it. Or see if another teacher or staff person at your school has experience in this area. If you've identified only one bully or potential bully in your classroom, ask other teachers if they have students who might benefit from belonging to the club.

Use meeting times to discuss inappropriate vs. appropriate behaviors, role-play various situations, teach empathy, reiterate the consequences of bullying behaviors, invite students to think about the consequences, practice prosocial skills, teach anger management, and more. All three sections of this book include activities you might try in the club; many activities in the "Helping Victims" section can be adapted to fit. *Tip:* From time to time, let students set the agenda.

HELP STUDENTS UNDERSTAND WHY THEY BULLY OTHERS

If you can help bullies to *recognize* that they behave inappropriately and take *responsibility* for their behavior,* you can start to help them *realize* why they do the things they do.

This activity and the "Reasons Why" questionnaire (pages 145–146) may not be appropriate for some students. Some questions may be too complex or confusing for their age or developmental level. Use your judgment and your knowledge of your students; adapt where appropriate—or come up with other questions you think will work better. If you use this questionnaire, be sure to tell your students that this isn't a test. There are no "right" or "wrong" answers—only answers that are true for them and may not be true for anyone else.

 Important: Consider inviting the school counselor or psychologist to join you for this activity. He or she will be a valuable resource. Also: This activity should precede "Help Students Stop Bullying" (following). If you decide to use the "Reasons Why" questionnaire, be sure to follow through with "Reasons Why (Guidance Questions)" (pages 147–148).

Depending on your students' ages and abilities, they can complete the "Reasons Why" handout and turn it in to you, or you might choose to go over the questions one at a time during a face-to-face meeting or small group discussion.

---

* See "Change Their Thinking" (pages 128–129).

HELP STUDENTS STOP BULLYING

This activity should follow "Help Students Understand Why They Bully Others" (preceding). If you haven't yet done that activity, please read through it carefully. If you choose not to do that activity, skip this one, too.

"Help Students Stop" returns to the questions in "Help Students Understand," with the addition of more questions designed to start students thinking about alternatives and solutions. If a student has identified one or more "Reasons Why" as true for him or her, you can refer to "Reasons Why (Guidance Questions)" (pages 147–148) for ideas on where to go next.

 Important: The "Guidance Questions" aren't meant to be comprehensive or conclusive, and you'll notice they don't have "the answers." Read them, think about them, then add your own notes and ideas. Be sure to consult your school counselor or psychologist; he or she will be a valuable resource.

STARTER TIPS FOR HELPING THEM STOP

A few possibilities to consider:

- Pair each student with a partner—an older student he or she respects, admires, and would like to be friends with. The older student can offer advice, just listen, and monitor the younger student's behavior (speech, actions, body language, etc.). The older student can praise positive changes and point out when the younger student reverts to bad habits or negative behaviors.

- When a student commits to making a change, suggest the "one-day-at-a-time" approach rather than a blanket promise for the future. *Example:* Instead of "I'll never pick on anyone ever again," try "I won't pick on anyone today."

- If possible, have students apologize and make amends to their former victims. Have them keep trying, even if the former victims are suspicious or don't believe the students are serious.

- Pair students with newcomers to your classroom or school. The newcomers won't know about the students' past, which will help clear the way for a possible friendship.

- Help students find and pursue interests outside of school and away from their former victims (and reputations). Encourage them to make new friends.

- Help students find and pursue physical sports or discipline (biking, blading, softball, martial arts) as a way to let off steam and use their strength in positive ways.

- Try to form a "safety net" of adults (teachers, administrators, playground supervisors, lunchroom supervisors) the students can go to when you're not available. These people should know that the students have had behavior problems and sincerely want to change. The students can go to their "safety net" people when they feel angry, upset, or about to lose control.

REASONS WHY

You know that you sometimes bully other people.
Have you ever wondered why? When we know the reasons
for our behaviors, this can give us the power to change our behaviors.

Maybe one or more of these reasons are true for you.
Read them, think about them, and decide for yourself.
Write answers only if you want to.

1. Is there someone in your life who picks on you?

2. Do you feel lonely at school?

3. Are you afraid of being picked on?

4. When other people hurt you, do you feel you have to get back at them?

5. Do you feel you have to prove that you're tougher and stronger than other people?

6. Do you just like to show off and get a reaction? Do you like lots of attention?

7. Do you always have to win at everything? Do you get angry when you lose?

8. Are you jealous of other people?

9. Is there someone who irritates you so much you just can't stand it?

CONTINUED

10. When you say or do something to hurt someone else, does that make you feel strong and important?

11. Is there something in your life that makes you feel unhappy or afraid?

12. When you feel sad, frustrated, angry, or afraid, does it seem like the only way to get rid of your bad feeling is to take it out on someone else?

13. Is there something in your life that makes you feel angry much of the time?

14. Is school really hard for you?

15. Do you feel like you're always letting other people down? Are their expectations just too high?

16. Are you bigger and stronger than other people your age? Does this make you feel powerful?

17. Do you hang around with other bullies? Do you feel you have to go along with whatever they do?

18. Is it very hard for you to control your temper? Does it seem impossible sometimes?

One more thing to think about . . .

Is there an adult you trust and respect—someone you think you could talk to? Would you be willing to talk to that person? OR: If you can't think of anyone, would you be willing to meet someone who's a really good listener?

REASONS WHY
Guidance Questions

1. Is there someone in your life who picks on you? *Go farther:* Do you want to tell me who it is? Would you like me to help you do something about it?

2. Do you feel lonely at school? *Go farther:* Would you like to feel less lonely and more like you belong here? Are you willing to try some ideas for fitting in?

3. Are you afraid of being picked on? *Go farther:* Do you feel the only way to protect yourself is to get other people before they get you? Would you like to learn other ways to feel safe and not worry so much?

4. When other people hurt you, do you feel you have to get back at them? *Go farther:* Would you like to learn other ways to deal with the hurt? And maybe avoid feeling hurt? Is it possible that people aren't hurting you on purpose?

5. Do you feel you have to prove that you're tougher and stronger than other people? *Go farther:* Are you willing to try other ways to feel powerful and important?

6. Do you just like to show off and get a reaction? Do you like lots of attention? *Go farther:* If you knew other ways to get attention—positive ways—would you try them?

7. Do you always have to win at everything? Do you get angry when you lose? *Go farther:* Would you like to learn how to enjoy things more and not worry so much about winning or losing?

8. Are you jealous of other people? *Go farther:* Why are you jealous? What do they have that you want? Is it really that important? Would you like to learn ways to be happy with who you are and what you have?

9. Is there someone who irritates you so much you just can't stand it? *Go farther:* Would you like to learn ways to avoid the person—or not let him or her "get to you" as much?

10. When you say or do something to hurt someone else, does that make you feel strong and important? *Go farther:* Are you willing to try other ways to feel good about yourself?

CONTINUED →

11. Is there something in your life that makes you feel unhappy or afraid? *Go farther:* What would make you feel better? Would you like someone to help you?

12. When you feel sad, frustrated, angry, or afraid, does it seem like the only way to get rid of your bad feeling is to take it out on someone else? *Go farther:* If you knew other ways to get rid of bad feelings, would you try them instead?

13. Is there something in your life that makes you feel angry much of the time? *Go farther:* Would you like to know how to handle your anger—maybe even get rid of some or all of your anger?

14. Is school really hard for you? *Go farther:* If you knew ways to make school easier and more fun, would you try them?

15. Do you feel like you're always letting other people down? Are their expectations just too high? *Go farther:* Would you like to tell them how you feel? Would you feel better if they backed off a bit and accepted you the way you are?

16. Are you bigger and stronger than other people your age? Does this make you feel powerful? *Go farther:* Do you ever wish you weren't so big and strong? Would you like to know positive ways to use your size and strength?

17. Do you hang around with other bullies? Do you feel you have to go along with whatever they do? *Go farther:* If you had a chance to get out of that group (or gang), would you?

18. Is it very hard for you to control your temper? Does it seem impossible sometimes? *Go farther:* Would you like to learn ways to control your temper, or how to get help when you can't?

Finally . . .

Is there an adult you respect and trust—someone you think you could talk to? Would you be willing to talk to that person? OR: If you can't think of anyone, would you be willing to meet someone who's a really good listener? *Go farther:* If you know someone and tell me who it is, I can help get the two of you together. Would that be okay? OR: May I suggest someone you might want to meet?

RESOURCES

BOOKS FOR ADULTS

Bullies & Victims: Helping Your Child Through the Schoolyard Battlefield by SuEllen Fried, A.D.T.R., and Paula Fried, Ph.D. (New York: M. Evans and Company, 1996). The goal of this book is to alert parents and other adults to the problem of bullying, to explain the difference between normal teasing and bullying, to help adults act effectively to help children, and to teach adults how to empower children to prevent and solve the problem themselves.

Bullying at School by Dan Olweus (Cambridge, MA: Blackwell, 1993). This psychologist, the world's leading authority on the topic, gives good practical advice on how to stop bullying in schools.

Bullyproof: A Teacher's Guide on Teasing and Bullying for Use with Fourth & Fifth Grade Students by Nan Stein (Wellesley, MA: Center for Research on Women; Washington, DC: NEA Professional Library, 1996). Eleven lessons, class discussions, role-plays, case studies, writing exercises, and more combine to give students the opportunity to explore and determine the distinctions between teasing and bullying.

Bully-Proofing Your School: A Comprehensive Approach for Elementary Schools by Carla Garrity, Kathryn Jens, William Porter, Nancy Sager, and Cam Short-Camilli (Longmont, CO: Sopris West, 1996). This excellent book presents a comprehensive, systematic approach for stopping bullying in elementary schools. It includes an overview of bullying, a variety of prevention and intervention strategies, and several reproducibles.

The Challenge to Care in Schools by Nel Noddings (New York: Teachers College Press, 1992). Noddings emphasizes that caring and being cared for are fundamental human needs, then calls on schools to address these needs and nourish students' growth.

Child Support Through Small Group Counseling by Lois Landry (Charlotte, NC: KIDSRIGHTS, 1996). Fourteen states (so far) have added this book to their mandated lists for elementary and middle school counselors. Designed to take the busywork out of planning small group sessions, it features more than 100 complete sessions covering the hottest topics in counseling today, including anger and aggression, death, decision-making, divorce, peer relations, responsibility, self-concept, and shyness.

Childhood Bullying and Teasing by Dorothea M. Ross, Ph.D. (Alexandria, VA: American Counseling Association, 1996). This book includes a review of literature and a variety of strategies that can be used by guidance counselors and others.

Emotional Intelligence by Daniel Goleman (New York: Bantam, 1995). This fascinating book discusses the importance of empathy, social deftness, and other forms of emotional intelligence for success in life, and includes information about how children develop these skills.

How to Handle a Hard-to-Handle Kid by C. Drew Edwards, Ph.D. (Minneapolis: Free Spirit Publishing, 1999). Clinical child psychologist C. Drew Edwards explains why some children are especially challenging, then spells out clear, specific strategies that parents can use to address and correct problem behaviors with firmness and love.

How to Talk So Kids Will Listen and Listen So Kids Will Talk by Adele Faber and Elaine Mazlish (New York: Avon Books, 1991). Filled with practical suggestions and examples, this is one of the best books ever written on how to talk with kids of all ages.

Learning the Skills of Peacemaking by Naomi Drew (Rolling Hills Estates, CA: Jalmar Press, 1987). This book teaches specific skills as well as a general problem-solving process by which elementary-age children can begin to create a peaceful future. The 56 lessons use creative writing, role-playing, the arts, music, and class discussion to teach children to resolve conflicts, accept themselves and others, and communicate effectively.

100 Ways to Enhance Self-Concept in the Classroom by Jack Canfield and Harold Wells (Needham Heights, MA: Allyn & Bacon, 1993). This is one of the most outstanding "how-to" books about the development of positive self-esteem.

Positive Self-Talk for Children by Douglas Bloch with Jon Merritt (New York: Bantam Books, 1993). Written for parents, teachers, and counselors, this book teaches adults how to speak more affirmatively to children and how to teach children to speak more affirmatively to themselves.

Quit It! A Teacher's Guide on Teasing and Bullying for Use with Students in Grades K–3 by Merle Froschl (New York: Educational Equity Concepts; Wellesley, MA: Center for Research on Women; Washington,

DC: NEA Professional Library, 1998). Ten lessons, class discussions, role-playing, activities, exercises, and connections to children's literature help children understand the difference between teasing and bullying. Also provides ideas for communicating with parents.

Reducing School Violence through Conflict Resolution by David W. Johnson and Roger T. Johnson (Alexandria, VA: Association for Supervision and Curriculum Development, 1995). The authors discuss how schools can create a cooperative learning environment where students learn how to negotiate and mediate peer conflicts.

Set Straight on Bullies by Stuart Greenbaum, Brenda Turner, and Ronald D. Stephens (Malibu, CA: National School Safety Center, Pepperdine University, 1989). The two sections of this book, "The Problem" and "The Solution," present research and statistics about bullying and ways to educate the public and prevent bullying from happening.

Tackling Bullying in Your School edited by Sonia Sharp and Peter K. Smith (New York: Routledge, 1994). This book provides teachers and others with step-by-step advice on developing a school-wide anti-bullying program, including sections on improving the playground environment.

Teaching Behavioral Self-Control to Students (second edition) by Edward Workman and Alan Katz (Austin, TX: Pro-Ed, 1995). This book was designed to turn around aggressive, withdrawn, unmotivated, absent, and uncontrollable youth, teaching them how to succeed in school emotionally and socially. For teachers and counselors of students grades 4–12.

Teaching Self-Management Strategies to Adolescents by K. Richard Young, Richard P. West, Deborah J. Smith, and Daniel P. Morgan (Longmont, CO: Sopris West, 1991). This program for students in grades 6–12 teaches children to develop new, productive habits to help them succeed in school and in life.

Teaching Your Kids to Care by Deborah Spaide (Secaucus, NJ: Citadel Press, 1995). The founder of the Kids Care Clubs, Deborah Spaide, believes that children have a natural instinct to help others. In this practical, inspiring book, she describes 105 projects that develop the charity instinct in children and youth from preschool through high school.

Waging Peace in Our Schools by Linda Lantieri and Janet Patti (Boston: Beacon Press, 1996). This practical guide to creating a peaceful classroom is based on the Resolving Conflict Creatively Program (RCCP), which has been used with more than 150,000 children in schools across the country.

What to Do When Kids Are Mean to Your Child by Elin McCoy (Pleasantville, NY: The Reader's Digest Association, 1997). In this practical book, parents of children ages 5–13 will learn about the painful topics of bullying, teasing, and rejection, and discover age-based, practical tactics for teaching kids to counter such behavior.

Win the Whining War & Other Skirmishes by Cynthia Whitham, M.S.W. (Los Angeles: Perspective Publishing, 1991). This step-by-step guide to increasing cooperation and reducing conflict will help eliminate all the annoying behaviors that drive you crazy. Easy-to-use techniques from the renowned UCLA Parent Training Program offer practical solutions to everyday problems. This is a book for anyone who lives, works, or spends time with children.

You Can't Say You Can't Play by Vivian Gussin Paley (Cambridge, MA: Harvard University Press, 1992). Paley, a kindergarten teacher at the University of Chicago Lab School (and a MacArthur fellow), describes her year-long classroom experiment with the rule "you can't say you can't play." Her classroom changes for the better, and her students develop real sensitivity to the feelings of others.

BOOKS FOR CHILDREN

All I Really Need to Know I Learned in Kindergarten by Robert Fulghum (Boston: G.K. Hall, 1988). This entertaining book says a lot about respect, sharing, playing fair, not hitting people, and saying you're sorry when you hurt someone. For all ages.

Bailey the Big Bully by Lizi Boyd (New York: Viking Kestrel, 1989). All the kids are afraid of Bailey, who's big and mean and always gets his way, except Max, the new boy in town. For grades K–3.

Best Enemies Again by Kathleen Leverich (New York: Greenwillow, 1991). Wealthy Felicity continues to complicate Priscilla's life both in and out of school, until one day the tables are turned. For grades 2–5.

Bootsie Barker Bites by Barbara Bottner (New York: Putnam Publishing, 1992). A little girl finds her life made miserable by the torments devised by the nasty, mischievous Bootsie Barker, until the terrible Bootsie receives her just punishment. For grades preschool–3.

Bullies Are a Pain in the Brain by Trevor Romain (Minneapolis: Free Spirit Publishing, 1997). This book blends humor with serious, practical suggestions to help children learn what to do if a bully picks on them. Also included are tips to help bullies get along with others. For grades 3–8.

Bully by Janine Amos (Tarrytown, NY: Benchmark Books, 1994). Different stories about kids being bullied or bullying others provide questions for a discussion about bullying. For grades K–4.

The Bully Buster Book by John William Yee (Toronto: Outgoing Press, 1997). This book provides boys and girls with hints on how to keep new bullies from bothering them as well as how to get rid of an existing bully. It is about how you can shift the odds in your favor by merely talking to the bully, making yourself more visible, and invading the bully's personal space. For grades 7–9.

The Bully of Barkham Street by Mary Stolz (New York: Harper & Row, 1963). Martin's parents are threatening to take away his dog Rufus, and Martin is having a rough time in school. Something must change. For grades 4–8.

Bully on the Bus by Carl W. Bosch (Seattle: Parenting Press, 1988). Jack is being teased by the fifth-grade bully on the school bus. Readers help Jack decide whether to ignore him, ask an adult for help, or fight back. For grades 2–6.

Bully Trouble by Joanna Cole (New York: Random House, 1990). Arlo and Robby, finding themselves the victims of a neighborhood bully, work out a red-hot scheme for discouraging him. For grades pre-school–3.

Cliques, Phonies, & Other Baloney by Trevor Romain (Minneapolis: Free Spirit Publishing, 1998). Cliques exist because everyone wants to have friends. This book explains what cliques are and why they exist, and gives important self-esteem tips that will help kids feel good about themselves. For grades 3–8.

Dear God, Help! Love, Earl by Barbara Park (New York: Knopf, 1993). Tired of being picked on and of having to pay protection money to Eddie McPhee, the school bully, wimpy Eddie Wilber and his friends, Maxie and Rosie, come up with an ingenious scheme to seek revenge. For grades 3–5.

The 18th Emergency by Betsy Byars (New York: Puffin Books, 1981). When the toughest boy in school swears to kill him, 12-year-old Mouse finds little help from friends and must prepare for this emergency alone. For grades 4–7.

Fighting Invisible Tigers by Earl Hipp (Minneapolis: Free Spirit Publishing, 1995). This book discusses the pressures and problems encountered by teenagers and provides information on life skills, stress management, and methods of gaining more control over their lives. For grades 6 and up.

First Grade King by Karen L. Williams (New York: Clarion Books, 1992). This book relates the experiences first-grader Joey King has at school: making friends, learning to read, and dealing with the class bully. For grades K–3.

Fourth Grade Rats by Jerry Spinelli (New York: Scholastic, 1991). Suds learns that his best friend is wrong. You don't have to be a tough guy to be a grown-up fourth-grader. For grades 4–7.

Freak the Mighty by W. Rodman Philbrick (New York: Blue Sky Press, 1993). Dumb, stupid, and slow. All Max's life, he'd been called these names, and it didn't help that people were afraid of him. So Max learned to be alone—at least until Freak came along. Together, they were Freak the Mighty. For grades 4–7.

Good Friends Are Hard To Find by Fred Frankel (Glendale, CA: Perspective Publishing, 1996). This book has step-by-step ideas to help children ages 5–12 make friends and solve problems with other kids. Includes concrete help for teasing, bullying, and meanness, both for the child who is picked on and for the tormentor. For grades K–6.

Harriet the Spy by Louise Fitzhugh (New York: Harper & Row, 1964). The revelation of Harriet's secret journal, recording the activities of her neighbors and schoolmates, causes chaos. For grades 4–7.

How to Handle Bullies, Teasers and Other Meanies by Kate Cohen-Posey (Highland City, FL: Rainbow Books, 1995). This book provides information on what makes bullies and teasers tick, how to handle bullies, how to deal with prejudice, and how to defend oneself when teased. For grades 6–10.

How to Lose All Your Friends by Nancy Carlson (New York: Viking Penguin, 1994). With colorful pictures and tongue-in-cheek humor, Carlson pokes fun at bullies, grumps, whiners, poor sports, and other kids who alienate others. For grades K–3.

I Am Not a Short Adult! by Marilyn Burns (Boston: Little, Brown, 1977). This nonfiction book talks about what kind of kid you want to be and has an excellent section on what your tone of voice, body language, and facial expression say about you. For grades 4–6.

I Like Being Me: Poems for Children About Feeling Special, Appreciating Others, and Getting Along by Judy Lalli, photographs by Douglas L. Mason-Fry (Minneapolis: Free Spirit Publishing, 1997). Simple rhyming poems and eloquent photographs explore issues important to the everyday lives of young children. A leader's guide is also available. For grades pre-school–3.

I Like Me! by Nancy L. Carlson (New York: Viking, 1988). By admiring her finer points and showing that she can take care of herself and have fun even when there's no one else around, a charming pig proves the best friend you can have is yourself. For grades preschool–3.

I'm Like You, You're Like Me: A Child's Book About Understanding and Celebrating Each Other by Cindy Gainer (Minneapolis: Free Spirit Publishing, 1998). Warm, simple words and appealing illustrations invite young children to discover, accept, and affirm individual differences. A leader's guide is also available. For grades preschool–3.

Joshua T. Bates Takes Charge by Susan Richards Shreve (New York: Knopf, 1993). Remembering how a mean gang of bullies used to tease him for being held back in the third grade, Joshua sees the same boys teasing a new student and fears that helping will bring the attention back to him. For grades 4–7.

King of the Playground by Phyllis Reynolds Naylor (New York: Atheneum, 1991). With his dad's help, Kevin overcomes his fear of the "King of the Playground" who has threatened to tie him to the slide, put him in a deep hole, or put him in a cage with bears. For grades K–3.

Liking Myself by Pat Palmer (San Luis Obispo, CA: Impact Publishers, 1991). This book introduces kids to the concepts of feelings, self-esteem, and assertiveness. For grades K–4.

Loudmouth George and the Sixth Grade Bully by Nancy L. Carlson (Minneapolis: Carolrhoda Books, 1987). After having his lunch repeatedly stolen by a bully twice his size, Loudmouth George and his friend Harriet teach him a lesson he'll never forget. For grades preschool–3.

Make Someone Smile and 40 More Ways to Be a Peaceful Person by Judy Lalli, photographs by Douglas L. Mason-Fry (Minneapolis: Free Spirit Publishing, 1996). Children model the skills of peacemaking and conflict resolution throughout this book. An ideal read-aloud book and discussion-starter. For all ages.

Nothing's Fair in Fifth Grade by Barthe DeClements (New York: Viking Press, 1981). A fifth-grade class, repelled by the overweight new student who has serious problems at home, finally learns to accept her. For grades 4–7.

Push & Shove by Jim and Joan Boulden (Weaverville, CA: Boulden Publishing, 1994). Bullies cannot exist without victims and both participate in the bullying relationship. The reader will discover how both a bully and a victim feel. For grades 2–4.

Random Acts of Kindness, More Random Acts of Kindness, and *Kids' Random Acts of Kindness* by the editors of Conari Press (Berkeley, CA: Conari Press, 1993 and 1994). Check out these books for inspiring true stories of people who have been the givers or recipients of caring and compassion. For all ages.

The Rat and the Tiger by Keiko Kasza (New York: G. P. Putnam, 1993). In Rat and Tiger's friendship, Tiger always gets the bigger piece and the most desired part. Rat, who is much smaller, finally has to stand up for himself. For grades K–3.

Reluctantly Alice by Phyllis Reynolds Naylor (New York: Atheneum, 1991). Disgusted with the seventh grade after only her first day, Alice finds her troubles compounded when she encounters Denise "Mack Truck" Whitlock. For grades 4–7.

The Shorty Society by Shery Cooper Sinykin (New York: Viking, 1994). Three seventh-graders, the victims of nasty pranks, turn the tables on their tormentors but run the risk of becoming bullies themselves. For grades 4–8.

Stick Boy by Joan T. Zeier (New York: Atheneum, 1993). During sixth grade, skinny Eric shoots up seven inches and becomes a misfit and the victim of the class bully. For grades 4–8.

Stick Up for Yourself! Every Kid's Guide to Personal Power and Positive Self-Esteem by Gershen Kaufman, Ph.D., Lev Raphael, Ph.D., and Pamela Espeland (Minneapolis: Free Spirit Publishing, 1999). Written for any kid who's ever been picked on at school, this book provides practical, encouraging advice through simple words and real-life examples. A teacher's guide is also available. For grades 3–7.

Stone Soup for the World: Life-Changing Stories of Ordinary Kindness and Courageous Acts of Service (Berkeley, CA: Conari Press, 1998). Inspiring stories by or about Nelson Mandela, Mother Teresa, Christopher Reeve, Ram Das, Steven Spielberg, and more than 100 others are included in this book, plus an extensive resource guide and directory to service groups and social organizations around the country. For all ages.

Teen Esteem by Pat Palmer (San Luis Obispo, CA: Impact Publishers, 1989). This book provides guidance on developing self-esteem and the positive attitude necessary to cope with such adolescent challenges as peer pressure and substance abuse. For grades 7–12.

We Can Get Along: A Child's Book of Choices by Lauren Murphy Payne, M.S.W., and Claudia Rohling (Minneapolis: Free Spirit Publishing, 1997). This book teaches essential conflict resolution skills—think before you speak or act, treat others the way you want to be treated—in a way that young children can understand. A leader's guide is also available. For grades preschool–3.

What a Wimp! by Carol Carrick (New York: Clarion Books, 1983). Although his teacher, mother, and older brother are sympathetic, Barney knows he'll have to find his own way to deal with the bully, Lennie. For grades 3–5.

What Do You Stand For? by Barbara A. Lewis (Minneapolis: Free Spirit Publishing, 1997). This book empowers children and teens to identify and build the character traits that are most important to them. True stories profile kids who exemplify positive traits and inspiring quotations set the stage for kids to think about, discuss, and debate positive traits. For grades 4–7.

What Do You Think? A Kid's Guide to Dealing with Daily Dilemmas by Linda Schwartz (Santa Barbara, CA: The Learning Works, 1993). This inviting book encourages young people to consider issues from more than one perspective. For grades 3–7.

What Would You Do? A Kid's Guide to Tricky and Sticky Situations by Linda Schwartz (Santa Barbara, CA: The Learning Works, 1991). This commonsense guide prepares children to handle more than 70 unexpected, puzzling, and frightening situations at home, school, or out on their own. For grades 3–7.

Why is Everybody Always Picking on Me: A Guide to Handling Bullies by Terrence Webster-Doyle (Middlebury, VT: Atrium Society, 1991). Stories and activities show how to resolve conflicts nonviolently. For grades K–5.

You're Dead, David Borelli by Susan M. Brown (New York: Atheneum, 1995). After his mother dies and his father absconds with company funds, David is sent to a foster home, an inner-city school, and a new life. Threatened by bullies and confronted by uncaring teachers, David must find his own way into a life that he can accept. For grades 3–5.

VIDEOS

Anger, Rage and You (23 minutes). This video teaches techniques for dealing with anger before it gets out of control. Pointing out that everyone feels anger at times, it explains the need to identify and handle misplaced and suppressed anger. A leader's guide is also provided. For grades 5–9. Available from The National Center for Violence Prevention, PO Box 9, 102 Highway 81 North, Calhoun, KY 42327-0009, toll-free telephone: 1-800-962-6662, fax: (270) 273-5844.

Beyond the Barriers (47 minutes). Mark Wellman and other disabled adventurers climb the desert rock towers of Utah, sail in British Columbia, scuba dive with sea lions in Mexico, and hang glide over the California coast. This film delivers the simple message: Don't give up, and never give in. For all ages. Available from Aquarius Health Care Videos, 5 Powderhouse Lane, PO Box 1159, Sherborn, MA 01770, telephone: (508) 651-2963, fax: (508) 650-4216, *http://www.aquariusproductions.com/*

Bridging Racial Divisions (30 minutes). This video explores how racial divisions affect everyone. Triggers to violence such as racial slurs and race-related graffiti are examined. Young people discuss how to build communication across racial and ethnic lines, the benefits of respecting others, and the value of diversity in our society. A leader's guide is also provided. For middle- and high-school students. Available from The Bureau for At-Risk Youth, 135 Dupont Street, PO Box 760, Plainview, NY 11803-0760, toll-free telephone: 1-800-99-YOUTH, *http://www.at-risk.com/*

Broken Toy by Thomas Brown (25 minutes). This is a powerful film that addresses the physical and emotional harm that bullying causes. Through dramatic storytelling, it educates children about the harm that is caused by tormenting and bullying other children. For students in grades 3–7. Available from the Educational Media Corporation, Box 21311, 4256 Central Avenue NE, Minneapolis, MN 55421-0311, telephone: (612) 781-0088, toll-free telephone (orders only): 1-800-966-3382, fax: (612) 781-7753, *http://www.educationalmedia.com/home.html-ssi*

Bully Breath: How to Tame a Troublemaker (19 minutes). Real-life situations are dramatized and then discussed, helping viewers understand the reasons behind a bully's behavior as well as specific steps to neutralize his or her power. A separate section for adults gives insight on helping children avoid being a victim and provides guidelines for managing the classroom, the playground, the home, and other areas where conflict can occur. For elementary-school students. Available from The National Center for Violence Prevention, PO Box 9, 102 Highway 81 North, Calhoun, KY 42327-0009, toll-free telephone: 1-800-962-6662, fax: (270) 273-5844.

BullySmart (31 minutes). This video teaches students how to say no to negative peer pressure and get away from a bully without fighting. For elementary-school students. Available from The National Center for Violence Prevention, PO Box 9, 102 Highway 81 North, Calhoun, KY 42327-0009, toll-free telephone: 1-800-962-6662, fax: (270) 273-5844.

Business as Usual by Sherry Kozak, Missing Link Productions (39 minutes). This video visits people from around the world with physical and mental disabilities who have created—and who own and operate—successful, profitable businesses which provide employment, income, and self-reliance for themselves and others. For middle-school students, high-school students, and adults. Available from Fanlight Productions, 4196 Washington Street, Suite 2, Boston, MA 02131, toll-free telephone: 1-800-937-4113, fax: (617) 469-3379, *http://www.fanlight.com/*

Conflict! Think About It, Talk About It, Try to Work It Out (15 minutes). In this video, two kids use the "Anger Commander" game when they find out that sometimes handling their anger appropriately isn't enough to avoid conflicts with others. The game teaches the kids a simple but effective three-step process for resolving conflicts. For grades 5–8. Available from The National Center for Violence Prevention, PO Box 9, 102 Highway 81 North, Calhoun, KY 42327-0009, toll-free telephone: 1-800-962-6662, fax: (270) 273-5844.

Coping with Fighters, Bullies, and Troublemakers (22 minutes). This video is helpful for all students, but especially for those who are frequently the target of bullies and troublemakers. The program also offers specific techniques for coping with disruptive classmates. Students learn how to avoid being a victim; the best defense against fighters, bullies, and troublemakers; how to stand up to bullies without making matters worse; and when to ask for help. For middle-school students, high-school students, and adults. Available from The National Center for Violence Prevention, PO Box 9, 102 Highway 81 North, Calhoun, KY 42327-0009, toll-free telephone: 1-800-962-6662, fax: (270) 273-5844.

Crimes of Hate (27 minutes). In an era when biased crimes are increasing in frequency and intensity, this documentary reveals the twisted thinking of perpetrators, the anguish of victims, and how law enforcement deals with these crimes. Be sure to preview this video before showing it to students. A teacher's guide is included. For middle-school students, high-school students, and adults. Available from the Anti-Defamation League, 823 United Nations Plaza, New York, NY 10017, *http://www.adl.org/*

Dealing with Anger plus *Cool, Calm and Collected* (two videos, 33 minutes total). This material teaches students to learn to identify the sources of their anger, where it comes from, what situations are most likely to arouse it, and the difference between justifiable and unjustifiable anger. Students also discover that it is possible to stay under control and stop anger from becoming dangerous. Included with the videos is a teacher's guide with lesson plans, student activities, and discussion questions. For grades 4–6. Available from The National Center for Violence Prevention, PO Box 9, 102 Highway 81 North, Calhoun, KY 42327-

0009, toll-free telephone: 1-800-962-6662, fax: (270) 273-5844.

Dealing with Bullies, Troublemakers, and Dangerous Situations, PeaceTalks with Michael Pritchard (30 minutes). This video discusses bullies and gangs, what to do when you feel afraid, how to protect yourself in threatening situations, how to help victims, and how to make our schools and neighborhoods safe. Students review street-smart tips that help prevent violent confrontations. A teacher's guide is included. For middle-school students, high-school students, and adults. Available from The Bureau for At-Risk Youth, 135 Dupont Street, PO Box 760, Plainview, NY 11803-0760, toll-free telephone: 1-800-99-YOUTH, *http://www.at-risk.com/*

Decoding the Rap: Gangs and Rap Music (30 minutes). This program examines the correlation between gang activity and "gangster rap." The program features Sgt. Ron Stallworth, who heads the unit dealing with gangs in the Utah Division of Investigation. For middle-school students, high-school students, and adults. Available from Films for the Humanities & Science, PO Box 2053, Princeton, NJ 08543-2053, toll-free telephone: 1-800-257-5126, *http://www.films.com/*

Disrespect, Rudeness, and Teasing (22 minutes). This video will help students learn what being disrespectful and rude tells us about a person and why teasing is never a good solution to a problem. They will also learn how to disagree without being rude. For middle-school students, high-school students, and adults. Available from The National Center for Violence Prevention, PO Box 9, 102 Highway 81 North, Calhoun, KY 42327-0009, toll-free telephone: 1-800-962-6662, fax: (270) 273-5844.

Don't Pick on Me! (20 minutes). This program examines the dynamics behind teasing and models effective responses to being harassed. A teacher's guide is included. For grades 3–8. Available from The National Center for Violence Prevention, PO Box 9, 102 Highway 81 North, Calhoun, KY 42327-0009, toll-free telephone: 1-800-962-6662, fax: (270) 273-5844.

Drugs, Alcohol, and Guns: Triggers to Violence (30 minutes). This video helps teens discover the link between alcohol and other drugs, weapons, and violence. The video emphasizes the consequences of one's actions and how to say no to drugs, alcohol, and violence. A leader's guide is provided. For middle- and high-school students. Available from The Bureau for At-Risk Youth, 135 Dupont Street, PO Box 760, Plainview, NY 11803-0760, toll-free telephone: 1-800-99-YOUTH, *http://www.at-risk.com/*

Frustration and Negative Feelings (19 minutes). Children learn the right way to communicate feelings of frustration and anger and how to stop bad feelings from building up inside. They also learn how to settle an argument so everyone wins. For middle-school students, high-school students, and adults. Available from The National Center for Violence Prevention, PO Box 9, 102 Highway 81 North, Calhoun, KY 42327-0009, toll-free telephone: 1-800-962-6662, fax: (270) 273-5844.

Gang Signs: How to Tell if Gangs are Influencing our Kids or Community (30 minutes). Karl Schonborn, Ph.D., explains what to look for if you suspect a child/teen is involved with a gang. Dr. Schonborn breaks down the age groups and what the slang terms and duties are for each group. He discusses how to reverse the hold gangs have on children and the rights of parents. Hate groups and substance abuse are also discussed. For adults. Available from The National Center for Violence Prevention, PO Box 9, 102 Highway 81 North, Calhoun, KY 42327-0009, toll-free telephone: 1-800-962-6662, fax: (270) 273-5844.

Gangs: The Fatal Attraction (21 minutes). The video introduces gang members who discuss initiation, nicknames, and specific retaliation methods. For adults. Available from The National Center for Violence Prevention, PO Box 9, 102 Highway 81 North, Calhoun, KY 42327-0009, toll-free telephone: 1-800-962-6662, fax: (270) 273-5844.

Gangs: Tags, Tacs, Terminology (20 minutes). In this video, gang members talk about how they got their names, the language of gangs, and the significance of religion, tattoos, scars, colors, hand signals, and clothes for gang members. For adults. Available from The National Center for Violence Prevention, PO Box 9, 102 Highway 81 North, Calhoun, KY 42327-0009, toll-free telephone: 1-800-962-6662, fax: (270) 273-5844.

Graffiti: The Language of Gangs (21 minutes). This video takes adults through the symbolism found in graffiti and provides insight into gang-related behavior. Included with the video is a leader's guide. For parents and teachers. Available from The National Center for Violence Prevention, PO Box 9, 102 Highway 81 North, Calhoun, KY 42327-0009, toll-free telephone: 1-800-962-6662, fax: (270) 273-5844.

Groark Learns About Bullying (28 minutes). Groark is a pleasant, childlike dragon puppet character playing with his friends when two of them start teasing and picking on a third friend. As the situation escalates, Groark gets drawn in, and before he realizes it, Groark is picking on his best friend. Groark then convinces his friends that they have been cruel and unfair, and they should make peace with the friend they teased. For elementary-school students. Available from The National Center for Violence Prevention, PO Box 9, 102 Highway 81 North,

Calhoun, KY 42327-0009, toll-free telephone: 1-800-962-6662, fax: (270) 273-5844.

Handling Dating Pressures and Harassment (30 minutes). This video discusses vital issues, including common misunderstandings between the sexes, when flirting crosses the line, sexual harassment, sexual coercion, and date rape. Kids learn how to say no to abuse and the importance of building healthy, positive relationships. This tape is an excellent discussion starter. For middle- and high-school students. Available from The Bureau for At-Risk Youth, 135 Dupont Street, PO Box 760, Plainview, NY 11803-0760, toll-free telephone: 1-800-99-YOUTH, *http://www.at-risk.com/*

Handling Peer Pressure and Gangs (30 minutes). This video requires teens to reflect on what peer pressure is and how it works. Pressures to join groups, cliques, and gangs are also discussed. Gang involvement, including why kids join, getting out, and dealing with friends who are gang members, is addressed. The qualities to look for in true friendship and how that differs from negative peer pressure are also presented. A leader's guide is provided. For middle- and high-school students. Available from The Bureau for At-Risk Youth, 135 Dupont Street, PO Box 760, Plainview, NY 11803-0760, toll-free telephone: 1-800-99-YOUTH, *http://www.at-risk.com/*

Hate Crimes (22 minutes). This video examines the bitter problem of hate crime and gives the viewer a hard-hitting look at the problem from its roots in stereotyping and prejudice all the way through the violence in today's headlines. Preview this video before showing it to students. A teacher's guide is included. For middle-school students, high-school students, and adults. Available from the Anti-Defamation League, 823 United Nations Plaza, New York, NY 10017, *http://www.adl.org/*

How I Learned Not to Be Bullied (16 minutes). This program presents two children's accounts of their success in learning not to be bullied. It includes a teacher's guide with eight student worksheets and English/Spanish send-home pages. For grades 2–4. Available from The National Center for Violence Prevention, PO Box 9, 102 Highway 81 North, Calhoun, KY 42327-0009, toll-free telephone: 1-800-962-6662, fax: (270) 273-5844.

How to Cope with School Violence (17 minutes). This video helps youngsters understand how to cope with violent confrontations that could arise in or around school. They learn effective ways to avoid violence and what to do when a confrontation seems unavoidable. For middle-school students, high-school students, and adults. Available from The National Center for Violence Prevention, PO Box 9, 102

Highway 81 North, Calhoun, KY 42327-0009, toll-free telephone: 1-800-962-6662, fax: (270) 273-5844.

How to Resolve Power Struggles (18 minutes). Students learn the best way to handle power struggles with siblings, parents, and teachers, and how not to let bullies and troublemakers take advantage of them. For middle-school students, high-school students, and adults. Available from The National Center for Violence Prevention, PO Box 9, 102 Highway 81 North, Calhoun, KY 42327-0009, toll-free telephone: 1-800-962-6662, fax: (270) 273-5844.

How We Play by Curtis Craven, Texas Parks and Wildlife (11 minutes). Most of the people in this short documentary are in wheelchairs, and one is blind, but they are anything but handicapped. Playing tennis, snorkeling, whitewater canoeing, practicing karate—they are living proof that a disability can be a challenge, not an obstacle. For all ages. Available from Fanlight Productions, 4196 Washington Street, Suite 2, Boston, MA 02131, toll-free telephone: 1-800-937-4113, fax: (617) 469-3379, *http://www.fanlight.com/*

Hurting with Words: Understanding Emotional Violence and Abuse (28 minutes). This program describes emotional violence as one person saying something that is harmful to someone else. These hurtful words may include threats, bullying, intimidation, and anything that causes feelings of humiliation, fear, or worthlessness. A leader's guide is also provided. For middle- and high-school students. Available from The National Center for Violence Prevention, PO Box 9, 102 Highway 81 North, Calhoun, KY 42327-0009, toll-free telephone: 1-800-962-6662, fax: (270) 273-5844.

Keeping Cool: Anger Management Tools (60 minutes). This video presents a series of specialized life skills that teach the viewer techniques of anger control, conflict resolution, effective communication, and problem solving. Teachers can view this video and present the content to students. Available from The National Center for Violence Prevention, PO Box 9, 102 Highway 81 North, Calhoun, KY 42327-0009, toll-free telephone: 1-800-962-6662, fax: (270) 273-5844.

Key Changes: A Portrait of Lisa Thorson by Cindy Marshall (28 minutes). This video profiles Thorson, a highly successful jazz singer who uses a wheelchair. Artfully weaving performance footage with interviews, it demonstrates how she challenges stereotypes and advocates for people with disabilities through her work. For middle-school students, high-school students, and adults. Available from Fanlight Productions, 4196 Washington Street, Suite 2, Boston, MA 02131, toll-free telephone: 1-800-937-4113, fax: (617) 469-3379, *http://www.fanlight.com/*

Names Can Really Hurt Us (26 minutes). Teenagers in an ethnically diverse urban middle school talk about their painful experiences as victims of bigotry and also reveal their own prejudices and stereotypes. Their revelations lead to healing, self-confidence, and courage to challenge bigots and bullies. For middle-school students, high-school students, and adults. Available from the Anti-Defamation League, 823 United Nations Plaza, New York, NY 10017, *http://www.adl.org/*

Nobody Likes a Bully (15 minutes). Children watch Fat Albert and the Gang to learn about bullies and how to build relationships that last. For elementary-school students. Available from The National Center for Violence Prevention, PO Box 9, 102 Highway 81 North, Calhoun, KY 42327-0009, toll-free telephone: 1-800-962-6662, fax: (270) 273-5844.

No More Teasing! (14 minutes). Students in this video introduce common teasing situations and offer solutions. Included with the video are seven student worksheets and a teacher's guide. For grades 2–4. Available from The National Center for Violence Prevention, PO Box 9, 102 Highway 81 North, Calhoun, KY 42327-0009, toll-free telephone: 1-800-962-6662, fax: (270) 273-5844.

The Old Gang of Mine: Incarcerated Gang Members Talking (50 minutes). This video portrays gang life and its dire consequences as seen through the eyes of actual gang members who have ended up behind bars. For middle-school students, high-school students, and adults. Available from The National Center for Violence Prevention, PO Box 9, 102 Highway 81 North, Calhoun, KY 42327-0009, toll-free telephone: 1-800-962-6662, fax: (270) 273-5844.

Peace on the Playground (27 minutes). This program teaches children and parents to deal with violence and the proliferation of guns. In the first segment, kids suggest ways to deal with anger, including counting, exercise, or doing something they enjoy. A second segment puts television violence into perspective and provides tips for parents on how to monitor what their children watch. A final segment discusses the dangers of guns in the home and at school. This video is best for elementary- and middle-school students. Available from Films for the Humanities & Science, PO Box 2053, Princeton, NJ 08543-2053, toll-free telephone: 1-800-257-5126, *http://www.films.com/*

Preventing Violence (30 minutes). This program paints a picture of teen violence today by identifying the types of violence schoolchildren face. The new pressures of guns and gangs and the grave emotional toll of teen violence is discussed. Three basic strategies for avoiding and reducing violence are presented: predicting consequences, cooling down, and walking away. For middle- and high-school students. Available from The Bureau for At-Risk Youth, 135 Dupont Street, PO Box 760, Plainview, NY 11803-0760, toll-free telephone: 1-800-99-YOUTH, *http://www.at-risk.com/*

Resisting Pressure to Join Gangs (22 minutes). This video will help students see the pressure to join gangs for just what it is—negative peer pressure—and offers them realistic alternatives. They will also learn how to feel like they "belong" without joining a gang. For middle-school students, high-school students, and adults. Available from The National Center for Violence Prevention, PO Box 9, 102 Highway 81 North, Calhoun, KY 42327-0009, toll-free telephone: 1-800-962-6662, fax: (270) 273-5844.

Resolving Conflicts (28 minutes). Tuggy and Rhonda learn that there are ways to resolve disagreement without fighting. When a dispute between them puts their class art projects in jeopardy, Tuggy and Rhonda learn to work out interpersonal conflicts in a peaceful and positive way. For grades 2–4. Available from The National Center for Violence Prevention, PO Box 9, 102 Highway 81 North, Calhoun, KY 42327-0009, toll-free telephone: 1-800-962-6662, fax: (270) 273-5844.

Respecting Yourself and Others (24 minutes). Disrespect for others is a common cause of violence. Kids review how to handle insults and put-downs nonviolently. In addition, teens discuss race and culture and how to respect differences in opinion. Finally, the importance of self-respect rather than depending on the opinion of others is emphasized. A leader's guide is also provided. For middle- and high-school students. Available from The Bureau for At-Risk Youth, 135 Dupont Street, PO Box 760, Plainview, NY 11803-0760, toll-free telephone: 1-800-99-YOUTH, *http://www.at-risk.com/*

Skinheads USA: The Pathology of Hate (54 minutes). This HBO production takes viewers for an extended look at the growth of white supremacy groups in the United States during the past decade. It covers the day-to-day activities of the Skinheads, their operation, and their headquarters. This program contains profanity and footage of violence and brutality against minorities, so be certain to preview this program before showing it to students. For middle-school students, high-school students, and adults. Available from Films for the Humanities & Science, PO Box 2053, Princeton, NJ 08543-2053, toll-free telephone: 1-800-257-5126, *http://www.films.com/*

Stepping Up to Peace (30 minutes). This video discusses how to break the chain of violence by developing concern for others and creating a positive sense of community. It explains the character traits of a nonviolent person: courage, tolerance, and

respect. Special emphasis is given to the value of compassion and community values, and how to turn enemies into friends. For middle- and high-school students. Available from The Bureau for At-Risk Youth, 135 Dupont Street, PO Box 760, Plainview, NY 11803-0760, toll-free telephone: 1-800-99-YOUTH, *http://www.at-risk.com/*

Stop It! Students Speak Out Against Sexual Harassment (17 minutes). Students, speaking out against inappropriate sexual behavior, make this program particularly effective in raising awareness of sexual harassment. For middle- and high-school students. Available from Films for the Humanities & Science, PO Box 2053, Princeton, NJ 08543-2053, toll-free telephone: 1-800-257-5126, *http://www.films.com/*

Tug of War: Strategies for Conflict Resolution (25 minutes). This fast-paced drama authentically portrays young people's anger and illustrates different ways of handling conflict without adult intervention. For middle- and high-school students. Available from The National Center for Violence Prevention, PO Box 9, 102 Highway 81 North, Calhoun, KY 42327-0009, toll-free telephone: 1-800-962-6662, fax: (270) 273-5844.

Without Pity: A Film about Abilities (55 minutes). This HBO documentary, narrated by Christopher Reeve, celebrates the efforts of the disabled to live full, productive lives. This video is best for middle- and high-school students. Available from Films for the Humanities & Science, PO Box 2053, Princeton, NJ 08543-2053, toll-free telephone: 1-800-257-5126, *http://www.films.com/*

Withstanding Ovation (24 minutes). In this video, viewers meet two capable young people with congenital amputations who have created active, full lives with only minimal reliance on mechanical prosthetics. Their physicians, therapists, families, and friends have learned from them to see people with physical differences as people with abilities. For all ages. Available from Texas Scottish Rite Hospital for Children, 2222 Welborn Street, Dallas, TX 75219-3993.

OTHER MATERIALS

Anger Management: From Mad to Worse. An activity book, reproducible activity pages, a facilitator's guide, and lesson plans in this package teach students positive ways to handle anger. For grades 3–4. Available from The National Center for Violence Prevention, PO Box 9, 102 Highway 81 North, Calhoun, KY 42327-0009, toll-free telephone: 1-800-962-6662, fax: (270) 273-5844.

Anger Management: Mad Me. The materials include an activity book, reproducible activity pages, a facilitator's guide, and lesson plans to help children learn to identify and handle feelings of anger. For grades K–2. Available from The National Center for Violence Prevention, PO Box 9, 102 Highway 81 North, Calhoun, KY 42327-0009, toll-free telephone: 1-800-962-6662, fax: (270) 273-5844.

"The Anti-Bullying Game" by Yvonne Searle and Isabelle Streng (London: Jessica Kingsley Publishers, 1996). This game includes a board, dice, counters, and four sets of color-coded cards arranged in categories corresponding to colored shapes on the board. The game is intended to help both victims and bullies understand what causes bullying behavior and help them learn to interact more effectively. This game should always be played with a therapist or another adult moderator. For ages 6–16. Available from Taylor & Francis Inc., 1900 Frost Road, Suite 101, Bristol, PA 19007, toll-free telephone: 1-800-821-8312, fax: (215) 785-5515.

Beyond Hate. This two-tape set includes *The Heart of Hatred* and *Learning to Hate.* The set takes us beyond hate by exploring its origins and dimensions, with perspectives from world leaders, human rights activists, students, youth gangs, Arabs and Israelis, and an American white supremacist group. For middle-school students, high-school students, and adults. Available from the Anti-Defamation League, 823 United Nations Plaza, New York, NY 10017, *http://www.adl.org/*

It's Not Okay to Bully. This program explains what bullying is and suggests ways to prevent bullying behaviors, including knowing when to stand up for yourself and when to tell an adult. The 12-minute video mixes real children and animation with a simple, original, easy-to-sing song. The 166-page coloring book (10 copies are provided with each video) includes stills from the video and song lyrics as text. For grades K–3. Available from The National Center for Violence Prevention, PO Box 9, 102 Highway 81 North, Calhoun, KY 42327-0009, toll-free telephone: 1-800-962-6662, fax: (270) 273-5844.

No-Bullying Curriculum. This program includes system-wide strategies to involve all school personnel, students, parents, and concerned community members. The kit includes a program director's manual; teacher's manuals for grades K–1, 2–3, 4–5, and middle school; 100 No-Bullying stickers; and 50 overview booklets. Available from The National Center for Violence Prevention, PO Box 9, 102 Highway 81 North, Calhoun, KY 42327-0009, toll-free telephone: 1-800-962-6662, fax: (270) 273-5844.

Scared or Prepared. This staff development video series includes a series of six videotapes ("Preventing Conflict and Violence in the Classroom," "Developing a School Safety Plan [and a Crisis Support System],"

"Dealing with the Potentially Violent Student," "Intervening Safely During Fights," "Preventing Gang Activity in School," and "Using Peer Mediation to Resolve Conflicts"), a copy of the book *Scared or Prepared: Preventing Conflict and Violence in Your Classroom,* and a leader's guide. The book and videos are also available separately. For school staff workers and teachers of grades 6–12. Available from Canter & Associates, Inc., PO Box 2113, Santa Monica, CA 90407-2113, toll-free telephone: 1-800-262-4347, *http://www.canter.net/cn/index.html*

Second Step. Empathy, anger management, and impulse control are the main lessons taught in this violence prevention curriculum. Age-appropriate lessons are available for students in preschool/kindergarten, grades 1–3, grades 4–5, and middle school/junior high. At all grade levels, the lessons include opportunities for modeling, practice, and reinforcement of the new skills. A guide for families can also be purchased. Available from the Committee for Children, 2203 Airport Way South, Suite 500, Seattle, WA 98134-2027, toll-free telephone: 1-800-634-4449, *http://www.cfchildren.org/*

Student Workshop: Handling Your Anger. A hands-on workshop designed to teach anger management techniques to middle-school students, this program helps students understand that while they cannot control angry feelings, they can control angry behavior. Includes a 33-minute video, 18 student handbooks, and a teacher's guide. For grades 5–9. Available from The National Center for Violence Prevention, PO Box 9, 102 Highway 81 North, Calhoun, KY 42327-0009, toll-free telephone: 1-800-962-6662, fax: (270) 273-5844.

Take Action Against Bullying. Included in this program are a book, video, bookmarks, and a poster set designed to teach students about the dangers of bullying. Visit the Web site for interesting facts and stories about bullying. For middle-school students. Available from Bully B'ware Productions, 1421 King Albert Avenue, Coquitlam, British Columbia, Canada V3J 1Y3, toll-free telephone: 1-888-522-8559, *http://www.bullybeware.com*

Teaching Students to Get Along. This staff development video package includes a series of ten programs on two videocassettes (including "Creating a Caring, Safe Classroom" and "Teaching Students to Respond to Conflict"), a copy of the book *Teaching Students to Get Along: Reducing Conflict and Increasing Cooperation in K–6 Classrooms,* a leader's guide, and an additional videotape with classroom scenes for students. The book is also available separately. For school staff workers and teachers of grades K–6. Available from Canter & Associates, Inc., PO Box 2113, Santa Monica, CA 90407-2113, toll-free telephone: 1-800-262-4347, *http://www.canter.net/cn/index.html*

Working with Hostile and Resistant Teens. This set of two 45-minute videos and a discussion guide teaches hands-on survival skills for dealing with hostile teens in any setting. The tapes include role-plays with actual at-risk teens, who in many cases are acting out their own personal histories. Dr. Steven Campbell leads the role-plays, then provides an analysis of each one, showing viewers how to work effectively with this challenging population. Appropriate for middle- and high-school teachers and staff members. Available from the Attainment Company, Inc., PO Box 930160, Verona, WI 53593-0160, toll-free telephone: 1-800-327-4269, *http://www.attainment-inc.com/*

ORGANIZATIONS

Angries Out
Talk, Trust & Feel Therapeutics
1120 Buchanan Avenue
Charleston, IL 61902
telephone: (217) 345-2982
fax: (217) 345-6314
http://members.aol.com/AngriesOut/

Talk, Trust & Feel and the Angries Out Web page were developed to give people alternatives to conflict and violence when they are upset. Their mission is to help people learn to use their anger in ways that empower them. From their Web site, you can download free articles about peace-building skills and learn more about bully behavior.

The Center for Effective Discipline (CED)
155 West Main Street, Suite 1603
Columbus, OH 43215
telephone: (614) 221-8829
http://www.stophitting.com/

Corporal punishment of children is unsupported by educational research, sometimes leads to serious injury, and contributes to a pro-violence attitude. CED provides educational information to the public on the effects of corporal punishment and alternatives to its use.

Center for the Prevention of School Violence
20 Enterprise Street, Suite 2
Raleigh, NC 27607-7375
toll-free telephone: 1-800-299-6054
http://www.ncsu.edu/cpsv/

The Center focuses on ensuring that schools are safe and secure, creating an atmosphere that is conducive to learning. Newsletters, research bulletins, and special feature articles provide current information about Center activities and school violence prevention.

Children's Creative Response to Conflict (CCRC)
PO Box 271
523 North Broadway
Nyack, NY 10960-0271
telephone: (914) 353-1796

CCRC provides conflict resolution training based on peer leadership to children, adolescents, teachers, and parents. This training emphasizes cooperation, communication, affirmation, problem solving, mediation, and bias awareness. The CCRC also conducts workshops and publishes other materials useful for training in conflict resolution.

Community of Caring, Inc.
1325 G Street NW, Suite 500
Washington, DC 20052
telephone: (202) 393-1250

Contact this organization for well-developed educational materials for grades K–12 and excellent consulting. Endorsed by the National Association of Secondary School Principals. A project of the Joseph P. Kennedy, Jr. Foundation.

Crisis Prevention Institute, Inc. (CPI)
3315-K North 124th Street
Brookfield, WI 53005
toll-free telephone: 1-800-558-8976
http://www.crisisprevention.com/form.html

CPI offers training in the safe management of disruptive and assaultive behavior, as well as other topics.

Educators for Social Responsibility (ESR)
23 Garden Street
Cambridge, MA 02138
toll-free telephone: 1-800-370-2515
fax: (617) 864-5164
http://www.esrnational.org/

ESR's primary mission is to help young people develop the conviction and skills to shape a safe, sustainable, and just world. The Resolving Conflict Creatively Program (see page 160) is ESR's largest initiative. ESR is nationally recognized for promoting children's ethical and social development through its leadership in conflict resolution, violence prevention, group relations, and character education. The Web site includes resources and activities for teachers and students.

The Giraffe Project
PO Box 759
Langley, WA 98260
telephone: (360) 221-7989
http://www.giraffe.org/giraffe

This powerful program helps teachers and youth leaders build courage, caring, and responsibility in kids from 6–18 years old, then guides kids in designing and implementing their own service projects. Businesses, service clubs, and other organizations can become Giraffe Partners.

Heartwood Institute
425 North Craig Street, Suite 302
Pittsburgh, PA 15213
toll-free telephone: 1-800-432-7810
http://www.enviroweb.org/heartwood/

This organization produces educational materials to support children's books about courage, loyalty, justice, respect, hope, honesty, and love. Mainly for elementary grades.

The National Association for Mediation in Education
205 Hampshire House
Box 33635
Amherst, MA 01003-3645
telephone: (413) 545-2462

This organization produces a newsletter called *The Fourth R.,* maintains a list of reprints on all facets of the field, distributes training materials in print and video, and sponsors conferences and training.

National PTA
330 North Wabash Avenue, Suite 2100
Chicago, IL 60611
toll-free telephone: 1-800-307-4782
http://www.pta.org/

The mission of the National PTA is to support and speak on behalf of children and youth in the schools, assist parents in developing the skills they need to raise and protect their children, and encourage public involvement in public schools. Visit their Web site for information on a variety of topics, including safeguarding children in schools.

National School Safety Center (NSSC)
141 Duesenberg Drive, Suite 11
Westlake Village, CA 91362
telephone: (805) 373-9977
http://nssc1.org/

The NSSC offers helpful booklets and videos addressing violence prevention, bullying, and conflict resolution for educators and parents. Call or write to request a free catalog.

PeaceBuilders
c/o Heartsprings, Inc.
PO Box 12158
Tucson, AZ 85732
telephone: (520) 322-9977
fax: (520) 322-9983
http://peacebuilders.com

PeaceBuilders, created by psychologist Dennis Embry, is a long-term, community-based program designed to help create a school environment that reduces violence. Four basic principles are at the heart of the program: praise people, give up put-downs, notice hurts and right wrongs, and seek wise people. This program

is in use in nearly 400 elementary schools across the country, and the number continues to grow.

Resolving Conflict Creatively Program (RCCP)
40 Exchange Place, Suite 1111
New York, NY 10005
(212) 509-0022
Fax: (212) 509-1095

An initiative of Educators for Social Responsibility (see page 159), RCCP is a pioneering school-based conflict resolution and intergroup relations program that provides a model for preventing violence and creating caring learning communities.

Ribbon of Promise
150 Seventh Street
Springfield, OR 97477
telephone: (541) 726-0512
http://www.ribbonofpromise.org/

Following the May 21, 1998, shooting at Thurston High School in Springfield, Oregon, local firefighters began the Ribbon of Promise campaign to increase awareness of school violence. Thousands of people across the country wear the brilliant blue ribbon of promise, representing sorrow for the victims of school violence, and hope for the future. Ribbon of Promise also provides educational materials and resources, and support for schools and communities that have been hurt by violence in schools.

Safe and Drug-Free Schools Program
1250 Maryland Avenue SW, Portals 604
Washington, DC 20202
telephone: (202) 260-6722
http://www.ed.gov/offices/OESE/SDFS/

This federal program supports initiatives designed to prevent violence in and around schools, and to strengthen programs that involve parents; the program also works to prevent the illegal use of alcohol, tobacco, and drugs. It is coordinated with other federal, state, and local efforts and resources.

Teaching Tolerance
400 Washington Avenue
Montgomery, AL 36104
telephone: (334) 264-0286
http://www.splcenter.org/teachingtolerance/tt-index.html

Teaching Tolerance is a national education project dedicated to helping teachers foster equity, respect, and understanding in the classroom and beyond. *Teaching Tolerance* magazine is available free to teachers.

WEB SITES

Bullies: A Serious Problem for Kids
National Crime Prevention Council (NCPC)
http://www.ncpc.org/10adu3.htm

This site provides characteristics that are commonly present in victims and bullies and also offers tips to parents and teachers about what they can do to help prevent bullying. More information about NCPC and their list of publications for children and youth is also available.

Family.com
http://family.go.com/

This site contains useful information for parents and other adults, including articles on helping children learn to face bullies and be kind to one another.

Family Education Network
http://create.familyeducation.com/

Search this site for the phrase "Back-to-School Safety." You'll find articles, a message board, and advice from experts on keeping children safe in school.

Kidscape
http://www.kidscape.org.uk/kidscape/

Visit this site for information about keeping kids safe. The ideas and materials here focus on preventing bullying before it happens.

Mental Health Net
http://www.cmhc.com/

This site is home to the oldest and largest online mental health community and indexes over 9,000 mental health resources, including articles on aggression and behavior disorders.

National Crime Prevention Council On-line Resource Center (NCPC)
http://www.ncpc.org/

NCPC is a national nonprofit organization dedicated to helping America prevent crime and build safer, stronger communities. Their Web site includes useful information about crime prevention, community building, and comprehensive planning, along with fun activities for kids.

INDEX

n indicates note; reproducible pages in **bold**

National Association for Mediation in Education (Web site), 160
National Association of School Psychologists (NASP), 5, 19n, 82, 117, 126–127
National Association to Advance Fat Acceptance (NAAFA), 98–99
National Center for School Safety, 82
National Center for Violence Prevention, 32
National Coalition to Abolish Corporal Punishment in Schools (NCACPS), 125
National Crime Prevention Council (NCPC) (Web site), 10, 107, 160–161
The National Mentoring Partnership (Web site), 106
National PTA (Web site), 160
National School Safety Center (NSSC) (Web site), 160
NCACPS (National Coalition to Abolish Corporal Punishment in Schools), 125
NCPC (National Crime Prevention Council) (Web site), 160–161
Nickelodeon (Web site), 74
No Blame Approach, 104
Nobody Likes a Bully (video), 156
No More Teasing! (video), 156
No-Bullying Curriculum (program), 158
Nonreward Retort Strategies response, 111–112
Nonviolent Crisis Intervention program (Web site), 112, 116
Nothing's Fair in Fifth Grade (DeClements), 152
New students, 36–37
NSSC (National School Safety Center) (Web site), 160

O

The Old Gang of Mine: Incarcerated Gang Members Talking (video), 156
Olweus, Dan, 8, 14, 149
100 Ways to Enhance Self-Concept in the Classroom (Canfield and Wells), 149
Opportunities for victims to shine, 107–108
Organizations, 159–160
Ostracism, 5
"Overcoming Bullying Behavior" (Clore and Hibel), 5
Overweight students, 98–99

P

Parents
    bringing out the best in kids, 122, **123–124**
    bully identification, 119, **120–121**, 122
    communication about bullying behavior, 129, 131
    consultation with, 14
    family relationships, encouraging strong, 105
    grandparents, encouraging relationships with, 105
    victim identification, 81
    victims, empowered to aid, 89, **90–92**
Passive victims, 6, 78, 103
Peace on the Playground (video), 156
Peace place, 58
Peacebuilders (Web site), 160
Peacemakers, lives of famous, 60
Peale, Norman Vincent, 50
Peers
    abuse by, 7
    conflict, normal *vs.* bullying, 82–83
    mediation by, 9, 60, **61**, 62
People with Disabilities Resource (Web site), 98
Persecution as early warning sign, 12
Photographs, 62
Pikas, Anatol, 99

Place to go for bullies, 142
Plan, comprehensive bullying prevention, 10–11
Planning skills, 109, **110**
The Points of Light Foundation (Web site), 74–75
Positive attitude, encouraging, 93
Positive classroom
    anger management skills, 32, 137–138
    assertiveness skills, 53–54
    conflict resolution skills, 58, **59**
    friendship skills, 34, **35**, 36
    "I" messages, 51, **52**, 58
    notes-to-the-teacher box, 31, 41, 45
    positive self-talk, 68, 71, **72**
    student affirmations, 65–66
    ways to deal with bullies, 41, **42–44**
Positive self-talk, 68, 71, **72**
Positive Self-Talk for Children: Teaching Self-Esteem through Affirmations (Bloch), 71, 149
Positive visualization, 97
Positive self-talk game, 97–98
Posters, 32n, 95, 136–137
Power issues
    equalization of, 107
    need for, 5–6
    positive ways to have, 141–142
    skills for, 109, 111–112
P/PV (Public/Private Ventures), 135
Prejudicial attitudes as early warning sign, 13
Preschool bullying, 1
Preventing Violence (video), 156–157
Principal, as essential leadership, 9
Privacy of grades, 49
Problem solving as a group, 54, 56
Protection
    by adults, 7, 8–9
    by schools, 14
    of teachers, 112–113
Provocative victims, 6, 78, 103
The Prudential Spirit of Community Initiative (Web site), 75
Public/Private Ventures (P/PV), 135
Punishment Retort Strategies response, 112
Push & Shove (Boulden), 152

Q

Quit It! A Teacher's Guide on Teasing and Bullying (Froschl), 149–150
Quotations as teaching tools, 49–50

R

Random acts of kindness, 50–51
Random Acts of Kindness (editors of Conari Press), 50
The Rat and the Tiger (Kasza), 152
RCCP (Resolving Conflict Creatively Program), 60, **61**, 62, 160
Reading, related to bullying, 57
Reasons Why for bullying, 143, **145–148**
Reducing School Violence through Conflict Resolution (Johnson and Johnson), 10n, 150
Rejection as early warning sign, 12
Reluctantly Alice (Naylor), 152
Reporting of bullying, 32, 34
Resisting Pressure to Join Gangs (video), 157
Resolution skills, 9–10
Resolving Conflict Creatively Program (RCCP), 60, **61**, 62, 160
Resolving Conflicts (video), 157

Troops, encouraging relationships with, 105–106
Tug of War: Strategies for Conflict Resolution (video), 157

U
Understanding, 56–57, 143

V
Victims
    blaming the, 7–8
    children as, 5, 6–7
    classroom expectations, 77–78
    clear message to, 88
    as early warning sign, 11–14
    helping
        adults, encouraging relationships with, 105–106
        Method of Shared Concern, 99, 101, **102–103**, 104
        positive attitude, encouraging, 93
        positive visualization, 97
        self-esteem building, 95, **96**, 97
        videos, 153–157
    identification, 78, **79–80**, 81
    interviewing, **103**
    number of, 19
    parents empowered to aid, 89, **90–92**
    power equalization, 107
    witnesses mobilized to aid, 89, 93
Violence, 8, 10, 11–13
Visualization, positive, 97
Vocabulary for feelings, 47, **48**
Volunteering, 73–75
Volunteering and Giving Among American Teenagers (-), 73n

W
Waging Peace in Our Schools (Lantieri and Patti), 8n, 150
Warning signs
    bullying, 119, **120–121**, 122
    victimization, 78, **79–80**, 81
Ways to deal with bullies, 41, **42–44**
Ways to stay bully free, 99, **100**
We Can Get Along: A Child's Book of Choices (Payne and Rohling), 152–153
Weapons, 10, 13
Web sites, 74–75, 159–161
    Angries Out (Talk, Trust & Feel Therapeutics), 159
    Big Brothers Big Sisters of America (BBBSA), 106, 135
    Boy Scouts of America, 105
    Boys & Girls Clubs of America, 105
    Camp Fire Boys and Girls, 106
    Campaign Against Workplace Bullying (CAWB), 112–113
    Center for Effective Discipline (CED), 159
    Center for Prevention of School Violence, 159
    Children's Creative Response to Conflict (CCRC), 159
    Community of Caring, Inc., 159
    Crisis Prevention Institute, Inc. (CPI), 159
    Educators for Social Responsibility (ESR), 159
    Family.com, 161
    Family Education Network, 161
    4-H, 106
    The Giraffe Project, 159
    Girl Scouts of the U.S.A., 106
    Girls Incorporated, 106
    Heartwood Institute, 160
    Institute for Global Communications, 98
    Kidscape, 161
    Mental Health Net, 161
    National Association for Mediation in Education, 160
    National Crime Prevention Council (NCPC), 160–161
    The National Mentoring Partnership, 106
    National PTA, 160
    National School Safety Center (NSSC), 160
    Nickelodeon, 74
    Nonviolent Crisis Intervention program, 112, 116
    Peacebuilders, 160
    People with Disabilities Resource, 98
    The Points of Light Foundation, 74–75
    The Prudential Spirit of Community Initiative, 75
    Resolving Conflict Creatively Program (RCCP), 160
    Ribbon of Promise, 160
    Safe and Drug-Free Schools Program, 160
    SERVEnet, 75
    Teaching Tolerance, 160
Weekly activities
    assessment, 68, **70**
    behavior profile comparison, 141
    goals, setting and reviewing, 57
    journals, 34, 38–39, 108–109
Welcome to new students, 36–37
What a Wimp! (Carrick), 153
What Do You Stand For? (Lewis), 153
What Do You Think? A Kid's Guide to Dealing with Daily Dilemmas (Schwartz), 153
"What If?" game, 107
What to Do When Kids Are Mean to Your Child (McCoy), 150
What Would You Do? A Kid's Guide to Tricky and Sticky Situations (Schwartz), 153
Why is Everybody Always Picking on Me: A Guide to Handling Bullies (Webster-Doyle), 153
Wilson, Woodrow, 50
Win the Whining War & Other Skirmishes (Whitham), 150
Without Pity: A Film about Abilities (video), 157
Withstanding Ovation (video), 157
Witness to bullying
    immediate intervention, 34
    mobilized to aid victim, 89, 93
    taking immediate action, 85–86
Working with Hostile and Resistant Teens (staff video program), 159
Worth the Risk (Erlbach), 93

Y
You Can't Say You Can't Play (Paley), 150
You're Dead, David Borelli (Brown), 153
Youth Service America, 75

Z
Zero tolerance, 10, 15, 127

ABOUT THE AUTHOR

Allan L. Beane, Ph.D., is a professor in the special education department at Murray State University in Murray, Kentucky. He develops bully prevention programs for schools and gives workshops on the topic. He also offers expert support to those who deal with school violence. Dr. Beane and his wife live in Murray, Kentucky. They look forward to visits from their two grown children.

Other Great Products from Free Spirit

Bully Free Zone Poster
Adapted from *The Bully Free Classroom* by Allan L. Beane, Ph.D., this big, bright poster sends a positive message: This is a place where everyone belongs and no one is bullied (or bullies others). *$6.95; 17" x 22"*

Bully Free Classroom Poster
$6.95; 17" x 22"

Bullies Are a Pain in the Brain
written and illustrated by Trevor Romain
Bullies are a pain in the brain—and every child needs to know what to do when confronted by one. This book combines humor with serious, practical suggestions for coping with bullies. For ages 8–13. *$9.95; 112 pp.; softcover; illus.; 5⅛" x 7"*

Stick Up for Yourself!
Every Kid's Guide to Personal Power and Positive Self-Esteem
Revised and Updated
by Gershen Kaufman, Ph.D., Lev Raphael, Ph.D., and Pamela Espeland
Realistic, encouraging, how-to advice for kids on being assertive, building relationships, becoming responsible, solving problems, setting goals, and more. For ages 8–12. *$11.95; 128 pp.; softcover; illus.; 6" x 9"*

A Teacher's Guide to Stick Up for Yourself!
A 10-Part Course in Self-Esteem and Assertiveness for Kids
Revised and Updated
For teachers, grades 3–7. *$19.95; 128 pp.; softcover; 8½" x 11"*

Growing Good Kids
28 Activities to Enhance Self-Awareness, Compassion, and Leadership
by Deb Delisle and Jim Delisle, Ph.D.
Created by teachers and classroom-tested, these fun and meaningful enrichment activities build children's skills in problem solving, decision making, cooperative learning, divergent thinking, and communication. For grades 4–8. *$21.95; 168 pp.; softcover; illus.; 8½" x 11"*

Being Your Best
Character Building for Kids 7–10
by Barbara A. Lewis
Written for children ages 7–10, this book invites them to explore who they are and who they'd like to be. Even elementary school kids can learn about and build important character traits like caring, citizenship, respect, and more—traits that will help them grow into capable, moral teens and adults. For ages 7–10. *$14.95; 148 pp.; softcover; illus.; 7¼" x 9¼"*

Leader's Guide
For grades 2–5. *$18.95; 128 pp.; softcover; 8½" x 11"*

What Do You Stand For?
A Kid's Guide to Building Character
by Barbara A. Lewis
Young people need guidance from caring adults to build strong, positive character traits—but they can also build their own. This inspiring book invites them to explore and practice honesty, kindness, empathy, integrity, tolerance, patience, respect, and more. For ages 11 & up. *$19.95; 284 pp.; softcover; B&W photos and illus.; 8½" x 11"*

To place an order or to request a free catalog of SELF–HELP FOR KIDS® *and*
SELF–HELP FOR TEENS® *materials, please write, call, email, or visit our Web site:*

Free Spirit Publishing Inc.
217 Fifth Avenue North • Suite 200 • Minneapolis, MN 55401-1299
toll-free 800.735.7323 • local 612.338.2068 • fax 612.337.5050
help4kids@freespirit.com • www.freespirit.com

Visit us on the Web!

www.freespirit.com

Stop by anytime to find our Parents' Choice Approved catalog with fast, easy, secure 24-hour online ordering; "Ask Our Authors," where visitors ask questions—and authors give answers—on topics important to children, teens, parents, teachers, and others who care about kids; links to other Web sites we know and recommend; fun stuff for everyone, including quick tips and strategies from our books; and much more! Plus our site is completely searchable so you can find what you need in a hurry. Stop in and let us know what you think!

Just point and click!

new! Get the first look at our books, catch the latest news from Free Spirit, and check out our site's newest features.

contact Do you have a question for us or for one of our authors? Send us an email. Whenever possible, you'll receive a response within 48 hours.

Win free books!
As a way of thanking everyone who's made our Web site a success, we often have book giveaways online. Stop by and get in on the action!

order! Order in confidence! Our secure server uses the most sophisticated online ordering technology available. And ordering online is just one of the ways to purchase our books: you can also order by phone, fax, or regular mail. No matter which method you choose, excellent service is our goal.